Colleges for Our Land and Time

Colleges for Our Land and Time

The Land-Grant Idea in American Education

by EDWARD DANFORTH EDDY JR.

Vice-President and Provost, University of New Hampshire

HARPER & BROTHERS　　　PUBLISHERS　　　NEW YORK

To

M S E

M H E

I V B

Contents

Foreword

BY RUSSELL I. THACKREY, *Executive Secretary,*
American Association of Land-Grant Colleges and
State Universities

It is timely that this first general account of the development of
the Land-Grant movement should appear as the Centennial of the
Morrill Land-Grant Act of 1862 approaches, and as the United States
may again face a period of revolutionary change in its system of
higher education.

The outlines of future changes in the pattern of higher education
are not now clear, just as they were not clear a century ago. But the
story of how a system of higher education that was clearly inadequate
to the needs of its society acquired a drastic redirection that was indigenous to America, of the movements and events that led up to the
change, and of the results that flow from it down to the contemporary
period, is a fascinating one whose lessons may be useful in a variety
of ways as we look to the future.

Much has been written about the Land-Grant institutions, but
little of it is currently available to other than research scholars. Much
does not cover the contemporary period or deals only with certain
phases of the Land-Grant movement. Thus the excellent *Democracy's*
College by Earle D. Ross of Iowa State College deals with the development of the Land-Grant system in its formative stage, down to
approximately 1890, and has long been out of print. The histories of
agricultural education, research, and extension work by the late A. C.
True of the United States Department of Agriculture end their story
in 1925, are likewise out of print, and deal primarily with the de-

velopment of agriculture in the Land-Grant institutions. A monumental survey by the United States Office of Education, published in 1930, is available only in research libraries.

Other published studies deal only with particular aspects of the story, and of these many are not readily available. There are excellent histories of individual institutions, and a few published analyses (such as the brilliant series of lectures by Carl Becker of Cornell), which interpret the story of an institution in terms of the national significance of the movement of which it is a part.

In this book for the first time the author has told the story of the Land-Grant movement from its beginnings to the present.

The men of broadest vision among the leaders of this movement dreamed of a system of colleges and universities in which the search for new knowledge in neglected fields of fundamental importance to the American people (and the application of this knowledge in practice) would have an honored place, though not to the exclusion of other traditional disciplines. They wanted at least one of these institutions in each state.

Some factual measure of the realization of their dream may be had in the knowledge that in 1955 the 69 Land-Grant institutions, enrolling slightly more than 20 per cent of all students in degree-granting colleges and universities, awarded 39.3 per cent of all doctoral degrees in United States colleges and universities, including more than half of all doctoral degrees in biology, 43.6 per cent in the physical sciences, 40.3 per cent in mathematics, and 38.4 per cent in the social sciences. Honoring a provision that they should give instruction in "military tactics" to provide a reserve of trained leaders for the nation's defense, they also furnished nearly half of all officers commissioned through the Reserve Officers' Training Corps program. Collectively they conduct the world's largest adult education program, its largest agricultural research program.

The above may create a picture of a group of institutions whose emphasis at all levels is primarily on scientific and professional education. Here the statistics are again revealing. At the undergraduate level more than 37 per cent of all students at Land-Grant institutions are enrolled in their colleges of liberal arts and sciences, and these figures exclude large numbers of students normally classified by separate arts colleges as arts and science students. At the graduate level they also in 1955 conferred 26 per cent of all United States doctorates in English; 30 per cent of all those in fine arts; 20 per cent of all those in foreign languages, modern and classical; and 46 per cent of all doctorates in geography; in addition to the 38.4 per cent in the social sciences referred to above. Their emphasis is, in short, as broad as the range of human knowledge.

Currently many of the Land-Grant institutions are heavily committed to working cooperatively with colleges and universities abroad. Here the problem is also one of building the educational, scientific, and technical bases essential to the survival and victory of the forces of political democracy against some form of totalitarianism. The struggle is literally one against time, with no question as to the nature of the disaster involved in failure. In this situation the "Land-Grant idea" of higher education in the service of all the people has become one of this country's most popular, and least controversial, exports. For those, here and abroad, whose responsibility it is to solve the great problem of using the time gained by defensive military measures to lay a sound basis for democracy in the uncommitted areas of the world, this book will be helpful.

It also sheds light on many other current questions, some new and some as hotly debated a century ago as today: How did this country establish and how can it best maintain its leadership in the natural sciences and engineering? How can our food supply keep up with our rapidly expanding population? Can the "liberal" and "practical" in higher education be successfully combined? Should post-high-school education be limited to an educational "élite" or include all those who can profit from advanced study? Does federal "control" inevitably follow federal aid to education?

The reader will be able to think about these and other problems with more understanding than before. One cannot, in fact, understand the past and present pattern of American higher education, or think intelligently about its future, without an understanding of the Land-Grant institutions—of their place in the pattern and their influence on the rest of the pattern.

This is a book which the author was peculiarly qualified to write. A graduate of a great Land-Grant institution combining the best of the old tradition exemplified by the earlier American universities with the democratic revolution of the Land-Grant movement which created it, he has since taught and done administrative work in a smaller Land-Grant university which also combines these traditions. He has had ample opportunity to mingle with and know the people from all over the United States who administer the various phases of work about which he writes, and to hear them discuss their problems and aspirations, formally and informally.

His devotion to the educational ideal which the Land-Grant institutions represent, and his recognition of accomplishment, have not blinded him to deficiencies and failures, of which he is a temperate but perceptive critic.

This is in no sense an "official" book, nor is it a sponsored book. It is the author's book. It is worth thoughtful reading by all those interested in the relationship of the development of American higher education to this country's past, present, and future.

Preface

In 1862 the Congress of the United States passed an act "to donate public lands to the several states and territories which may provide colleges for the benefit of agriculture and the mechanic arts." The legislation, known as the Morrill Act because of its sponsorship and promotion by Representative Justin Smith Morrill, caused the founding or further development of sixty-nine leading American colleges.

Each state accepting its benefits was obligated to establish "at least one college where the leading object shall be, without excluding other scientific and classical studies, and including military tactics, to teach such branches of learning as are related to agriculture and the mechanic arts . . . in order to promote the liberal and practical education of the industrial classes in the several pursuits and professions in life."

An attempt has been made in these pages to outline the development of the philosophy and program of these institutions which have become universities in the true sense, offering study for thousands of American youth in almost every field of endeavor. Probably no other single group of colleges has so affected American higher education. In addition, their work has contributed substantially to the progress of the nation of which they have become an integral part.

Five men in particular have influenced profoundly the content of this volume, although of course they cannot be held responsible for what has been written. To these men the author is deeply indebted for interest and guidance. Dr. Arthur S. Adams, President of the American Council on Education, first suggested such a study and watched its progress with the continual encouragement which it so often needed. Three good friends and former associates at Cornell University, Professors A. L. Winsor and A. M. Drummond and the late President Edmund Ezra Day, contributed in more ways than the study could possibly reflect. The author wishes to thank particularly Dr. Russell I. Thackrey, Executive Secretary of the American Association of Land-Grant Colleges and State Universities, for his friendly assistance and helpful criticism.

In ways large and small many others have assisted and encouraged. Among those whose helpful comments strengthened the writing were Professor Robin M. Williams, Jr., of Cornell University, and Dean Edward Y. Blewett and Mr. Harry R. Carroll of the University of New Hampshire. My special and personal thanks are extended to my patient and competent secretary, Mary Frances Marshall.

The quality of institutions is measured best by the quality of the men and women who serve them. This volume, though it speaks in terms of institutions, in reality tells the story of the thousands of men and women who, through the years, devoted their lives to the development of the institutions of which they were a part. I wish it were possible to mention all of the past and present pioneers of the land-grant movement. To each of them ultimately must go the credit for whatever quality this story of their efforts contains.

EDWARD DANFORTH EDDY JR.

Durham, New Hampshire

Colleges for Our Land and Time

I

The Background

Into the first half of the nineteenth century the American nation was still clinging to its inhibiting concepts; then a new freedom—an American type of freedom—began to emerge. It was to take many years and a great interplay of ideas and experiments before it would find its educational expression in the so-called Land-Grant Colleges. To understand these institutions, which reached maturity in the twentieth century, one must first examine the conditions out of which they arose, including this emerging and uniquely American type of freedom.

The America of the early nineteenth century could be characterized as simple and agricultural. The population, 85 per cent of which was rural, lived on farms and in small towns along the Eastern seaboard. The center of knowledge was the church and the growing academy. The average person found little reason or desire to learn to read or write. Life was made secure by a strong agricultural economy and a strong religious faith. To the West lay vast miles of uninhabited territory. The conquering of this frontier became the stimulus to a gradual revolution out of which emerged the new form of American independence.

One of the phases of the revolution about to take place, and one of significance to education, was the break from the hold of orthodox religion on the minds of the people. It took its most dramatic form in the emergence of a fixed belief in materialism as the credo of American life. The words *more* and *better* became the guiding symbols of men who believed that anything was possible in the new nation. Man was considered both capable and close to perfect. He needed only the

1

methods and the institutions by which to work out his ultimate perfection. Materialism gave vent to the concept of utilitarianism and to the final test of a process or an institution in its workability.

The inevitable result was a dislocation of classes and society, a process which began with the Revolution, took discernible shape in the 1820's, and extended throughout the century. The country became conscious of the great discrepancy between actual life and the noble sentiments espoused in the Constitution. Perhaps the single most dramatic illustration of the breakdown of class was the election in 1828 of Andrew Jackson, espouser of the right of the common people to be ruled by their representatives and not by the "gentleman-statesmen" who "knew how." The supreme worth and dignity of the individual was becoming a political credo as well as a religious and democratic concept. It followed that the people should be given opportunity and means to develop their latent talents. Benefits available to one must be the right of all.

America, the sleeping giant, had begun to stir. It would no longer depend entirely upon the Old World for its thinking and examples. The frantic fight to make democracy work had begun. The fight would be waged in all quarters. Education must change, too, for working democracy depended on the intelligent understanding of the common people. Looking back a century later, Charles and Mary Beard found that "all in all the epoch of 'Jacksonian democracy,' the 'era of the common man,' the 'fabulous forties' and the fermenting fifties, was a time of dramatic mental activity and creative thinking in respect of everything human." [1]

THE COLLEGES THEN EXISTING

Well-entrenched institutions are usually the last to respond to change which occurs all about them. This was particularly true of the colleges which "Jacksonian democracy" had inherited from the Colonial period. These fortresses of knowledge, termed such because little of the changing times passed over the drawbridge, had been patterned, like most modes and institutions of early America, after the European examples. Professor Carl Becker sounded the lament that such could happen in that particular time:

Among the ideas . . . brought to America were the ideas then prevailing in England about schools and universities. In this respect the seventeenth century might be thought a bad time for the United States to begin its institutional career. At almost no other time . . . could the first settlers have brought to these shores a set of ideas more restricted or less promising for the promotion of learning in the new world. In seventeenth-century England, as in Europe generally, the prevailing idea was that schools and universities should teach nothing that would discredit the established religion or the authority of kings and magistrates.[2]

As a gathering ground for refugees from religious persecution on the continent, America had accepted no single religious sect or denomination to represent the higher aspirations of its people. The result was a multiplication of organized church bodies. Since the church represented most of the learning in its day, it was natural for these bodies to found and support what colleges then existed. The principal purposes of the institutions should be the expounding of theology and training for the ministry. Just as all the early colleges were church-connected, so the great majority of those founded between 1800 and 1860 were denominationally-inspired. As the frontier was pushed west the church followed, often in bitter competition with other denominations, to establish its right to disseminate the truth as it saw it.

The classical colleges were the source also of the needed men of learning: schoolmasters, doctors, lawyers, and occasional men of business and commerce. Knowledge gained in the colleges was the mark of respectability. Prestige came automatically. The academic aristocrat was not anxious to question or change that which gave him his place in the community. In fact, his educational experience was so rigid as to discourage change of any kind. The term "higher education" does not describe these early institutions. Most of the students entered in their early teens and were graduated at the age now considered close to minimum for a college freshman. Louis Agassiz characterized the Harvard College of the 1850's as "a respectable high school where they taught the dregs of learning." [3]

For a period of two hundred years, since the inception of the first college, the curriculum had remained the same. It was narrow, restricted, and adhered so to the concepts of the Middle Ages that it refused to entertain any subject which its tradition had refused previously to honor. The content consisted of philosophy, theology, the dead languages, and mathematics. Even literature was not approached as a living representation of man's thoughts, but as rote training for the disciplined mind.

Basic to the rigid curriculum was this concept of education as mental discipline. The student was expected to train his sights on the glories of the past. Adequately trained, the mind could then deal with the problems of the present. Authoritarian and empirical teaching developed in the student a loyalty to tradition to such extent that tradition could not and should not be questioned. The college was thus designed to preserve and transmit tradition. Professor Becker comments:

Rarely troubled by doubt, and always disposed to rely on the recognized authorities, their chief distinction was to know and to enforce all of the right answers rather than to know or to ask any of the right questions. "I would rather have ten settled opinions, and nine of them wrong," Professor Taylor of Yale was accustomed to say, "than to be like my brother Gibbs with none of the ten settled." [4]

Much of the teaching was done by tutors who were recent graduates "very poor and very pious," [5] sitting in a box three times a day to hear the words of the textbook as committed to memory by the students. Education was recitation, not interpretation. Looking back on his Yale experience, Andrew D. White observed, "The minds of the students were supposed to be developed in the same manner as are the livers of the geese at Strasburg—every day sundry spoonfuls of the same mixture forced down all throats alike." [6]

The college had no concern for research to improve the future. Another university president of a later day recalled the college library of the 1850's:

This consisted mainly of old theology books and other lumber, with a sprinkling, however, of some books that a student could use. It was opened once a week by the professor of Latin and Greek and kept open for half an hour. So far as I remember, I never saw any other student in the dusty, ill-lighted, unheated room. I think the custodian was pleased when I went off and left him to turn the key. [7]

Although the curriculum included smatterings of science, such subjects were seldom taught in the scientific manner. As late as 1850 not a single college had a laboratory, or anything like a laboratory, in its physical plant. Equipment and apparatus for teaching were nonexistent. This would smack of the experimental, and experiments were intolerable to the prevailing educational thought. The undergraduate curriculum constituted all that a man needed to be educated, hence graduate work was not a part of collegiate function. Finally in 1861 Yale conferred the first degree of Doctor of Philosophy, but the real development of graduate work awaited the further expansion of knowledge.

The classical college, then, was a vested interest in the midst of a rapidly expanding and almost radical America. It can be credited with serving as a necessary conservator of at least some of the enduring values of academic life. In its own way it prepared some of the outstanding leaders of the nation and most of the faculty later to be engaged in the "new education." But it did all of this in terms of the few rather than the many of an enlarging and awakening population.

THE PRESSURE BUILDS

Forces were at work in the first half of the nineteenth century which, when channeled, would finally lead to the establishment of a new type of collegiate education. Across the country the free school movement had begun. In this period, too, came the important assumption that education was a public obligation. This was to cause great ramifications on all levels of the educational system. Since the Constitution had established the principle of the separation of church and state, it was only a matter of time before the government sought to break the educational stronghold of the churches. The church and state must part company in the classroom as well as in the halls of government. The decision in the Dartmouth College Case made clear that church institutions were to be free from state control. In like manner, state-supported educational enterprises were to be immune from religious commitment.

Extension of educational opportunity to all included women for the first time. Although this movement would not mature until the twentieth century, this period found many crusaders, including Mary Lyon, Emma Willard, and Catherine Beecher. In 1837 Oberlin College risked public censure by opening its doors to both sexes. The pressure was to build until coeducation became an accepted part of the educational pattern in the latter half of the century.

Outside the college walls in this period, the sleeping giant raised his head. Thwing described it well:

The time was favorable to . . . enrichment and enlargement. The successive decades of the century from 1820 to 1860 were, with brief intervals, periods of intellectual and ethical quickening. The decade beginning with 1831 and the following years were the era of the seer and the prophet. The time was one of beginnings; it was a period of newness. The westward movement of population was slowly pressing its way between the mountains and the great river and passing beyond. Mighty anticipations of mighty powers were filling the hearts and minds of men. . . . Visions of wealth were filling the public eye. Values in certain lands reached a figure which they have never since touched. Reforms were in the air. Apostles of newness abounded. . . . Everybody had a mission; and, as Lowell says, his mission was spelled with a capital M.[8]

Intellectual Awakening

Perhaps the single most dramatic illustration of this intellectual awakening is found in the vast growth of the American Lyceum movement, beginning in 1826 and extending for decades thereafter. It is the forerunner of collegiate extension services of the present century. The lyceum was a device for popular education at a time when the demand was great to improve common education. Millions of people throughout the country came together in their towns to listen to lecturers on almost every conceivable subject. One of the early lyceum lecturers, Wendell Phillips, gave his lecture on "The Lost Arts" two thousand times before town audiences. When education at the lower level began to improve, the lyceums concentrated on adult improvement. Their objective was the spread of useful knowledge and their process was open to all who might wish to benefit.

While the average American was seeking self-education in his hometown, the scholars and thinkers were journeying to Europe. The steamers crossing the Atlantic carried men intent on discovering for themselves the reverence for scholarship and research which Germany, in particular, had to offer. A later pioneer of the land-grant movement, Thomas Clemson, went to Europe in 1826 in despair because, as he said, "there is not a single scientific institution on this continent where a proper scientific education can be obtained. Those who wish to cultivate science are compelled to resort to institutions maintained by the monarchial governments of Europe." [9] The lasting effect of these journeys to Germany was not to be felt, however, until later in the century.

Dissatisfaction Without Remedy

Such movement and such forces were illustrative of a growing dissatisfaction. They stemmed in part from earlier expressions, such as the futile attempt to establish a national university early in the century. Throughout the period when the new nation was taking shape, its leaders had expressed an interest in the possibility of a national university. In his message to Congress in January 1790, Washington urged public interest in science and literature and then concluded, "Whether this desirable object will be the best promoted by affording aids to seminaries of learning already established, by the institution of a national university, or by any other expedients, will be well worthy of a place in the deliberations of the legislature." [10] In 1806 Joel Barlow found so much enthusiasm for the project that he drew up a prospectus and drafted a bill, but it failed to elicit the majority interest of Congress. One of its chief purposes was to further scientific study, particularly of husbandry.

Jefferson was an ardent advocate of scientific farming, of military training within the colleges, of free choice of curriculum, and of public education at a higher level for those with exceptional talents and virtues. In his message to Congress in 1806, he suggested grants of land as a method for endowing a national university. Jefferson's ideas, properly adjusted to the Jacksonian theories, were accepted increasingly in many quarters during the early nineteenth century. But his concepts were sufficiently ethereal for the age that few could translate them into practical measures. Many raised voices against the domination of the curriculum by the classics and the dead languages, but an acceptable substitute to serve as a new type of education could not be found. The trend was toward reason rather than memory. There was still lacking the economic emphasis which was later to make vocational education attractive.

Early efforts to reform the curriculum were doomed to failure. It took time, increased pressures, and a growing scientific age to remodel the ancient pattern of the colleges. The Brown report of 1850 was said to foreshadow the state university movement, but it did not cause

Brown to change. This report of Francis Wayland to the Brown corporation commented, "Our colleges are not filled, because we do not furnish the education desired by the people. . . . We have produced an article for which the demand is diminishing. We sell it at less than cost, and the deficiency is made up by charity. We give it away, and still the demand diminishes." [11]

The growing distrust of the church colleges took shape first in the attempt to bring them under state control. That movement ended in dramatic failure with the decision in the Dartmouth College Case. Even the state universities founded before 1860 were religious either in structure or control. Their independence, as we now know them, awaited the stimulus of the Morrill Act of 1862. Nonetheless, there were mighty beginnings of publicly-supported higher education even in those early days. The first state universities seemed to be founded on genuinely democratic aspirations, but some fell to the revival of religious enthusiasm which followed early in the 1800s. The new states were the leaders in the public university movement, largely because even then Congressional grants of land were sufficiently attractive. Altogether, twelve of the seventeen new states before 1860 had state universities. The South and the West were leaders in the faltering movement, but all were handicapped by lack of teachers, students, and funds.

EMERGENCE OF SCIENCE

One of the chief causes of eventual educational reform was the emergence of science and the subsequent development of industry and vocations. It took time for the passing of the age of religious dogma so that one cannot claim the sudden revelation of the age of inquiry. The booming of the new civilization slowly began to sound louder than the cries of orthodox traditionalism. Darwin's *Origin of Species* was published in the same year in which President Buchanan vetoed the first Morrill bill. That was a long step forward, preceded by a half-century of struggle. W. J. Kerr offers a delightful illustration:

The classic record [of skepticism] is that of the school board at Lancaster, Ohio . . . in 1829. In response to a request for the use of the school building for a discussion concerning the practicability of railroads, the board announced, "You are welcome to use the school house to debate all proper questions, but such things as railroads are impossibilities and rank infidelity. God never designed that His intelligent creatures should travel at the frightful speed of fifteen miles an hour." [12]

In spite of the school board's fears, railroads were to have the right of way. Their expansion is an illustration of the increasing industrialization of the country. Eventually when the East and West were joined by the Union Pacific Railroad, the important incorporation of the road was to occur just one day before the final passage of the Morrill Act. The number of patents each year increased from two hundred in 1820 to thirteen thousand by 1870. Across the length and breadth of the land, the booming of the grist mills was heard. The use of steam power in manufacturing gave rise to the great industrial cities. In the twenty years from 1837 to 1857 the wealth of the country quadrupled and the per capita income more than doubled. The sleeping giant was now sitting up. He was about to stand.

Inevitably, with the pressure of democratic thought and the industrial revolution, the demand for vocational education would start. Farm and labor groups became class conscious and wanted to share the educational wealth. Utilitarianism found no satisfaction in existing patterns of education. "Progress" was a practical concept and needed a practical education to help it realize its aims. In identifying "the only hope" for his beloved South and for civilization as well, Thomas Clemson wrote in 1859:

I have long been of the opinion that the time would surely come, when in this country, more than in any other, the demand for scientific instruction, and that in its highest grade, would be imperative. I have seen the subject rolling on and gathering daily strength, with the diffusion of general information. It appears to me that it would be a consequence of information and reflection. [13]

These were the words of a man who was one of the few reputable scientists of his time.

Chemistry was the first real science of the new age. A few experimentalists were engaged in experimenting with the mysterious. A few stout-hearted men gave a sincere place to research. Occasionally a curious university professor would astound his students and colleagues by the magic of these new devices. But, as one commentator of the passing scene has observed, "when the land grant act was passed, even Harvard taught less botany than is now taught in almost any good high school." [14] Much of the early teaching of sciences was governed by a fear of breaking with orthodox Christianity.

The First Scientific Institutions

In 1802, the establishment of West Point Academy by Congress was the start in a series of collegiate attempts at a more practical curriculum. A handful of colleges, and schools within colleges, in the first half-century became important milestones on the path toward the land-grant institutions. The first application of engineering was military. For a decade it was the only type of engineering practice known. The subject at West Point was confined to fortifications until 1812, when a department of engineering was created with one professor to teach the art "in all its branches." A former commandant, Captain Alden Partridge, established in 1819 the first private engineering institution in an academy at Norwich, Vermont.

By far the most significant step in this direction was taken by an amazingly far-sighted man, Steven Van Rensselaer, who founded an Institute in Troy, New York, in 1824. The benefactor and founder wished to apply "science to the common purposes of life." He wrote, "My principal object is to qualify teachers for instructing the sons and daughters of farmers and mechanics, by lectures or otherwise, in the application of experimental chemistry, philosophy, and natural history to agriculture, domestic economy, the arts, and manufactures. . . ." [15] Begun primarily as an agricultural institute, it developed soon after into the first genuine engineering college. It was a complete break with the traditions of the past and a clear forerunner in many of its aspects of the coming Land-Grant Colleges.

A number of years were to pass before the general movement caught up with the older classical institutions. Finally, in 1846, the Yale corporation established two new professorships—one in agricultural chemistry and animal and vegetable physiology, and the other in practical chemistry. At the same institution in 1859 James B. Sheffield began the school which bore his name. And to Harvard in 1847, Abbott Lawrence left a sizable fortune, giving a place and purpose to the Lawrence Scientific School. By 1862 perhaps twenty institutions could be classified as scientific. In most colleges, however, science was studied for its own sake. With the exception of the several pioneers of the land-grant movement, the colleges treated science in somewhat the same manner as they treated literature—to be studied but not used.

AGRICULTURE BEGINS TO MOVE AHEAD

The movement in agriculture paralleled and often crossed the development of science. The history of agriculture seems to be one of incredible ups and downs. Farm income and interest in farming dip and soar with the changing times and the changing economy. At the beginning of the nineteenth century many felt that agriculture was on the dip side. Henry Adams drew an amazing picture of its sorry conditions:

The plow was rude and clumsy; the sickle as old as Tubal Cain, and even the cradle not in general use; the flail was unchanged since the Aryan exodus; in Virginia, grain was still commonly trodden out by horses. Enterprising gentlemen-farmers introduced threshing machines and invented scientific plows; but these were novelties. Stock was as a rule not only unimproved but ill-cared for. The swine ran loose; the cattle were left to feed on what pasture they could find, and even in New England were not housed until the severest frosts, on the excuse that exposure hardened them. Except among the best farmers, drainage, manures, and rotation of crops were uncommon. The ordinary cultivator planted his corn as his father had planted his, sowing as much rye to the acre, using the same number of oxen to plow, and getting in his crops on the same day. He was even known to remove his barn on account of the manure accumulated around it. . . .[16]

Despite their apparent isolation and ignorance, farmers were not immune to the growing concepts of democracy. Everywhere—in speeches, letters, editorials—they began to voice dissatisfaction with their economic plight, their social inequality, and their political infirmity. When crops failed in 1838, agricultural need became a pressing issue not only to the farmers but to the country as a whole. The period was followed by an amazing economic recovery—the ups and downs of agriculture once again illustrated—and by intense concern over the exhaustion of the soil in the East.

Agricultural scientists joined the exodus to the Continent where the pioneers in agricultural research were already at work. Edward Hitchcock's vivid report in 1851 on what he had seen overseas stirred the imagination of those who wanted to do something but knew not what to do. Limited attempts had been made throughout this period to establish experimental farms and analysis laboratories, but none was comparable to the great Rothamstead station opened in England by private enterprise in 1843.

Farmers, too, wanted education for their children but they had no concept of what the education should constitute. The general idea was there, but few of the specifics. In 1838, Solon Robinson wrote in the *Albany Cultivator:*

We should have . . . in every county and principal town in the United States a well founded agricultural school, in which young men and girls can acquire such an education as will be USEFUL. Not a piano, French, Spanish, or flower daub education, but one that will make the men of scientific farmers and mechanics, and intelligent public officers . . . and the women fit to become the honored wives of such citizens—who will never be ashamed to tell their daughters that they obtained the education that has since been able to render them ornaments to society, in a manual labor school, where, by their daily toil, they earned their daily requirements.[17]

Thus, in an attempt to meet the demand, a large number of manual-labor schools sprung up throughout the country. In 1831, Theodore Weld established the Society for the Promotion of Manual Labor in Literary Institutions.

The first school devoted exclusively to agriculture was established in 1823 as the Gardiner Lyceum in Maine. It closed in 1832 after ten years of valuable work for its time. It was followed by numerous other attempts, particularly in the Northeast. One year after the founding of the Gardiner Lyceum the first publication designed for use in the schools, an Agricultural Reader, appeared in Boston. Its introduction contained the following statement: "Agriculture and the Gospel are the two great instruments of Divine Providence to check the voluptuousness and exercise the virtues of man." [18] Among its other subjects, it contained chapters on lightning rods, brief hints to parents, the way to make money plenty in every man's pocket, the mode of making and refining cider adopted by the religious society called Quakers, and poems on rural felicity and female felicity.

The first mention of the need for agriculture in the collegiate curriculum evidently came in a prospectus of King's College (later Columbia University) as early as 1754. In 1792, the Trustees of

Columbia confessed "the necessity for Professorships of Law; Ancient and Modern History; Natural History; Chemistry; Agriculture, and other arts depending thereon. . . ." [19] And in that same year the New York Legislature granted the college funds for a professorship in agriculture.

This was followed some years later with the bequest of Benjamin Bussey to Harvard College in 1835 for "a course of instruction in practical agriculture, in useful and ornamental gardening in botany, and in such other branches of science as may be tried to promote a knowledge of practical agriculture and the various subservient arts thereto." [20] Because of legal difficulties, nothing resulted from the bequest until 1870. In 1837, the Act chartering the University of Michigan provided specifically for instruction in "practical farming and agriculture." During the decade 1840 to 1850 movements for the teaching of agriculture were well under way in a number of states. Louis Agassiz' popularization of science is credited with great importance in the years following 1848 when he first came to Harvard.

The first half of the nineteenth century witnessed also the spread of local, state, and even national agricultural societies and organizations for the promotion of the interests of agriculture. As early as 1744, Benjamin Franklin had given leadership to the organization of the American Philosophical Society which held agriculture among its concerns and which published articles related to farming. In March of 1785 the first organization in America devoted solely to agriculture was founded in Pennsylvania and became known as the Philadelphia Society for Promoting Agriculture, with its chief purpose being "greater increase of the products of the land within the American States." [21] Articles were printed and prizes offered for experiments, improvements and essays. State organizations, beginning with Massachusetts in 1792 and Connecticut in 1794, became the pattern in many states. The movement came to a head in 1852 with the establishment of the United States Agricultural Society with headquarters in Washington. True estimates that, by this time, there were some 300 active organizations in 31 states and 5 territories, and by 1860 the number had increased to 941 on the books of the United States Agricultural Society.[22] Ross reports, in addition, that the number of agricultural papers reached a score in 1840 and increased to three dozen by 1850.[23] Both the societies, which brought together influential citizens concerned with farm progress, and the papers, which voiced the sentiments then prevalent, were to play an increasingly important role in the concern to "do something" which reached a climax in 1862.

From as early as post-Revolutionary days, sentiment was voiced in favor of Congressional support of agricultural education and "help for the farmer." The state legislatures and the Congress were frequently petitioned in behalf of professorships, schools, or the schemes of men who saw a way to help. John S. Skinner, a long-time editor of agricultural and industrial journals, for instance, in 1848 asked Congress for subsidies to the states for colleges of agriculture and mechanic arts. Congress did not act, but in the meantime the states had adopted a number of varying practices, such as the establishment of state boards of agriculture and appropriations to assist agricultural societies.

Popular support of schemes for agricultural education was not overwhelming. The average farmer had no interest in and was even inclined to oppose efforts to assist him. There was widespread concern over the dangers involved in mixing the practicalities of farming with the prevailing methods of education. The farmer probably did not understand what was intended. We can understand his conclusions by noting what constituted the educational processes of that time. How could one possibly expect to reconcile the methods associated with achieving mental discipline with the down-to-earth toil of the agricultural "artisan"? The farmer's skepticism was not to be conquered until he was given proof in the form of successful and respectable institutions. Such proof was, unfortunately, many years away, in spite of the organizational progress made in several states before the Civil War.

THE FIRST OF THE NEW COLLEGES

A number of agricultural schools and colleges were founded in the decade from 1850 to 1860. A few were successful enough to withstand the difficulties encountered by inadequate funds, some open opposition, and widespread public apathy. Most of these early institutions had disappeared by the time of the passage of the Morrill Act in 1862. Nevertheless, they are important as illustrations of the agitation as well as imagination of the period.

The best known and best conceived project was the People's College in upstate New York. The scheme for its operation brought together all of the incipient ideas of the times. It was initially the result of the vision of Harrison Howard, whose broad charter is described by Ross as follows:

Agriculture, manufactures, and industrial arts were to be organized as a regular part of the course, and every student and teacher was to devote from ten to twenty hours each week "to bona fide useful labor in some branch of productive industry." Women's education was not specifically mentioned in the charter, but the prospectus of the previous year had promised that all studies should be "open equally to both sexes" and that special provision would be made for their instruction in household and industrial arts.[24]

Howard's dream for a central or state college of practical science was sufficiently appealing to attract a number of supporters, not the least of whom was the famous Horace Greeley. In the *Weekly Tribune* of May 11, 1850, Greeley editorialized, "The university shall embrace agriculture as well as mechanical instruction and the farmers should be invited to cooperate in founding it. It should . . . be rendered in time the Model Farm of the State." [25]

Charles Cook of Havana, New York, set a precedent for later land-grant benefactors by providing some of the necessary funds and a farm for a site if the college were to be located in his home town. He was the first of a distinguished long line, including in later years Ezra Cornell of New York, Benjamin Thompson of New Hampshire, and Thomas Clemson of South Carolina, among many others.

Plans and agitation for the People's College reached a climax after almost ten years of spade work when The Reverend Amos Brown was chosen first president and the cornerstone was laid in 1858. It was reported that some eight thousand people attended the opening exercises and were edified by the new president, as well as by Mark Hopkins and Mr. Greeley. Brown's thinking extended far enough into the future to believe that agricultural instruction by itself was not enough; it should and must be combined with liberal studies. But he had little opportunity to practice what he preached. The College, which finally opened in 1860, was forced shut before the end of the first year by the beginning strife of the Civil War. It had served the purpose, however, of attracting attention to a practical plan for agricultural and technical instruction. Its failure was due in part to inadequate private support, which served the additional purpose of making evident the need for public assistance.

The People's College was not alone in its time. One can point to such examples as the Ovid, New York, Academy begun in 1860, and the Farmers' College near Cincinnati, Ohio, founded as early as 1846 and which, according to Ross, "remained a center of agitation rather than demonstration." [26]

During this period, a Michigan dream was about to become a far more important reality. The agitation started in 1849 and reached a first climax in 1850 when, in revising the state constitution, the following provision was added: "The Legislature shall encourage the promotion of intellectual, scientific, and agricultural improvement, and shall as soon as practicable provide for the establishment of an agricultural school . . ." [27] The Legislature did not find it "practicable" until 1855 when the Governor signed a bill creating the first State Agricultural College in the nation. This was a major victory for the farmers, who had been fighting for the establishment of a separate institution in opposition to the many who thought that the teaching of agriculture should be added to the existing state university. The State Agricultural Society played an important and determining role. In 1854 it had taken a stand for a separate college in the fear that agriculture would not receive its due share of attention otherwise. Andrew D. White concluded later that the location of the college in East Lansing was an attempt to keep it far away from the state university. Vocational education was hardly a respectable method for preparing youth for leadership.

At the dedication of the college in 1857, its first president, Joseph R. Williams, gave a remarkably clear picture of the objectives as well as problems. Kuhn summarizes:

Details of the course of instruction would be developed from experience, Williams explained, but its principles were clear. "First, we would begin with the farmer himself . . . Morally, physically, intellectually, he must be a man, before he can be a farmer." Because he is also a citizen, he should be able to execute "the duties of even highly responsible stations, with self-reliance and intelligence." He should be qualified to keep his accounts, survey his land, and speak and write his native tongue "with

ease and vigor." He should be a chemist, a student of physiology, entomology, mechanics, electricity, and the veterinary art. He must learn,
above all, to "subordinate himself, and all animal and vegetable life
around him, to those inexorable laws, moral and physical, the violation
of which meet with swift retribution." [28]

President Williams had only to look about him at the mud and
the desolation to realize that the harsh realities of the situation were
bound to temper any such noble plans. He was certainly not one to
ignore the problems ahead:

We have no guides, no precedents. We have to mark out the Course of
Studies and the whole discipline and policy to be followed in the administration of the Institution. There are numerous Agricultural Schools in
Europe, but while an inspection would afford important vital suggestions,
they would afford no models for us.

Again, the Institution commences here, almost in a virgin forest, to be
subdued and subverted, before it becomes an instrument to maintain the
self-sustaining character of the Institution, or a means of ample illustration. . . .

The want of a permanent endowment will act as a discouragement. In
its infancy, the Institution must rely on the caprice of successive Legislatures. The adoption of a permanent policy requires a stable and reliant
support that will carry it through adversity, regardless alike of the frowns
or smiles of indifference, ignorance, or malice.

Friends and enemies will demand too much and that too early. The
acorn we bury today, will not branch into a majestic oak tomorrow. The
orchard we plant this year, will not afford a harvest of fruit the next.[29]

The important fact was that the acorn was buried. In its first plant-
ing in Michigan, no one could possibly conceive of the majestic oak a
hundred years hence. To each generation in succession, only a few
sproutings would appear important. For the first generation "its
corduroy roads, its chills and fevers" predominated. Beal describes the
first schedule of work:

They rose early in those days. Chapel exercises were at five-thirty A.M.;
breakfast was at, or near, six. Labor for the first section of students began
at six-thirty and lasted till nine-thirty. Meanwhile classes for the other
two sections were going on, beginning at seven A.M. At nine-thirty the
second section went to work, mainly logging and clearing up land. At
twelve-thirty all took dinner, and from one-thirty till four-thirty the third

division labored. After two years, all recitation and lectures ceased by twelve o'clock, and after dinner the manual labor occupied all students for three to four hours.[30]

The requirement for manual labor had been established by legislative law in 1855. It was continued for nearly forty years.

The curriculum was a matter of some hits and many misses. The catalogue of 1861 enumerates its strange mixture of the old and the new.

PREPARATORY

Higher Arithmetics
Physical and Mathematic Geography
English Grammar

Algebra
Natural Philosophy
Rhetoric

COLLEGE COURSE

First year

Geometry
Meteorology
History

Trigonometry & Surveying
Elementary Chemistry
English Literature
Book-keeping

Third year

Drawing and Rural Engineering
Geology
Mental Philosophy

Astronomy
Zoology

Second year

Physics
Vegetable Physiology, Horticulture
Rhetoric

Civil Engineering
Botany, Horticulture, Mineralogy
Inductive Logic

Fourth year

Analytical Chemistry
Animal Physiology
Political Economy

Agricultural Chemistry
Entomology, Veterinary Medicine,
    Economy of Domestic Animals
Agricultural and Geographical Bot-
    any, Technology, Household and
    Rural Economy [31]

One could conclude that a student would be well prepared for a life of farming, until he realizes that the content of many of these courses was ill-defined and sometimes nonexistent. This was just a beginning.

In 1861 the Legislature empowered the faculty to confer degrees for the first time. In that same reorganization of College legislation, the possibility of efforts beyond the confines of the campus was mentioned for the first time. The governing board of the College (the State Board of Agriculture) was authorized to "institute winter courses of lectures for others than students of the institution." Another acorn was planted, from which the oak of extension might later grow.

Across the country in another state, a man was fashioning an institution for the Commonwealth of Pennsylvania. No one person had left his imprint on the early years of the Michigan Agricultural College, but it was Evan Pugh who fought, sometimes alone, for his Pennsylvania scheme. The Pennsylvania Legislature in 1854 had authorized the start of the Farmers' High School which, guided by Pugh, would become a college by 1862. Pugh's ideal plan included "a central college with branch schools in each county, investigation stations in each township, and observers on every farm. The college was to train not only farmers and farmers' wives but research specialists and teachers for the rural schools." [32] Pugh was opposed to manual labor in spite of the prevailing sentiment in its behalf. He wanted an institution which would be professionally scientific in the best known sense of that term. He wanted, too, to combine agriculture and the mechanic arts in one college. He argued, "Both are branches of industrial education, both associate the idea of manual labor and study, and both represent interests so inseparably connected, that it would be most injudicious to separate them." [33]

The venture was a success, in contrast to many of its day. With the passage of the Morrill Act, Pugh led the fight to make this the sole land-grant institution for the Commonwealth.

In certain other states, too, a start had been made. As early as 1825, a four-year Massachusetts Agricultural College had been proposed. The report of Edward Hitchcock recommended the establishment of an agricultural college with some state support. In 1856, the Massachusetts Legislature created the "Trustees of the Massachusetts

School of Agriculture," to be headed by Marshall Wilder, and charged with "holding, maintaining, and conducting an experimental farm and school . . . with all needful buildings, library, apparatus, and appurtenances, for the promotion of agricultural and horticulture art within this Commonwealth." [34] But it remained for the stimulus of the Morrill Act to bring the institution into being.

The movement in Iowa in this period was somewhat typical of the activity in other states of the mid-West. It began two years after Iowa became a state when in 1848 the General Assembly "memorialized Congress for the donation of the site and buildings of Fort Atkinson in Winneshiek County, together with two sections of land, for the establishment of an agricultural college." [35] The state as such, however, did not take action until 1858, when a law was passed appropriating $10,000 and creating a Board of Trustees for the Iowa State Agricultural College and Farm. A location was chosen, but again the actual opening awaited Federal assistance.

In Maryland, on the other hand, the college, established in 1856, actually opened in 1859 on a 428-acre farm some ten miles from Washington. It suffered the same handicaps as Michigan and Pennsylvania. These three, however, became the first triad of a new era in agriculture and the mechanic arts. They were pioneers in every sense of the word. It could not be claimed that the national movement was substantial or widespread. The 1860 census recorded only 3 per cent of 397 American colleges with departments of science and agriculture.

Nevertheless, it was a beginning. In 1860 Thomas Clemson wrote, "Agriculture, therefore, now stands upon a basis far different from what it has hitherto occupied; and not working as we have heretofore, in the dark, but knowing where to look for causes and effects, we may expect the next century to make a stride that will give to this art, or rather convocation of arts, a place among the exact sciences." [36] The sleeping giant had risen to his feet and now began to stretch. He was awake at last.

THE PRECEDENT OF LAND GRANTS

Before concluding this examination of the influences leading to the land-grant concept, we pause at the last to glance at the growing tradition to use land for the stimulus of education. When the Revolutionary days were over and the new nation had become an entity, the American people were concentrated on a thin line along the

Eastern seaboard. To the West, including much of what we now regard as East, lay the national bounty. The United States, as a governmental unit, came into possession of countless acres of land. This was the great national resource. It became the incentive for much of the improvement in life during the first three-quarters of the nineteenth century. It was also the chief component of the public treasury.

Dipping into the public domain to aid a cause as close to the people as education was not a purely American practice. Oxford and Cambridge had received their initial endowment in this fashion. So, too, Gustavus Adolphus had bestowed land and its derived income on the University of Upsala. In America as early as 1618, King James had instructed the Virginia Company "to reserve ten thousand acres in the territory of Henrico, Virginia, of which nine thousand acres were to be used to endow a university, and one thousand acres for a college." [37] Harvard had received a maintenance grant of five hundred acres from the Massachusetts colonial government in 1640, and, in somewhat similar fashion, William and Mary, Yale, Dartmouth, and Princeton were recipients of varying amounts.

The action generally cited as setting a precedent came in 1785 when the Continental Congress inserted in the Northwest Ordinance of May 20th the provision that "there shall be reserved the lot No. 16, of every township, for the maintenance of public schools." Two years later, in the Ordinance of July 13, 1787, appeared a clause which, practically speaking, has become the motto of American education: "Religion, morality, and knowledge being necessary to good government and the happiness of mankind, schools and the means of education shall be forever encouraged." Of this clause Daniel Webster was later to write, "I doubt whether one single law or any lawgiver, ancient or modern, has produced effects of more distinct, marked, and lasting character than the Ordinance of 1787." [38]

In that same year, on July 23rd, Congress wrote into the Bill of Sale to the Ohio Company the provision that "not more than two complete townships . . . be given perpetually for the purposes of an University . . . to be applied to the intended object by the legislature of the state." This date may well be considered the birthday of the state university movement in America. These were the first donations of the nation to higher education. With the precedent once established, the national government continued to grant land for a university in the charter of each of the twenty-one states established before the Civil War, with the four exceptions of Vermont, Kentucky, Maine, and Texas. It is safe to assume that many states would have left to the church the task of higher education had it not been for such a provision.

Indirect educational grants also were made throughout the early nineteenth century. Income from areas reserved for the working of salt springs, swamp lands, Half Million Acre Grants, and the Five Percent Plan, went to education in many states.

The precedent being established, Congress was the recipient of frequent requests for aid in the establishment of universities, seminaries, institutions for the deaf and dumb, and even for the purpose of cultivating tropical plants. Congress seemed to feel, however, that each state, at the time of its admission, had shared in the public bounty. It was the responsibility of the individual state to carry on from there.

Altogether by 1857 sixty million acres of public land had been set aside for the support of common schools. In addition, four million acres had been granted to fifteen states to endow state universities. None of the grants was specific; none included direction as to the purpose or character of the institutions to be aided or established. Nevertheless, it was evident that the national government, by its own action, had placed itself in the business of education. By no means had it adhered strictly to the concept that education was purely the function of state and local governments. It was logical, therefore, for the agitators on behalf of agricultural and industrial education to look to the national government for assistance. The Morrill Act and subsequent Land-Grant College legislation were but a development of a precedent established many years before.

By the middle of the century, it remained only for a few men to crystallize the thinking of the many. The elements were there: a wealthy nation with a new concept of democracy, dissatisfaction with the existing education, the new science, the growth of industry, the precedent of the grants of land, and the urge to help the farmer by realizing some of the potentiality in the relationship of science to agriculture. Two men in particular sensed the national possibilities and were to play the leading roles in shaping the course of the immediate future.

2

The Foundation Stone, 1862

THE Land-Grant College movement may be likened to the growth of a river. At the start it is but a mountain spring. Along its course other springs join it until it begins to resemble something more formidable than the brook. It is fed from the streams of the countryside and becomes a river. But, to be a major means of transportation, it must await the time and the place when it is joined by other rivers. Then the water is ready to carry the devices of men.

We consider first a disappointed schoolmaster and an academic jack-of-all-trades. Jonathan Baldwin Turner, who was early in his clear and insistent demand for a new education.

JONATHAN TURNER

Jonathan Turner's daughter later observed that as early as 1833 her father became interested in extending the opportunities of education to more than the few. In his growing enthusiasm, he began to talk and to write about the need to adapt education to the times and to the people. He coupled this with the writing of exploratory pieces on the relationship of science to farming. Certainly he did not originate the concept of industrial education, but just as certainly he became its loudest and strongest advocate. By the middle of the century his ideas had begun to take shape in a master plan for a state industrial institution in Illinois. He outlined it in full first in a speech given at Griggsville, Illinois, on May 13, 1850. At a meeting in Granville, Illinois, in November 1851, he set forth his thoughts, which were expanded in the published proceedings of the meeting. Favorable re-

23

sponse was immediate. Resolutions were passed. Turner's plan appealed to those who wanted to do something but knew not what to do.

By March of the succeeding year, he was ready to write of a scheme for support through federal land grants. In a letter to the *Prairie Farmer,* he exuded his confidence:

And I am satisfied that if the farmers and their friends will now but exert themselves they can speedily secure for this State, and for each State in the Union, an appropriation of public land adequate to create and endow in the most liberal manner, a general system of popular Industrial Education, more glorious in its design and more beneficent in its results than the world has ever seen before. There is wisdom enough in the State, and in the Union, to plan and conduct it—there are students enough to patronize it—there is useless land and wealth enough to endow it—and there are hearts enough that want it. . . . But let us, by all means, strive together, as one man, for the glorious end of the liberal and appropriate practical education of every class, of whatever name, throughout the State, and throughout the Union.[1]

By 1853, after several more conventions had been held to promote the Turner plan, the Illinois Legislature was ready to respond to the overtures. A set of Industrial League Resolutions were adopted for presentation to the Federal Congress. The resolutions seemed to sum up all the most cogent ideas thus far presented:

Whereas, the spirit and progress of this age and country demand the culture of the highest order of science; and will not continue to increase without calling into requisition all the elements of internal thrift arising from the labors of the farmer, the mechanic, and the manufacturer, by every fostering effort within reach of the government; and Whereas, a system of Industrial Universities, liberally endowed in each State of the Union . . . would develop the people, tend to intellectualize the rising generation and eminently conduce to the virtues, intelligence, and true virtue, intelligence and true glory of our common country; therefore be it resolved. . . . That our . . . Congress be instructed . . . to use their best exertions to secure the passage of a law. . . . donating to each State of the Union an amount of public lands not less in value than five hundred thousand dollars, for the liberal endowment of a system of industrial universities, one in each State in the Union, to cooperate with each other

and with the Smithsonian Institution in Washington, for the more liberal
and practical education of the industrial classes . . .[2]

Horace Greeley was quick to call the legislative action "a notable
step forward" which has "materially hastened the coming of scientific . . . education for all who . . . are willing to work for it." [3]
In spite of the support of thinking men, the Illinois Legislature was
shouting in the dark. It would take more than a resolution to move
Congress. The cry was heeded by some and ignored by many. It
remained an idea for almost a decade, but it is such a worthy idea
that it would be well to examine it more closely.

The Turner Plan

The early pressure for agricultural and industrial education had not
taken into account the possibility of entirely new institutions devoted
to such purposes. Most agitators felt that the existing colleges might
absorb this important new function. As we have noted previously, in
Michigan the Legislature deliberated for some time before ignoring
the existing state university. At the heart of the Turner plan lay a
strong dissatisfaction with the educational institutions of the first
half of the nineteenth century. Turner is quoted as saying that the
old colleges "have hauled a canoe alongside their huge professional
steamships and invited the farmers and mechanics to jump on board
and sail with them; but the difficulty is, they will not embark."
Turner could not imagine a combination of the new with the old.
He dismissed it in scathing terms:

No wonder such educators have ever deemed the liberal culture of the
industrial classes an impossibility; for they have never tried, nor even conceived of any other way of educating them, except that by which they
are rendered totally unfit for their several callings in after life. How absurd
would it seem to set a clergyman to plowing and studying the depreda-
tions of blights, insects, the growing of crops, etc., in order to give him
habits of thought and mental discipline for the pulpit; yet, this is not half
as ridiculous, in reality, as the reverse absurdity of attempting to educate
the man of work in unknown tongues, abstract problems and theories,
and metaphysical figments and quibbles.[4]

In setting forth his ideas for the new education, Turner first took
note of the division of society "into two distinct, cooperative, not

antagonistic classes." The first and the smaller of the two was composed of those "whose proper business it is to teach the true principles of religion, law, medicine, science, art, and literature." But the second class, the much larger one, was far closer to his heart. These were the laborers in agriculture, commerce, and the arts who were in need of educational assistance dealing with the realities of life.

Turner's plan has been called the "common man's educational Bill of Rights." It called for innovations later to be considered essential to the Land-Grant College idea: education for the working man, practical education in the pursuits and professions of practical life, experimentation and research, the college reaching into the community through institutes and lyceums, opportunity to study in almost any subject, the use of land to support the endeavor, the concept of a definite endowment given to each state on an equal basis. Some of these ideas were new; many had grown slowly over a period of fifty years. But here they took shape and relationship. The call went out in the first of three resolutions, all backing Turner, adopted at the Granville convention in 1852: "As representatives of the industrial classes, including all cultivators of the soil, artisans, mechanics, and merchants, we desire the same privileges and advantages for ourselves and our posterity in each of our several pursuits and callings, as our professional brethren enjoy in theirs." [5]

Several states away, in a rural section of Vermont, the ideas of another man were beginning to take shape. A second tributary was about to flow into the mighty river.

JUSTIN SMITH MORRILL

On the third of December, 1855, the man whose name was to become synonymous with a great new system of colleges first walked into the halls of Congress. He came from a small state but his contribution to many affairs in a growing nation were to be large. His influence was felt in as great a fashion in other areas of national concern as it was in the new education. Morrill was a member of the House of Representatives until 1867; thereafter, until his death in 1898, he served in the Senate. Throughout his forty-three years of public service he championed the cause of land-grant education.

By 1840 the movement for vocational education had reached the State of Vermont. Perhaps some of it rubbed off on the country storekeeper. We know that Morrill watched with interest the struggling and nearby Norwich University. He, too, was dissatisfied with the time-honored. In 1848 he described in a letter his feeling that it might be well to "lop off a portion of the studies established centuries ago as the mark of European scholarship and replace the vacancy—if it is a vacancy—by those of a less antique and more practical value." [6] His interest in agricultural affairs had always been strong. By 1856 he was representing his county at the annual meeting of the United States Agricultural Society. It is safe to assume that the growing pressures for a new type of education converged on this man, as it had on so many others, by the mid-fifties.

The fact that the eventual Morrill bill contained some of the Turner language has led many to believe that Morrill was but an instrument for the Turner plan. The 1856 Agricultural Society meeting which Morrill attended was devoted in part to a full discussion of the Turner ideas. We must suppose, therefore, that he was at least acquainted with the Turner plan. There is no record, however, of any intimate relationship between the two. Too many men and too many movements were involved to credit the Land-Grant Colleges to one man. In any case, it was Morrill's political acumen and keen parliamentary ability which brought the legislation into being. As Kandel points out, for instance, the first college bill was never considered by a House committee, was discussed only briefly by two speakers, and soared through the House in almost record time.[7] It was this same leader, too, who would not give up until his measure was finally passed five years after its first introduction, and who attempted continually to assist the first struggling colleges with additional aid in spite of the apathy and opposition of the times. Often in a democracy an idea needs a statesman, if not a politician, and Morrill was the man.

Morrill's Purpose

To attempt to define Morrill's purpose in introducing first his bill of the late fifties and then his successful measure of 1862 is like reading the mind of a man one hundred years after it is made up. Some writers feel that Morrill himself knew not what he thought within twenty years after he thought it. Morrill concluded that a new and vigorous type of education was necessary because of certain conditions:

1. *The rapid dissipation of the public land by donations to local and private interests.* The great public bounty was disappearing—not through any well-organized plan for its investment in projects bringing profitable return to all, but through Congressional indulgence in petty petitions. Soon the nation would have to rely on taxation as its principal source of income. Public lands would be gone. Before it was too late, Congress should cease this wasteful indulgence and make wise use of the remaining lands.

2. *The soil deterioration and wastage engendered by the cheapness and easy acquirement of these lands might be lessened by more thorough and scientific knowledge of agriculture and by a higher education of those devoted to its pursuits.* Morrill had watched the short occupancy of the new settler who gained all he could from the soil and, when it was exhausted, moved on to new land to repeat the process. He felt that if only science could be applied systematically to agriculture, the life of the soil could be prolonged. So, in discussing his first bill, he commented, "We need a careful, exact, and systematized registration of experiments—such as can be made at thoroughly scientific institutions, and such as will not be made elsewhere." [8] To achieve this marriage of science and agriculture, it would be necessary to expose young men to its possibilities in a practical collegiate setting.

3. *The need of a useful education for the man who will use it.* Morrill felt that education should be much closer to the needs of the average man. Looking back, he commented, "The fundamental idea was to offer an opportunity in every State for a liberal and larger education to large numbers, not merely to those destined to sedentary professions, but to those much needing higher instruction for the world's business, for industrial pursuits and professions of life." [9]

4. *The inadequate existing scheme of collegiate education which ignored the needs of farmers and mechanics.* Morrill, the politician, was never one to be caught in stinging criticism of the "existing scheme." In more gentle rebuke than most of his day who joined in his thinking, he was to say:

The object of the laws was not to injure any existing classical institutions, but to reinforce them and bring liberal culture within the reach of a much larger and unprovided for number of the industrial classes in every state. It was designed to largely benefit those at the bottom of the ladder who want to climb up, or those who have some ambition to rise in the world, but are without the means to seek far from home a higher standard of culture. This and more was sought to be accomplished by bringing forward at less cost of time and money, courses of study, and of greater use in practical affairs than those then largely prevailing, which seemed to offer little of lasting value beyond mere discipline imposed.[10]

Morrill was anxious that classes not become stratified in the new society as they had in the old. Equal opportunity to an adequate education would help prevent this. Even the poor boys might attend college by working on neighboring farms.

5. *The fact that several states were quite unable, unless federally aided, to provide adequate educational facilities.* Morrill had in mind a concept which is of great concern to Congress even to our day. It was not one which would be prominent in the debates on the bills, but rather an extension of the concept of equal opportunities.

6. *America must seek to realize what Europe had already demonstrated: the benefits from agricultural and industrial schools.* One of Morrill's chief interests was the protection of American production. He did not want to witness the loss of leadership of a growing nation. This was one way to arrest a disturbing trend. In a speech in 1862 he commented:

Should no effort be made to arrest the deterioration and spoilation of the soil of America, while all Europe is wisely striving to teach her agriculturists the best means of hoarding up capital in the lands on that side of the Atlantic, it is easy to see that we are doomed to be dwarfed in national importance, and not many years can pass away before our ships will be laden with grain not on their outward but homeward voyage.[11]

It must be remembered that Morrill was a practical man, not an educational theorist. His intentions, practical as they might be, were happily combined with theory as he went along.

7. *And politics was not entirely apart from the picture.* Morrill was a good Republican and he recognized early the need of his party to woo and win the agricultural interests. The tariffs had been devised to protect American commerce and industry. Something must be done for the farmer. This he was frank to admit when, in introducing

his first bill, he commented that Congress was quick to protect other interests whereas "all direct encouragement to agriculture has been rigidly withheld." He noted further that "when commerce comes to our doors, gay in its attire and lavish in its promises, we 'hand and deliver' at once our gold. When manufactures appear, with a needy and downcast look, we tender, at worst, a 'compromise.'" His concern for the farmer was a mixture of honest desire and political wisdom.

Morrill was aware of the growing ideas around him. The bills to which he gave his name (the first unsuccessfully and the second triumphantly) were a collation of the most widely accepted plans of his time. He brought together all the ideas in a form which first would be unpalatable to a president and then edible by a majority. Ross has concluded that his effort was "a generalized synthesis of all [of the numerous past proposals], the epitome of two decades of regional agitation and experimentation." [12]

Before attempting to examine the essential elements of this all-important piece of legislation, let us review how it came about. The politics of the situation have bearing on the intent of the legislation and on the success of the venture in the years afterward.

THE UNSUCCESSFUL EFFORT OF THE FIFTIES

Morrill began his efforts in behalf of agricultural colleges within three months of becoming a member of Congress. On February 28, 1856, he introduced the following resolution in the House:

That the Committee on Agriculture be . . . requested to inquire into the expediency of establishing . . . one or more national agricultural schools upon the basis of the U. S. Naval and Military schools, in order that one scholar from each congressional district and two from each state at large, may receive a scientific and practical education at public expense.[13]

The resolution was lost by the objection of a Representative from South Carolina. This was not the scheme which would gather around Morrill the support necessary for passage. It was an early, ill-conceived, and justifiably unacceptable possibility.

The following year, on December 14th, the first Land-Grant College bill was introduced by Morrill: "An act donating public lands

to the several States and Territories which may provide colleges for
the benefit of agriculture and the mechanic arts." The purpose was
to provide

the endowment, support, and maintenance of at least one college in each
State where the leading object shall be, without excluding other scientific or classical studies, to teach such branches of learning as are related
to agriculture and the mechanic arts, as the legislatures of the states may
respectively prescribe, in order to promote the liberal and practical education of the industrial classes in the several pursuits and professions of
life.[14]

There was included a provision for granting, to this end, 6,340,000
acres of the public land, apportioned on the basis of 20,000 acres for
each member of Congress.

By April 20th, Morrill was ready on the floor of Congress to lead
the fight for his measure. In his speech he admitted that the law
might be accused of unconstitutionality, but he pointed to the many
previous efforts of Congress either to protect or promote special interests. He lamented Congressional inactivity in behalf of agriculture.
He pointed to the need for improvement of farming and to the widespread interest of farmers in improvement. He cited the need for field
and laboratory experiments and for special schools for farmers and
mechanics, but was quick to claim that these would not be in competition with the existing literary colleges. He emphasized what
European countries were doing and how, by contrast, America was
dangerously apathetic. Congress, he noted, had already encouraged
education in the states by grants of land, and the states believed the
Federal government was obligated to provide more for worthy purposes. Congressional actions in the past demonstrated that "the power
of Congress to dispose of the public lands at its discretion is plain,
absolute, and unlimited."

The opposition to the measure was swift and pointed. It came
largely from the mid-West and South. Senator Rice of Minnesota
sneered, "We want no fancy farmers; we want no fancy mechanics,"
while Senator Mason of Virginia cried out, "It is one of the most
extraordinary engines of mischief . . . misusing the property of the
country . . . an unconstitutional robbing of the Treasury for the
purpose of bribing the States." Senator Clay felt that "the honest

tillers of the soil (do not) desire the patronage of Congress . . . all
they ask is sheer justice and no favor. They ask that you let them
alone to work out their own progress; that you will keep your hands
out of their pockets."

Despite the opposition, the passage through the House was swift
and sure. The final vote in the Senate on February 7, 1859, was 25 to
22. Eighteen Southern senators and four Northern Democrats were
in the minority.

But it was not that simple. James Buchanan was in the White
House. He is said to have bowed to Southern pressure. His veto
message came back on February 24, 1859. Ross calls it "a classic of
individualistic reasoning." Buchanan found the bill financially in-
expedient because of poor economic conditions, confusing as to the
relationships between the Federal and state governments, injurious
to the new states because of the danger of speculators seizing large
portions of the land, without Federal power to compel the execu-
tion of the trust, prejudicial to the existing colleges because of its
inclusion of science and liberal studies already taught by them, and,
most important of all, unconstitutional because Congress does not
possess the power to appropriate money for education.

Morrill arose immediately in indignation. He spoke again of all
the arguments in its favor; he attempted to counter the President's
opposition. "Many literary universities had already been established
with the approval of James Buchanan. . . . If we can legislate for the
deaf and dumb, may we not legislate for those who can hear and
speak? If we can legislate for the insane, may we not legislate for the
sane?" [15] He asked immediately for the previous question, but it was
to no avail. The veto was upheld by a lack of the necessary two-thirds
majority. In the process, however, Morrill had not lost one supporter.
Thus ended, for the time being, the effort in Congress. Meanwhile,
the pressure was to grow and to be reinforced by the attempts of
several states to accomplish on their own the establishment of the
institutions which Morrill and his supporters so desperately wanted.

THE ACT OF 1862

While Morrill bided his time, the country was changing in such
drastic fashion as to make the opportunity come earlier than perhaps
he dreamed possible. The effect of the Civil War had been felt in

Congress by 1861. The Southerners had withdrawn and with them had gone much of the insistence on the rights of individual states. In a riper time, therefore, Morrill stepped forward once again. On December 16, 1861, a new bill was presented in the House of Representatives.

It was "new" because it contained several substantial changes from the one previously vetoed by Buchanan. The major differences were: (1) the omission of the territories; (2) the increase of the land grant for each member of Congress from 20,000 to 30,000 acres; (3) the exclusion of benefits to States while in the act of rebellion; and (4) the requirement to teach military tactics. This last important feature was an obvious result of Civil War concern. The North had found itself at a strong disadvantage in the first battles of the War because of the Southern superiority of trained officers, a tradition which the South had long emphasized.

The heart of the measure appeared in Section 4:

That the moneys so invested or loaned shall constitute a perpetual fund, the capital of which shall remain forever undiminished (except so far as may be provided in section five of this act), and the interest of which shall be inviolably appropriated, by each State which may take and claim the benefits of this act, to the endowment, support, and maintenance of at least one college where the leading object shall be without excluding other scientific and classical studies, and including military tactics, to teach such branches of learning as are related to agriculture and the mechanic arts, in such manner as the legislatures of the States may respectively prescribe, in order to promote the liberal and practical education of the industrial classes in the several pursuits and professions in life.[16]

The law, in brief, provided that each state was to select first its lands for this purpose from those public lands available within the state. If the amount were not sufficient, then the Secretary of the Interior was directed to issue land scrip "to the amount in acres for the deficiency of its distributive share." The states would sell the scrip and allocate the proceeds entirely "to the uses and purposes prescribed in this act and for no other use or purpose whatsoever." All expenses were to be paid by the states. The moneys so earned should be invested in safe stocks yielding not less than 5 per cent interest, and were to constitute "a perpetual fund, the capital of which shall remain forever undiminished." The state must make up any deficit or loss. Ten per cent of the moneys could be "expended for the purchase of lands for sites or experimental farms," if authorized by the state.

The purpose of the fund was specified as support and maintenance of operation, not buildings. Within five years of state acceptance, at least one college, as provided, should exist or the state must return the funds. An annual report was required to be written and distributed. All states must express legislative acceptance within two years of the enactment.

Morrill, in 1867, gave his own summary:

The bill proposed to establish at least one college in every State upon a sure and perpetual foundation, accessible to all, but especially to the sons of toil, where all the needful science for the practical avocations of life shall be taught, where neither the higher graces of classical studies, nor that military drill our country now so greatly appreciates, will be entirely ignored, and where agriculture, the foundation of all present and future prosperity, may look for troops of earnest friends, studying its familiar and recondite economies, at last elevating it to that higher level where it may fearlessly invoke comparison with the most advanced standards of the world. The bill fixes the leading objects, but properly, as I think, leaves to the States considerable latitude in carrying out the practical details.[17]

Since the bill contained so many features attractive to diverse interests, the support was broad. The agricultural interests were concerned with the possibility of doing something for the farmers. The United States Agricultural Society gave its approval, but it is not clear how forceful and significant this was. Educators and college presidents were ardent in behalf of the bill, because of the educational possibilities and the provision for endowment income. Among those prominent in working for its passage were Marshall Wilder of the Massachusetts Agricultural College, Amos Brown of the People's College, John Kennicott of Illinois, and Evan Pugh of Pennsylvania. The older states were interested in its provision for land. They were anxious to share in the Western wealth. The political leaders saw an opportunity to obtain political support from the farmers. Chief among those who helped Morrill in Congress was Senator Benjamin Wade, described as "a good opportunist, a grand strategist, and a clever tactician [whose] influence was tremendous." [18]

The opposition was vocal, based on two factors—sectionalism and speculation. The South had walked out of Congress so the Morrill Bill fell to a squabble between East and West. The West saw in the passage of the act an Eastern attempt to place valuable land in the hands of speculators. The Western states, still left with large areas of public land, were particularly defensive. They feared the unlimited and unfair character of the Morrill-proposed distribution. More than any other factor, however, they feared the specter of speculation. The Morrill Bill would encourage an already unfortunate situation.

The Senate passed the measure on June 11, 1862, by a vote of 32 to 7. The House concurred on June 19th with 90 in favor and 25 opposed, of whom 21 were from Western states. This, it should be noted, came during one of the darkest hours of the Civil War. It remains a remarkable example of forward-looking legislation in the midst of calamity.

Once again the Land-Grant College bill made its way to the White House. But this time a different man sat in the presidential chair. Some claim that Abraham Lincoln was the product of the forces and traditions which led to the culmination of a long movement in the act itself. As a Whig, Lincoln believed the Constitution to be far more flexible than Buchanan's rigid interpretation. He was not inclined to oppose federal measures for interests close to the common people. Lincoln was a man undoubtedly far ahead of his times, but a new education in agriculture and the mechanic arts had never been one of his strong concerns. Nevertheless, it was a part of the progressive legislative pattern and philosophy to which he gave leadership. He signed the bill on July 2, 1862.

The Morrill Act contains such significance for the colleges and universities which it fostered that it is well now to examine in detail its major provisions.

The Grant of Land

The land feature of the act was of great importance. Some would have us believe that it was the only reason for the legislation and the only guarantee of its passage. Becker calls it "an ordinary political bargain—give us a share-plus in the public lands, and we will give you your agricultural colleges." [19] It is important to note, however, that land was practically the only endowment which the Federal government could bestow at the time. There were no funds to be set aside for collegiate education in the states. The land-grant, therefore, was essential to the whole scheme of providing for a new education. In a sense, the government acted as a real estate promoter. It was anxious to find settlers to occupy the public surplus property. In the same year as the passage of the Morrill Act, Congress had passed the Homestead legislation which transferred approximately 234 million acres to private ownership. This, too, had important implications for agriculture. Through it, the owner-occupied family farm became the pattern of the West.

The method of distribution of public land emerged as the controversial feature of the Morrill legislation. It broke precedent with previous grants by its varying method of distribution according to the population (considered a barometer of the needs) of the individual states. It provided also definite conditions and supervision in the expenditure of the funds derived.

The Morrill land-grant amounted to 17,430,000 acres and is reported to have realized a sum of $7,545,405. In the year 1953, the states received an income totalling $1,774,666 from the original grants. The funds thus derived represent today a tiny portion of the total income, but their significance in the years following 1862 cannot be overlooked. Other provisions of the Morrill Act may have been of more lasting importance, but without the land feature the passage of the act and the establishment of many of the resulting colleges would have been impossible.

"The Industrial Classes"

We have noted the slowly changing structured society of the nineteenth century. We have seen how education was limited to the aristocratic and professional—the clergyman, physician, and lawyer. In contrast, all others were a part of a vast laboring group which included farmers, mechanics, artisans, and pure laborers under the nomenclature of "industrial classes." Jonathan Turner had used the term to designate those who were not professional. In his later years, Morrill was to claim that the new education was not intended to be limited only to the laborer:

It was to be a liberal education for the industrial classes, and the professions also, and nothing less can be a legal compliance with the terms of

the original act. The offer of great advantages to the industrial classes to
seek a higher education was manifestly not to exclude them or any others
from Land Grant Colleges, even if they proposed to train their faculties
for any of the "professions." [20]

Ross concludes that the term "industrial classes" was a general
designation for "all groups of the educationally underprivileged. And
this objective applied to social no less than to economic disparity." [21]
For our time the term is not a good one, but it was accepted without
question in the 1860s. In the twentieth century, the social and economic disparity has disappeared to a large extent. It is true that
many, if not all, of the present day land-grant institutions serve the
farmer and the laborer but it is principally because they are citizens
eligible for equal opportunity. Thus the Morrill Act did not create
overnight the true democratization of education, but, like many other
features, it gave the impetus so badly needed.

Educational Intentions

In any discussion of the educational intentions of the Morrill Act,
it is well to recognize that the word "college" in 1862 was synonymous with practically all instruction above the level of the common
schools. In most communities high schools did not exist. Private
academies were furnishing the instruction, but no attempt was made
to reach a majority of the youth.

President Day has concluded with many others that "Morrill himself was quite indefinite about the educational purposes of the legislation until he was well along in years and had had time to organize his
memory." [22] On the floor of Congress during the discussions of the
bill, there was infrequent mention of the educational provisions or
even of what was contemplated educationally. Kandel observes:

It is no depreciation of the merit of Senator Morrill's service to education
to say that he builded better than he knew. Whatever his motives in
undertaking the advocacy of the measure to secure federal aid for agricultural education, it is difficult to resist the opinion that he had no
definite picture in mind of the kind of institution that he was helping to
build up. Indeed, the whole subject of agricultural education and policy
forms but a meagre portion of the many hundreds of pages given to the
discussion of the subject of federal aid for colleges of agriculture and
mechanic arts.[23]

We shall have to trust to Morrill's honesty in later years to discover what he intended in the establishment of such colleges. In an interview with the faculty of Sheffield Scientific School at Yale in 1867, he commented that he did not expect the colleges to be "agricultural schools," but schools of science as distinct from the existing classical colleges. They were not to be institutions of lower grade or academies. By 1888 he found the opportunity in an address before the Vermont Legislature to outline in full what he had wanted and still desired:

Only the interest from the land grant fund can be expended, and that must be expended, first—without excluding other scientific and classical studies—for teaching such branches of learning as are related to agriculture and the mechanic arts—the latter as absolutely as the former. Obviously not manual, but intellectual instruction was the paramount object. It was not provided that agricultural labor in the field should be practically taught, any more than that the mechanical trade of a carpenter or blacksmith should be taught.

Secondly, it was a liberal education that was proposed. Classical studies were not to be excluded, and, therefore, must be included. The Act of 1862 proposed a system of broad education by colleges, not limited to a superficial or dwarfed training, such as might be had at an industrial school, nor a mere manual training, such as might be supplied by a foreman of a workshop, or by a foreman of an experimental farm. If any would have only a school with equal scraps of labor and of instruction, or something other than a college, they would not obey the national law . . .

Whatever else might be done . . . scientific and classical studies, as already stated, were not to be excluded, were, therefore, to be preserved, and this is set forth at the very starting point, but the national bounty act brought to the front "branches of learning related to agriculture and the mechanic arts"—learning in the broad fields of the practical sciences, and none are broader than those related to agriculture. The useful was to have greater prominence in the eyes of students, as it will have in all their after-life, and not stand unequal and shame-faced even in the presence of ancient literature.[24]

The act represented, therefore, for the first time, a collegiate attempt to combine the liberal with the vocational. It was not to be done at the expense of the existing system and philosophy:

I would not diminish by a hair's breadth the prestige or prosperity of our other State institutions of liberal learning. They are in a large sense kinsmen and co-workers in the same field in behalf of humanity, and no one of them could fail to be harmed by the depreciation of any other . . . By no means was it designed to curtail the usual extent of a collegiate education, but to add thereto such essential and practical sciences as were then almost universally neglected by literary colleges, although indispensable to the advancement of the American people in their industrial and diversified life.[25]

Intelligence would be combined with daily labor in such a way as to make life more pleasant, more meaningful, and of greater service. The emphasis was largely on agriculture; little or nothing was said of the mechanic arts.

Many historians have pointed out with some amazement the lack of substantial discussion of the educational provisions of the act. By 1862 the need for agricultural and mechanical instruction was accepted. The arguments centered only about the method of meeting the need. The purposes of the subsequently emerging institutions evolved *from* the legislation rather than being specifically provided *within* it. No man alone could envisage the magnitude of the scope and task of the coming Land-Grant Colleges. The colleges were, rather, the result of thought and action, of experiment and direction over a period of years. Each man would contribute to the movement in his own time and in his own way.

Something for Agriculture

Coupled with the concern over equal educational opportunity for the farmer's son was the more realistic distress over agricultural conditions. Farm lands were being stripped quickly of their fertility and usefulness. The soil was rapidly exhausted of plant food because of inadequate conservation knowledge. The Morrill Act became a popular measure not only to do something for the farmers but for farming. The possibilities of growing scientific thought being applied to the age-old problems of agriculture were enticing. Congress, too, had submitted to the pressures of business and commerce. The business interests were obviously favored, and this distressed not only the agriculturists but the political leaders who wanted to please them.

The Morrill Act proved an attractive combination of high-minded help and political expediency.

The concern for agriculture is demonstrated also by the establishment of the United States Department of Agriculture in the same year as the passage of the Morrill Act. It may be assumed that the same general movement was responsible. Thus, together, the Land-Grant Colleges and the Federal Department were to grow, prosper, and serve increasingly well.

The Mechanic Arts

When the Morrill Act was before Congress, American industry had only begun to develop. The production of raw materials, grains, cotton, lumber, and minerals was the chief enterprise. The engineer of that day was more concerned with construction than with industry. The technical colleges then in existence prepared the student mainly for such type of work. Pearson reviewed the meaning at mid-century of the terms "engineering" and "mechanic arts" and concluded, "If Senator Morrill really intended that work in mechanic arts or engineering in land grant institutions should represent the highest and best, and that these institutions should help to train leaders, then in his day it would have been a mistake to have used the term 'engineer' or 'engineering,' and it was right to use the term 'mechanic arts'. . . ." [26]

Pearson based his conclusions on a study of the dictionaries of the time. Worcester's dictionary of 1855 stated that an engineer is "one who constructs engines and cannons," and a civil engineer is "one who constructs canals, docks, railroads, etc." Webster's dictionary of 1862 referred to an engineer first as a military engineer and then added that engineers were also employed in delineating plans and superintending construction of other public works, as aqueducts and canals. Such men were called civil engineers. If Morrill had used the term "engineering" rather than "mechanic arts," he would have intended largely military engineering "and beyond that a very narrow field in modern engineering" as we know it.

Since Morrill's interests were agricultural and since his later speeches dealt with agricultural education, we have little on which to base a conclusion regarding his mechanic arts intentions. Presumably he was acquainted with the work of such existing schools as Rens-

selaer, West Point, Norwich, and others which had begun to make
their appearance. He knew also the failures of the Civil War, and he
had watched the slowly developing industrial revolution in its early
stages. Obviously he could not foresee the coming great demand for
engineering skills and training. There were those who argued, too, that
he intended mere manual training. By 1909, however, the land-grant
Association had concluded otherwise in a resolution stating, "That it
is the sense of this association that the national laws which constitute
the charter of the land-grant colleges, distinctly prescribe work of collegiate grade in agriculture and mechanic arts, including engineering
in all its branches and the science related to industries. . . ." [27] The
final definition of mechanic arts awaited the extensive growth of the
curriculum and the demands of the times upon the colleges.

". . . and including military tactics"

The requirement of military tactics had not been included in Morrill's original bill of the late 1850s. Presumably it had occurred to no
one. But the days of 1862 were different. The first battle of Bull Run
had been fought in 1861. Then, while the East and West fought the
political battle of sectionalism and speculation in Congress, the North
and South fought the military battle at Fort Henry and Fort Donel-
son in Kentucky, and at Pea Ridge and Shiloh. On June 6, 1862,
while Morrill was making his major speech in favor of the legislation,
McClellan was engaged in his Peninsular Campaign. Morrill pointed
to "that military drill our country now so greatly appreciates."

The lessons of the Civil War had been bitter. The lack of Northern
military knowledge, experience, and leadership had been astounding.
Few were fit to become officers, and the troops were to suffer from
incompetence and inexperience. The "educated soldier" was needed
badly. Those who had experience were not educated; those who were
educated had no experience. The nation was possessed of neither the
funds nor the philosophy to support a large standing army. Morrill's
plan was intended to fill the gap without creating the cost or violating
the tradition. He called it "military schooling" for those whose
principal occupation would be to serve the peaceful arts. Should the
need arise again, the kind of tragedy which the North had experienced
might be averted.

As in all else, Morrill could not be expected to see much beyond his present. He "builded better than he knew."

Relations with the States

The fact that Congressional action was the stimulus to the establishment of many of the Land-Grant Colleges and Universities is an indication of their national character. Morrill frequently mentioned their potential value to the national welfare. If they had been intended as engines of the state alone, Congress would not have acted in their behalf. Their purpose and nature were of national concern and significance. National land was used as a kind of educational trust to supply their beginning endowment. The economy and the quality of agriculture and the mechanic arts were and are of national concern. No state could ever exist of and by itself, producing and consuming its own food and materials for living. Military tactics was provided to benefit and defend the nation as a whole. Each, then, of the features of the Land-Grant College bill was designed to benefit the United States, not just the single state.

In spite of this national origin and character, however, the majority of the Land-Grant Colleges as established became essentially state institutions. They continue to be integral agencies of the state government. Thus the intent of the Morrill Act was in keeping with the American tradition for local control of education which had begun in the isolated communities of the raw frontier and had been reinforced by the Constitution.

The state was expected to adapt the nationally-sponsored college to local conditions. Professor Brewer reported Senator Morrill as saying, "The general wants and local conditions were very different in the different towns and for the best use of this fund there must be much variety allowed in the details, although all the colleges should be the same in spirit and essentially in grade, that is, colleges in which science and now classics should be the leading idea." [28] Relatively simple obligations were put upon the states, and these, again, in outline only. The college must teach agriculture, mechanic arts, and military tactics among its offerings. It must not exclude other scientific and classical studies. The South Dakota Supreme Court in 1933 was to render the opinion that the college had authority to teach any subject not specifically forbidden by state law, but the state had a moral and legal obligation through the Morrill Act to teach agriculture, mechanic arts, and military tactics.

The state must protect the funds derived from the grants of land so that the capital remains undiminished. This, according to the Klein study, "carried the far-reaching implication of future financial support by the State governments themselves." [29] Since no funds were to be used for construction or maintenance of buildings, the states accepted the implied obligation to make such provisions.

Another simple responsibility was the rendering of an annual report of operations and progress and an accounting of the Federal funds received. Finally, in order to be eligible, the state must enact enabling legislation pledging itself to these ends. This was the outline; nothing more was intended or required. There was omitted even a provision for fixing standards. The states were free to move within this bare framework.

The action of the Federal Congress and the requirement of specific acceptance by the states has been a healthy influence in controlling the number and character of colleges of agriculture and mechanic arts within each state. These subjects had been concentrated by governmental directive and not left to develop and spread by inadequate attempts to meet the need.

In spite of its apparent looseness, the Morrill Act did go beyond previous grant legislation, with its specific establishment of the type of college, something of the curriculum, and details for the management of funds. The next step would have been to set the standards. Ross credits the traditions of state rights and the practices of frontier individualism with causing a lack of sufficient sentiment for centralization to make it possible. The wonder is that so little was fixed. Congress could have bowed to the pressures of special interests. An article in the *North American Review* in 1867 commented on the advantage of freedom from restraints:

Many persons, aiming to benefit the industrial classes, would have insisted on some particular form of institution to be adopted in every State, and would have hampered the bill with objectionable features. . . . Even if there were no danger that . . . extravagances . . . would find place in legislation, it would not have been surprising if a spite had been shown against Latin and Greek, or a predilection for manual labor, or a determination that a farm should in all cases be secured. Some advisers would have thought it essential that the general government, in providing the endowment, should perpetually exercise the right of inspection or direction. Military men might have been tempted to insist on a military organization for the discipline of students. But all such objectionable restrictions are happily omitted from the act of Congress.[30]

No provision was made for a racial division of students. With the subsequent offer to and acceptance by returning Southern states, the funds went to white institutions. Four Southern states set aside part of the endowment for Negro Land-Grant Colleges. The rest were to ignore the Negro until forced to change in 1890.

The Significance and Effect

The passage of the Morrill Act met with no burst of enthusiasm except, perhaps, in the already existing and feeble agricultural colleges which saw in it their principal hope for salvation. Educational circles generally, however, were indifferent. There was not a single reference made to it in the proceedings of the American Institute for Instruction during the sessions of 1862 and 1863. Becker sums up the reaction of the times:

It is scarcely an exaggeration to say that in 1862 the Morrill Act was less well known as a land grant college act than as a land grant grab act . . . even the avowed friends of agricultural education found singularly little to say in commendation of the Morrill Act. It was in no sense played up in the newspapers, or even much commented upon in the agricultural journals. . . . As late as 1891 the founders of Poole's *Index to Periodical Literature* could find no more than six articles on the subject that were worth listing. . . . Horace Greeley . . . could only say that the act would have been worth while if even five states took advantage of its provisions.[31]

It remained for the institutions created by it to prove its value. According to James, it marked "the beginning of one of the most comprehensive, far-reaching . . . schemes for the endowment of higher education ever adopted by any civilized nation." [32] And Morison and Commager were to call it "the most important piece of agricultural legislation in American history." [33] But these were later opinions. Proof was necessary first.

We can come in retrospect to some conclusions on its significance and effect. It forced education to fit the changing social and economic patterns of an expanding nation. It helped to create equality of educational opportunity by offering education at public expense to the industrial classes; it gave some measure of dignity to the vocations pursued by such classes. It placed science in relation to everyday work. It provided a marriage certificate for agriculture and engineering, of which W. M. Riggs was later to remark, "Their progeny is now too multitudinous, and their mutual responsibilities too heavy for either of them ever to turn longing eyes to the divorce courts." [34] In this marriage it began, too, the movement toward equality of studies so necessary for education to meet the changing times. With its vocational emphasis, it forced education to conform to the growing American outlook of utilitarianism. Finally, it gave birth or renewed life to sixty-nine institutions of higher education during the course of the following fifty-four years.

Andrew D. White later would claim, "In all the annals of republics, there is no more significant utterance of confidence in national destiny out from the midst of national calamity." [35] The Foundation Stone had been laid.

3

The Struggle, 1863-1879

THE Morrill Act was an educational revolution, but not of the kind to happen overnight. It would take almost one hundred years to complete. It would be accomplished in periods of twenty years more or less. We shall now examine the first period—the most difficult, the least rewarding: the struggle.

The Civil War in America was followed by a period of unprecedented growth. Although some of the frontier was still to be conquered, the growth was not so much in land and territory as in "things." In a short period of time the War had both dislocated and unified the nation. The South would take several generations to recover, but the North and the West were ready to blossom.

In this strange period of "things," the occupation of Western land was completed and with it came a remarkable expansion of transportation facilities. In 1860 only 30,000 miles of railroad track had been constructed in the entire country. By 1890, when the peak had been reached, 163,000 miles of track stretched from coast to coast and connected thousands of hitherto isolated communities and states. Then came the human flood from Europe. The population increased by five million from immigrants alone. The number and size of cities increased tremendously. With cheap labor available, with a demand for goods, and with rapid transportation now possible, industry flourished. Factories jumped in number and size, and out of industry and transportation came the growth of large corporations. The organization of labor started in a movement of lasting significance to the character of the "industrial classes."

The "boundless" resources of mine, land and forest were to be ex-

ploited in such drastic fashion as to make them bounded within a
short time. In the North and West agriculture would respond, too, to
the material growth. In the ten years from 1860 to 1870 alone, the
population of the grain states jumped over 40 per cent. Over 297,000
square miles (an area said to equal that of France and Great Britain)
were added to the lands under cultivation throughout the country.
With transportation easier and with a reduction in freight rates, farm
produce began to move beyond the immediate area. For the first time,
farmers started to serve a national and even worldwide community on
a large scale. All would not be prosperity, however. At least three extended panics or depressions were to occur in the twenty-five years
from 1873 to 1898. With all the rapid growth and intercommunica-
tion, it was natural for provincialism to melt away. Nationalism was
to rise in its place. The prerogatives of the Federal government were
extended into such areas as interstate commerce, conservation, and
sanitary conditions.

Into this time of renewed and greatly strengthened materialism and
utilitarianism came the Land-Grant Colleges. They emerged in time
to collide with the new demands on education to meet a rapidly
changing America. Rogers observes, "This period, roughly from 1860
to 1890, might well be called the critical period in American higher
education, for the rapid transformation of society rendered obsolete
much of the older learning, producing new and strident demands for
a new education for the new world." [1] Hardly able to crawl, much less
walk, the Land-Grant Colleges would soon be asked to justify their
existence in the light of society's needs in the same manner as were all
colleges of the times. On assuming his duties as president of Yale in
1871, Noah Porter was to speak of the "breeze of public interest and
public criticism which is now blowing so freshly through the halls of
ancient learning." [2] The national changes and demands would be too
rapid for the slow-moving education. It would take all the strength of
the Land-Grant College to survive with their new concepts of education, much less attempt to fill all the requests made of them. They
were born in a period of turmoil and change; it is a wonder their childhood was not even more unhappy and frustrated.

ACCEPTANCE AND FORM

Scarcely two months after President Lincoln had affixed his signature to the Morrill Act, Iowa became the first state to accept its conditions. Vermont followed a month later and Connecticut by the end of 1862. Fourteen states passed legislation in 1863, three in 1864, one in 1865, six in 1866, four in 1867, three in 1868, one in 1869, and two in 1870. By the end of the eighth year after its passage, thirty-seven states had agreed to establish state-sponsored teaching of agriculture, mechanic arts, and military tactics.

Controversy and bitterness characterized the fight which followed in practically every state. Though the new subjects lacked "academic respectability," there were many interested in the bank account which accompanied them. Pressures were exerted in at least three directions —to establish the new curriculum as a part of an existing private institution, or as a part of an existing state university, or within a new and separate college. The presence of an ill-equipped, poorly managed, and entirely classical private or church college was a signal for its supporters to conclude that here, of course, was the logical recipient of the national funds. In some states when it appeared that no one denominational institution had sufficient strength in the state legislature to gain the designation, the private colleges banded together to propose a division of the funds among all. Harried and desperate in 1864, Evan Pugh in Pennsylvania commented, "That Literary Institutions should, with such undignified haste, grasp at resources . . . to which they had not the slightest legitimate claim, is a melancholy illustration of the terrible extremities to which they are driven in the struggle for existence." [3]

Equally strong in some states was the demand that the courses be added to the curriculum of the existing state university. This, it was pointed out, would save funds, promote efficiency of management, and concentrate the state's interests in higher education. The farmers and mechanics, for whom the new education was obviously intended, would gain from the contact with the literary and classical. The friends of agricultural education rallied immediately to counter with the argument that the state university had shown little interest in these new fields until the possibility of funds loomed on the legislative horizon. They concluded that the new education would succeed only in an institution devoted solely to its promotion with proper facilities and staff.

With the possibility of the founding of a college in their midst, local communities began to fight over the location of the new institutions which were to be separate. In Illinois alone at least fifteen different communities and agencies were said to be at work to secure the benefits. Observing it nationally, Ross commented, "The location of these colleges, whether as divisions of established or as new institutions, involved political and regional logrolling which differed mainly in the degree of crassness and discrimination." The end results of the arguments over location were the reason why many Land-Grant Colleges eventually found themselves off the beaten track—on a hillside or a plain far from the centers of population and commerce. The location in Massachusetts, New York, Maine, Virginia, Illinois, Indiana, and Colorado are examples. An interested farmer or an ardent community effort often prevailed.

The initial scramble was the cause, too, for a great variety of resulting patterns of organization and affiliation within the land-grant scheme. In general, three plans were followed: assigning funds to a private or church-related college, or to a state university, or establishing a new and separate institution. Individual instances varied widely. In general classifications only, the grant went to these institutions already established or just beginning to operate by 1862:

Five private colleges
  Rutgers in New Jersey
  Vermont (with agriculture as a state supported college)
  Sheffield at Yale (from 1863 to 1895)
  Brown in Rhode Island (until 1892)
  Massachusetts Institute of Technology (for mechanic arts)

Eight state universities or colleges
  Georgia
  Tennessee
  Delaware
  Missouri
  Wisconsin
  Minnesota
  Florida
  Louisiana

Four agricultural colleges founded by the state
  Michigan

Pennsylvania
Maryland
Iowa

Within the period from 1862 to 1879, the general pattern continued:

One private college
Cornell in New York (a combination of state and private)

Eleven state colleges or universities
Massachusetts
Kentucky
Maine
New Hampshire (affiliated with Dartmouth until 1893)
Illinois
California
West Virginia
Nebraska
Arkansas
Ohio
Nevada

Eight separate agricultural and mechanical colleges
Colorado
Mississippi
Kansas
Oregon
Purdue in Indiana
Texas
Alabama
Virginia

Six separate colleges for Negroes
Alcorn in Mississippi
Lincoln in Missouri
Arkansas
Alabama
Prairie View in Texas
Kentucky

Thus the variations continued, until today the sixty-nine land-grant institutions may be divided into three general and somewhat arbitrary classifications: thirty-two state or territorial universities, twenty colleges or universities separate from the state university, and seventeen institutions primarily for Negroes.

In almost all states, the institutions were separated from the existing state government organization. A separate board of trustees was created, responsible to the state administration and legislature. This was a significant action in the early days. Historically, by and large, it has prevented political control and influence and has kept state-supported higher education sufficiently isolated from the machinations of changing political regimes.

The Land Endowment

The dreams of Turner, Morrill, and their supporters of a sufficient endowment for the new colleges were soon to be shattered. The congressional opponents who argued speculation could have the satisfaction of knowing that, though they lost in 1862, they won in the years immediately following. In order to support the new colleges or the new curriculum in existing colleges, the states had to have the funds. The Morrill Act had provided that only the interest could be used, so the movement began to turn the scrip into immediate cash. The Homestead Act, passed also in 1862, had bestowed land without charge upon settlers. The Morrill Act restricted the type of sale to be made. A buyer's market was created with speculators dominating the small group really interested. With few exceptions, the states couldn't delay. Some were swindled; others suffered from lesser degrees of poor management. Few realized what they had hoped. Undoubtedly this situation of speculation and waste, of disappointed advocates, of meager endowment, was one of the chief causes of the struggle for survival within the years to follow.

What to Teach

The first and most basic problem confronting the newly established institutions was a decision on the curriculum. The example of the pioneer European schools would not suffice for a different and expanding country. Of course there was Michigan as a faltering example, but Michigan was struggling in the dark, too. In spite of this, the Michigan policies were copied widely and not infrequently the first duty of a new president was to travel to East Lansing to observe and note.

We have seen that curricular changes were not widespread in the first two-thirds of the nineteenth century. Science had not yet established a place. The methods of teaching in general had not changed. But the purposes of the new institutions were different. The question on the minds of all associated with them was simple: How could they accomplish their objectives? They were there to promote the welfare of the farmer and the mechanic by relating education to daily life. They were there to promote the scientific interests of agriculture so that it might more fully benefit the nation. They were there to bring education to the masses without sacrifice of quality. But, in terms of course offerings, how? Institutional objectives were clear, but curricular details were not.

The first presidents and faculties were handicapped immediately by a lack of clear understanding of the educational intentions of the Morrill Act. Educational administrators were not yet ready to travel distances for group conferences on curricular objectives. An article in the *North American Review* in 1867 lamented:

We cannot but regret that an educational problem so important as that which is involved in the establishment of these National Schools of Science is to be settled, at any rate for a time, with so little comparison of views among the educators of the country, and so little discussion of the principles of mental training . . . there is no public conference of scholars or statesmen respecting the legitimate scope of the institutions; no inquiry in regards to the wants of this country or the experience of others; no sharp and clear announcement even, in the act of Congress which confers the grant, of the character to be aimed at in the new establishments; no thorough discussion in the periodicals of the day respecting the changes which are possible and desirable in the national education. . . .[4]

Only one aspect was clear and not to be denied: the college must teach agriculture and the mechanic arts, as well as military tactics. It must include these, but on the other hand it might include any others. Liberal studies were not to be omitted, probably as a concession to the prevailing opinion that these constituted the only true education. Beyond these basic essentials there was nothing fixed, nothing settled. Presidents and faculties knew only that they didn't want to carry over the traditional, classical education against which they were rebelling. The early thinking was, then, largely a negative reaction.

The nineteenth-century liberalism, of which Andrew D. White, first president of Cornell University, was among the vocal champions, was based on the belief that "there existed a body of abstract truth, an objective verity which might be grasped by men if only they would seek it unceasingly." [5] This was coupled with the confidence that man, the human animal, had the intelligence and skills to find and understand such truth. The liberal approach was to become the basis of Land-Grant College teaching, even though it would take years to formulate and systematize. From the beginning, the break from the orthodox was desired and attemped.

In an early letter to White, Professor Goldwin Smith of England urged the new colleges to consider themselves not bound by tradition and free to set their own educational pattern. He said:

I know too well the difference between the old and the new world. At least the only advice I should give you would be—without ignoring the educational experience of Europe, to act quite independently of it, and to remain uninfluenced either in the way of imitation or of antagonism, by our educational institutions or ideas. The question of academical education on this side of the water is mixed up with historical accidents and with political struggles to which on your side there are happily no counterparts. . . . What I would say is—adapt your practical education, which must be the basis of the whole, to the practical needs of American life, and for the general culture take those subjects which are most important and interesting to the citizen and the man.[6]

White became the effective spokesman for "an industrial, scientific, and general education suited to our land and time." To suit the land and time meant to take cognizance of the rapidly expanding economic life. As a result, a belief in the validity and wisdom of vocational education at the college level began to emerge. Looking back years later, Eugene Davenport recalled, "We called it the 'New Education' in those early days as distinct from the traditional. In the narrowness of our enthusiasm we called it practical and useful as distinct from the classical and useless. For of what good is it when a man can say 'I am hungry' in six or seven languages, but cannot earn his own bread and butter?" [7]

Even the rapidly growing conviction for the *useful* as against the *useless* led to disagreement. On the one hand, there were those who thought it meant a "trade" education with emphasis on such handicrafts as blacksmithing and carpentry. Out of this would grow the emphasis on manual labor as integral to the college schedule. On the other hand, there were those who held it should be strictly "higher" education, with the new subjects taught by methods similiar to the old. This, it was thought, would give the new subjects academic respectability. The inevitable result was a new and strange combination of the two. The evidence of eventual extension of the university idea from one extreme to the other can be noted in the modern Land-Grant College with its highly specialized graduate school and its thoroughly practical short course. Both extremes, and all that lay between, came to have an important place in the land-grant scheme. This would serve well the college of the future.

The new education was to differ from the old not only in subjects offered but in the approach to the subjects. Instead of memory and rote, the power of observation was encouraged. Instead of acceptance, the power of reasoning. Instead of dogmatism, conclusions based on practice. The new educators were convinced that such an approach was more conducive to mental discipline than the outmoded method of the traditional college. The transactions of the Illinois Farmers' Association in defending the colleges summarized the new thinking: "The most natural and effectual mental discipline possible for any man arises from setting him to earnest and constant thought about the things he daily does, sees and handles and all their connected relations and interests." [8] The student, it was believed, would gain far more from his study if it were related to those subjects and objects which interested him, rather than to literature and language long since dead.

In spite of the free thinking of the period, the new colleges had to depend heavily upon the old, both for subjects and for faculty. Until they could evolve a body of truth in the new sciences and until they could graduate their own teachers, they were bound in no small measure to that from which they wished to break. The mixture was so strange that by 1873 President Anderson of Kansas State College was led to observe, "Whatever else yet need to be tried there is no use of repeating the experiment of flying a literary kite with an agricultural tail, so often made in various quarters." [9] Again the result was integration—the liberal would be combined with the practical not only in the same college but in the same classroom.

Since Turner and Morrill had already stressed the need to do something for the industrial classes, and since they referred frequently to the individuality of the farmer and mechanic's son, the new education already had its basis in an emphasis on the student rather than the subject matter. The Land-Grant Colleges even in their earliest years, did as much to discover the individual in educational method as did any other single force. So White was to exclaim in 1869, "Make your student a master-farmer, or a master-mechanic; but make him also a master-man." [10] And the Trustees of the Ohio Agricultural and Mechanical College in their second annual report, published in 1873, expressed the earnest desire not just "to educate those confided to them simply as Farmers or Mechanics, but as men, fitted by education and attainments for the greater usefulness and the highest duties of citizenship."

The *American Agriculturist* in 1867 urged the colleges to start simply and to move slowly:

Set a number of earnest men, capable of teaching agriculture, down upon a good farm, with a good large house and barns upon it, and the cooperation of a good farmer; put up a few temporary buildings, if need be, for lecture rooms now, and perhaps for stables by and by; give the Faculty a little money to spend upon books, apparatus and fitting up; let them know that they shall have more as fast as they can show results; let all permanent improvements be made with a view to the future and leave the Faculty as unhampered in regard to matters of instruction and discipline as possible, and success of the most gratifying character will be almost certain in any State of the Union.[11]

In many colleges this is exactly what happened. The 1875–77 catalog of Kansas State listed typical "industrials" of a purely practical nature, including The Farm, The Nursery, Carpentry, Cabinet Making, Turning, Wagon-Making, Painting, Blacksmithing, Dress-Making, Printing, Telegraphy, Scroll-Sawing, Carving, Engraving, and Photography. Not all colleges were this intensely practical. Cornell presented its high aims in a description of the "Features of the University" contained in the First General Announcement of 1867:

First. Every effort will be made that the education given be practically useful. The idea of doing a student's mind some vague general good by studies which do not interest him, will not control. The constant policy will be to give mental discipline to every student by studies which take practical hold upon the tastes, aspirations and work of his life.

Second. There is to be University liberty of choice. Several courses, carefully arranged will be presented, and the student, aided by friends and instructors, can make his choice among them. . . .

Third. There will be no Fetichism in regard to any single studies. All good studies will be allowed their due worth. . . .

Fourth. Historical studies and studies in Political and Social science will be held in high honor, and will have more attention than is usual in our higher institutions of learning. . . .

Fifth. There will be no petty daily marking system, a pedantic device which has eaten out from so many colleges all capacity among students to seek knowledge for knowledge's sake. Those professors will be sought who can stir enthusiasm, and who can thus cause students to do far more than under a perfunctory piecemeal study.

Sixth. It enters into the plan adopted by the Board of the Cornell University to bring about a closer and more manly intercourse and sympathy between Faculty and students than is usual in most of the colleges.

Seventh. The study of Human Anatomy, Physiology and Hygiene, with exercises for physical training, will be most carefully provided for.

Eighth. The Cornell University, as its highest aim, seeks to promote Christian civilization. But it cannot be sectarian. . . . By the terms of the charter, no trustee, professor or student can be accepted or rejected on account of any religious or political opinions which he may or may not hold.

The Teaching of Agriculture

Since little concern had been evidenced for the mechanic arts and since the nation was not yet in the throes of the coming industrial expansion, agriculture was the first interest of most of the new colleges. The country was still primarily rural, and the Morrill Act had received its greatest single share of support from farm groups. It was natural, therefore, for the new colleges to attempt to respond to the challenge of "something for the farmer." If one were to examine only the statements of aims in the early catalogs, he would soon gain the impression that the colleges existed solely to train farmers in a trade-school approach and atmosphere. The announcement of the University of

Wisconsin in 1868–69, for instance, stated, "It is the design of the University to give in this department a thorough course of instruction directly pertaining to agriculture, which will enable our graduates to conduct the operation of a farm both intelligently and profitably." [12] Beyond the rudiments of farming, however, there was little else, so the first schedule of courses fell back on the old subjects to fill the curriculum. Here was a strange combination of "How to Plow" with "Mental and Moral Philosophy."

The failure to provide more agricultural science, as we know it now, was a logical one: there was no agricultural science. In spite of all the centuries of farming, there did not yet exist an adequate body of knowledge from which the faculty could offer adequate instruction. The term "agriculture" meant simple farming.

To find something to teach, the colleges relied on the operation of a model farm. Here the few students would have the opportunity for observation and practice. The model farm loomed as one of the important, if not the most important, parts of the college. Michigan State College was often called the "state farm" in the sixties and seventies. And President A. J. Smith of Maryland later remarked, "When I became president of the Maryland Agricultural College the main thing that seemed to be required of me to demonstrate my fitness for the position was my ability to have a model farm." [13] The maintenance cost of the farm was high and the expectations of its producing great results even higher. Severe criticisms were later to cause the disbanding and sometimes the sale of these units which had provided the link for agricultural instruction from handicraft to science.

Agriculture not only had little to teach but it also had little place of its own. Isaac Roberts at Iowa State reported suffering "a sort of social neglect . . . in an alien atmosphere." [14] There was still enough of the classical hold on the colleges to deny the new vocational a place in the sun. Not only was there difficulty in gaining respectability among the scholars, but Roberts reported little interest even among the trustees who had been charged by the state to carry out the national directive for agricultural instruction. By now it was evident that higher education in agriculture would have to await the development of science. This came to be recognized widely. A committee of the Iowa State Horticultural Society appointed to report on the college in 1873 wrote, "The results heretofore attained have not fulfilled the just

expectations of the friends of agricultural education." [15] The emergence of the laboratory method, of research, and of experimentation
were to give agriculture that "dignified place in the world of higher
education" which so many desired.

The Teaching of Mechanic Arts

The beginning years of the Land-Grant Colleges paralleled the start
of the so-called Industrial Revolution. With an unlimited supply of
raw materials, the extension of more rapid transportation, and the increase in market possibilities, industry came into its own. The total
value of manufactured products in 1860 was approximately $1,900,-
000,000. By 1894 it had risen to $9,500,000,000. Products manufac-
tured from iron and steel were valued at $36,500,000 in 1860 and at
$479,000,000 in 1890. The period witnessed a tremendous develop-
ment in the production of flour, meat, lumber, clothing, boots and
shoes, as well as all textiles. There was no doubt that some form of
"mechanic arts" at the college level was needed and even demanded.
Its teaching would be less sensational than that of agriculture, chiefly
because other institutions had pioneered in its field. There was no
suspicion of engineering "book-learning" as there was of "book-
farming."

The tremendous industrial expansion resulted in a desperate
struggle to employ trained men for the new machine-operated civilization. The demand was to give a place for the mechanic arts which was
denied agriculture. By 1874 White was led to comment, "What is the
great want of our Western States at this moment? Greater agricultural
production? No. What they want is, the development of great and
varied manufacturing industries, so near them that it shall no longer
take two-thirds of a bushel of corn to carry the other third from producer to consumer." [16] The farmers needed no systematic help. If the
land wore out, there was still enough new land left to find and cultivate. But industry could not afford such wastage. It recognized the
necessity for trained men, and it was willing to pay for them. It
couldn't afford mistakes. Many educators saw the needs as did President White when he said:

. . . it is no exaggeration to say that millions on millions of dollars have
been lost by the employment of half-educated engineers. Proofs of this
meet us on every side—lines of railway in wrong positions, bad grades and

curves, tunnels cut and bridges built that might have been avoided, water-supply systems made failures for want of proper calculation as to friction, whole districts sickened by badly managed drainage, fearful catastrophes on railways caused by the falling of bridges devised by men who had not been properly trained but had shown skill on the purely "practical" side.[17]

Due to the demand as well as the glamour and novelty, students came to the Land-Grant Colleges to be experimented upon in the growing mechanical arts curriculum.

In the beginning, mechanic arts education was submitted to the same argument as agricultural education: what did it mean? Some thought it implied preparation for the trades; others considered it technical education at the highest possible level. There were even those who tried to link the terms "mechanic arts" and "agriculture" together so that it would mean "mechanic arts as applied to agriculture." The designation "master mechanic" was frequently used. It meant one thoroughly and scientifically trained to accomplish the practical.

The early curriculum centered around shop practice and practical training. The output of the college shops—castings, forgings, and machinery—was displayed in order to convince the public of the value of the training. The work included a large measure of drawing and surveying. Until 1870 when mechanical engineering began to appear in the college catalogues, all engineering was civil. Electrical engineering did not appear as a separate field until the eighties. As the sciences developed, chemistry, mathematics, and physics found important places in the engineering course list. By building on a scientific foundation, the Land-Grant Colleges exerted a dominant influence in engineering education. Engineering needed science; science needed to be needed. The two grew together.

Engineering enrollment in the Land-Grant Colleges grew steadily through the seventies and was to jump even more rapidly as the course of study became valued and respected. Many of the Land-Grant Colleges survived the period of struggle because of the interest in mechanic arts. As the needs of industry arose, the colleges responded by adding more courses and then subdividing the field so that eventually from the one root of civil engineering sprang a number of majors and then schools. Here was an early example of the colleges responding to both national and local needs.

Equality of Studies

The new education was to be partly responsible not only for breaking the monopoly of the classical colleges but also the stranglehold of
the completely fixed and prescribed curriculum. Two interrelated
movements were to run simultaneously through this period—equality
of studies and the elective system. President Charles W. Eliot of Harvard is credited with the introduction of the important elective
principle. By 1872 the senior year at Harvard had become completely
elective, then the junior year in 1879, and sophomore in 1884. By
1894 only one requirement remained—English A—which could be
waived by an entrance examination. The Harvard idea was to take
hold in many colleges and universities.

Its counterpart in the developing Land-Grant Colleges was an
emphasis on equality of studies, forced in part by an attempt to give
recognition to science, agriculture and engineering, and by the broadened curriculum which made prescription sometimes impossible.
Equality of studies became the wedge by which science and the other
subjects could thrust a foot into the educational door. Once again
President White of Cornell was its most able spokesman. In his autobiography he summarized his inaugural address of 1868 and concluded:

. . . I especially developed ideas which had occurred to me as far back
as my observations after graduation at Yale, where the classical students
belonging to the "college proper" were given a sort of supremacy, and
scientific students relegated to a separate institution at a considerable
distance, and therefore deprived of much general, and even special, culture which would have greatly benefited them. Indeed, they seemed not
considered as having souls to be saved, since no provision was made for
them at the college chapel.[18]

White was determined that there should be meaning to this phrase of
the Morrill Act—"the liberal and practical education" in the same
institution. Naturally, the arguments for equality did not set well with
the adherents to the classical. They were quick to recognize that it
foreshadowed the end of domination of the curriculum by the dead
languages.

One inevitable result of making studies equal and open to choice
was a growth in the individualization of education. It began with the

necessity as well as desirability of closer contact between the professor and the student. Later it would lead to the provision for counseling and guidance as an accepted part of the university process.

Coeducation and Home Economics

The "industrial classes" as defined by Turner and used by Morrill did not include women. Their place was considered to be the home where higher education was not necessary. The changing social pattern of the tumultuous days to follow was responsible for giving women a prominent place in the educational scheme. Scattered experiments with coeducation had been made in the first half of the century. By the 1850's, several state universities of the West, such as Utah and Iowa, had opened their doors to women students. Washington followed in 1862. But it remained for the land-grant movement to give genuine acceptance to the notion that women could and should study on the same campus as men. Many of the Western Land-Grant Colleges were open to women from the start; others soon followed. By 1870, for instance, Michigan, Illinois, California, and Missouri all had a few women students enrolled. During the seventies a majority of the Eastern institutions adopted the practice. Penn State as early as 1871 enrolled six women, and the number there increased to forty-nine by 1879. That, however, was the maximum for the next thirty years.

The idea was not accepted without opposition. Indeed, many of the administrators and faculties were openly skeptical and had some difficulty convincing themselves that they were right, especially in the face of fantastic charges. Housing presented one problem. Many colleges were struggling to provide dormitories for the men. Women, if they chose to come, would have to find quarters with faculty or in private homes "in town." There were those, too, who wondered whether women were strong enough physically to undertake the rigors of academic training. This was a man's work. Women might well collapse from overwork and worry, leading inevitably to a lowering of academic standards. The lack of courses to suit the needs and interests of women was an important consideration, too. Few could conceive that women might want or find need to study the same subjects as men.

These were considerations to worry the presidents and faculties.

The general public was far more concerned with the moral issues involved. This became a heated and much debated subject of the day. Schaffter and Woody describe the issues:

The opposition proclaimed the inevitable loss of "the delicate bloom of womanhood" in the "enforced familiarity" of the mixed college; the "corruption of manners and morals"; it would destroy romance, bring disillusionment, fewer marriages, hence race suicide; it would produce too many and too ready marriages; it would lower intellectual standards, for woman was a "weaker vessel"; again, when girls have proved stronger than expected, coeducation was opposed on the ground that one must safeguard the boys' scholarship; it was detrimental to physical health, emasculated boys, stunted girls; in sum, coeducation, to opponents, seemed the epitome of "reform against nature," for what God had differentiated, man should not strive to make the same.[19]

In spite of the charges and denunciations, the Land-Grant Colleges and the state universities took the leadership in admitting women.

With women in their midst, the colleges were forced to find something to teach to suit their interests and needs. This led to the first offerings in what is now termed "home economics," a field in which the Land-Grant Colleges were indisputably the pioneers. The first record of a course in this new field comes from Iowa State College in 1869. By 1871 the Iowa "Ladies Course" listed "Domestic Economy" as a subject offered for the women students. The wife of the first president delivered lectures on cooking for two or three years prior to 1875. In that year she convinced the trustees to establish a department of "cookery and household arts." This led to the development of an experimental kitchen, the first of its kind in any college. Kansas began its "Domestic Economy" curriculum in 1873 with lessons in sewing and instruction on the application of chemistry to foods. Illinois started in 1874 and developed a systematic and thorough program. Other colleges followed suit in the same halting way, but the extended development of home economics was to await the introduction of the research method as well as a demand for trained graduates.

Manual Labor

In the beginning years of the Land-Grant Colleges, great emphasis was placed on student labor as an essential and desirable part of the educational process. Practically every new college including those connected with existing universities adopted the requirement. Professor Roberts reported that, at Iowa State, "All college students were then required to work two and one-half hours daily, being paid an average wage of about eight cents an hour. From forty to fifty were detailed each morning to the farm." [20] The agricultural students spent time clearing fields, caring for livestock, and helping to plant and harvest crops on the "model farm." The students in mechanic arts were expected to spend an equal number of hours in the shop, as well as helping with outdoor efforts to build and beautify the campus. Women students were detailed to the dining room and kitchen.

The practice of requiring manual labor was instituted and then defended on several counts. The students who came to the new colleges were from the "industrial classes." Up to this time higher education had been open only to the moneyed class. Not only was there a necessity to provide as costless an education as possible for the sons of farmers and mechanics, but the opportunity to help "pay their way" would be an added inducement to get them to come to college. The requirement was advanced, too, on the grounds of its practical application of course content. By working directly on problems discussed in the classroom, the student would understand better the relation of reality to learning. The colleges were also faced with the necessity of convincing their farmer-support as well as their farmer-opposition that the students would not lose touch with practical matters by attending college. They would not be "educated away from the farm" by this new method of "book-farming." The Michigan Agricultural College Catalogue in 1871 stated, "It is believed that the three hours' work that every student is required to perform on the farm or in the garden, besides serving to render him familiar with the use of implements and the principles of agriculture, is sufficient also to preserve habits of manual labor and so foster a taste for agricultural pursuits." [21]

But the practice was never made perfect. It proved neither satisfactory nor workable. The students came to regard it as drudgery and, without their interest and cooperation, it could not be successful. The faculty found that it actually provided no intellectual benefits and had little, if any, relation to "higher" education. In addition, most of the students coming to college were well schooled in manual labor. They had performed such functions all their lives and were not interested in the meager returns of financial assistance from such hard labor. The practice fell into disrepute and was dropped by most institutions, although Michigan State held its students to the requirement, frequently unsuccessfully, until the 1890's.

Military Training

The Morrill Act had specified "and including military tactics" as a requirement for the Land-Grant Colleges. Beyond this it did not go. Neither the Congress nor the Army in the years stretching from 1862 to 1916 made any serious attempt to define what the original legislation meant. One can imagine the consternation of the new colleges in their attempt to live by the letter of the law without knowledge or guidance of what was intended or sought. There were no previous examples of military training in civilian institutions. West Point had long been operating, but this was a *military* academy as distinct from the new colleges devoted to the peaceful pursuits of agriculture and the mechanic arts. On one point everyone agreed: no one intended the new institutions to place military tactics above the other specified subjects. Without guidance, then, the colleges were left to develop what they considered desirable. Because of the traditional emphasis on discipline of mind and body, military tactics was welcomed in some quarters as a practical method of achieving this long-pursued objective, as well as providing healthful exercise. It sounded like rationalization, but the colleges had no other course in the face of the requirement.

Congress in 1862 had made no attempt to provide officers or leaders of any kind to instruct in military tactics. A supplementary act in 1866 detailed army officers to the land-grant institutions as military instructors. In 1888 and 1891 further provision would be made for their number and duties. But an act of Congress does not always produce the desired results. Out of indifference, the military began its long-heard plea of poverty which would be repeated so many times in subsequent years. Though Congress gave its blessing to the provision of officers, the officers did not arrive. Consequently, the colleges began military training by appointing in its charge some member of the faculty who had, somewhere in his background, military experience. In the first years this was not difficult because of the recent Civil War. In 1865 Pennsylvania, for instance, employed General John Fraser as professor of mathematics and lecturer on military tactics.

The man in charge was left upon his own to invent a program as best he knew. No outlines of study were available, no equipment, no uniforms. As a result, the "teaching" consisted mostly of drill. In many of the colleges it was required of all male students. In some, the military commandant was placed in charge of all student discipline. The faculties were described as tolerant of, rather than sympathetic to, the military effort. There is little reason why one should expect more, in the light of the almost total indifference of the Army.

Nonsectarian

The Land-Grant Colleges, together with the often parallel state universities, were the first to make the strong initial break from the traditional mixing of education and the church in the United States. Founded by national and state governments which, by constitutional provision, had separated them from the church, the colleges were morally bound not to promote any particular sect or creed. Here was the beginning of the ever-increasing movement toward the secularization of American higher education. In his inaugural address, Cornell's President White enunciated the protest:

Perhaps no one thing has done more to dwarf the system of higher education in this land than the sectarian principle. As the result of such observation and thought I declare my firm belief that, but for our enslavement to this unfortunate principle, we would long since have had great free universities, liberal and practical, the largest, the most ample in equipment, most earnest in effort, the most vigorous in thought the world has yet seen.[22]

The new colleges sought truth for truth's sake, or, in the phrase which President Edmund Ezra Day of Cornell was later to use frequently, "the disinterested pursuit of truth." In the opinion of the founders and first presidents, these must not be institutions where "the main purpose of the faculty [is] to stretch or cut Science exactly to fit 'Revealed Religion.' "[23]

Except in principle, the break was not as great as it would appear to be. Teaching and campus activity both were based on the accepted and rigid moral traditions. Most institutions made daily chapel compulsory. A good share of the extra-curricular activities of the times were religiously centered. The social life was frequently built around near-by churches or the campus Y.M.C.A. And the students were often engaged in the same evangelical arisings as those which occurred in numerous American communities of the times. Nevertheless, here was the beginning of the scientific spirit breaking from orthodox Christianity. The colleges were charged almost constantly with being Godless institutions. They helped set the pattern, however, for a reconciliation of religion and science at the college level. Ross concluded that "the tolerant secularization, following slowly but surely, was not the least valuable of the contributions of the land-grant idea and movement to American education." [24]

Adhering to no one church or creed and thus considering all equally acceptable, from the earliest days the colleges made a practice of avoiding any semblance of religious discrimination in the selection of students. As a result, for the first time there emerged an American college community which was a melting pot of all creeds and kinds. This, too, was akin to the growing national unity and an important part of the developing democratization of higher education.

CONDITIONS OF THE PERIOD

Enrollment

Not the least of the struggles of the early period was the difficulty in attracting students of sufficient number and sufficient caliber. In many states the public school movement was just beginning. It would take some time before the principle of state support was established and compulsory attendance laws passed. In the meantime, in the words of a land-grant scholar, "democracy's college awaited democracy's high school." [25] The institutions would not grow in size until the public high school became an accepted part of the local community.

As a result, the early colleges were forced to take two steps: lower the admission standards and consequently academic standards, and offer preparatory courses on their own. From 1857 to as late as 1890, Michigan State required for admission to the freshman class only bare essentials, including the satisfactory passing of an examination in arithmetic, geography, grammar, reading, spelling, and penmanship. To this was added a desirable but not necessary knowledge of elementary algebra. At Kansas State, until 1873, a student who had completed district school could earn his bachelor's degree in six years. To fit the needs of the times, many of the colleges were, in effect, state high schools. The new colleges found their students wherever they could and at whatever level. The dreams of offering a "higher" education had to be postponed until students were prepared to undertake such advanced work. In spite of low standards, during the first thirty years of Michigan State only one of every ten matriculants in agriculture actually graduated.

Chief among the enrollment problems was the inability to interest students in the agricultural course. It was far easier to find those who wanted mechanic arts. Most young men could see neither the reason nor the wisdom of spending four years in college studying a subject learned by practical farm experience in much less time. Farming was no difficult operation requiring higher learning; anyone could do it. Unfortunately many of the college professors had yet to learn more than the intelligent farmer. In 1874 Cornell registered only three senior students in agriculture. It was as late as 1889 before the first student matriculated in agriculture at the University of Minnesota. Illinois had forty-five students in 1875–76 and the number dropped to twenty-three by 1879. One agricultural graduate emerged from the University of Wisconsin prior to 1880. In its first eight or ten years, Iowa State contented itself with preparing the traditional—doctors, lawyers, clergymen, and teachers—who constituted nearly 60 per cent of the enrollment.

The colleges would not be blessed with student numbers for some time to come. In his report for 1876–77, the United States Commissioner of Education issued the following statistics:

College	Number of Faculty	Number of Students	Library Books
University of California	31	177	13,324
Delaware College	7	40	6,000
Illinois Agricultural College	4	41	500
University of Kentucky	9	80	Not given
Louisiana State University	5	3	11,500
University of Minnesota	15	107	10,000
University of Missouri	31	117	10,000

University of Nebraska	9	75	2,000
Cornell University	40	304	39,000
University of Vermont	8	66	16,827
West Virginia University	13	39	4,500
University of Wisconsin	19	225	7,500

The Commissioner did not bother to gain statistics from many of the new Land-Grant Colleges, particularly those not a part of state universities.

The Faculty

The new education was forced to depend upon the old for its initial supply of teachers. Undoubtedly many faculty attempted to adjust themselves to the new subject matter and approach, but others were to make a mockery of Morrill's noble scheme. A correspondent for the *Chicago Tribune*, M. L. Dunlap, writing in 1868, found "the institutions present a most singular anomaly, a school for the industries in the hands of the learned professions." Several months later he was even more irate, "We have had enough of quackery in the subject of agricultural education. Let us have a few grams of good common sense. If the legislature had a desire to aid, then let them put this school in the hands of those for whom it was designed instead . . . of clergymen, lawyers, and doctors, who know little of the real wants. . . ." [26] His intentons were good but it would not be that easy. The trustees of Michigan State confessed that they "knew not where to find a man for this work" in the practical instruction of agriculture.[27] The situation was confounded by a complete lack of material on which to base the courses. Textbooks were irrelevant or nonexistent. The instructor was forced to derive his lecture material almost entirely from his own personal experience. This resulted in a strange conglomeration of the classical and the practical.

The situation would be remedied only by the slow creation of a body of teachable material as well as teachers in both agriculture and the mechanic arts. Teachers would come in time but the texts would have to await the maturing of the faculty member who felt himself sufficiently informed to write. Isaac Roberts recalls in his autobiography his first consternation and his delightful way of solving the problem, one which must have been followed frequently in the early period:

When the subject of the horse—breeding, age, care and management— came up, I went again to the library for help. But the horse books were all out of date, chiefly filled with information about hunters, jumpers, and racers and their wonderful feats, and a little about the European draft breeds which were then in process of formation. . . .

It appeared to me that farmers should know how to tell the age of a horse with a reasonable degree of certainty; and hearing that many rather young horses had recently died of an epidemic in the immediate neighborhood, I had two farm hands dig them up and preserved the heads and some special parts and such limbs as had been malformed by disease. By careful inquiry. I was able to fix accurately the ages of most of these animals. Arranging my material on a workbench in the open, I placed the class on the windward side and taught them the fundamental principles of horse dentition.[28]

We can imagine that many of the early classes were placed "on the windward side."

Much was asked of those first faculties. Funds were not sufficient to employ a man versed in each of the subjects offered, so a frequent "doubling up" took place. At Michigan, according to Beal, no member of the faculty had a chair to himself, but "occupied a whole settee." [29] The Florida State College of Agriculture listed a professorship of "Agriculture, Horticulture, and Greek" which was held by a master of arts. New Hampshire's first professor, who suffered from epilepsy, was the business manager of the college, prepared the annual reports, planned and supervised the construction of buildings, organized and taught most of the courses (including the chemistry courses at Dartmouth), lobbied at the legislature, gave lectures throughout the state, and recruited students. It was the rule rather than the exception for the president of the college to teach a number of courses in addition to performing administrative duties. The faculty lot was continually complicated by low pay, internal conflict, and uncertainty of tenure.

These were the men, however, who struggled to keep alive the land-grant dream and to whom credit for the quality of its early life must be given. This was not so much a time of institutions as of men. The power of personality rather than of knowledge pervaded the campus. As Liberty Hyde Bailey observed, "It was not then a day for erudition, or for high technical scholarship, but a time for clear faith, homely, and direct relations with the people, wisdom in giving advice. . . ." [30]

The Bare Necessities

The majority of the new colleges were located in isolated sections of the state, sometimes near the geographic center as a means of satisfying or pacifying all. The campus was frequently miles from the nearest railroad and city. Ross observes, "Undeveloped transportation facilities intensified isolation; campuses were snow-bound in winter and mud-bound in spring. The long winter vacation, in addition to other advantages claimed for it, brought relief from drifted, wind-swept spaces where natural forces were little tempered by architectural and landscaping moderations and adornments." [31] Since the Morrill funds constituted an endowment of which neither the capital could be used nor any part spent on buildings, the first structures were built either at minimum cost to the state or donated by some interested farmer. One building often sufficed and became, in effect, the entire campus, including classrooms, offices, dormitories, and dining hall. A typical student, recalling in later years his "campus experience," would remember it in terms of a single structure standing in the midst of virgin woods or wide prairie, lonely and looming. This was the feeble physical start.

From the viewpoint of instruction, even more of a hardship was the lack of equipment. The classical colleges had found little use for "apparatus." Few understood the new education well enough to realize that equipment was essential to teaching. Dunaway relates that Waring, the professor of chemistry at Penn State, was able to obtain $1000 from the Board of Trustees for laboratory equipment only after proving that the course was a worthy addition to the curriculum. Finding this sum not enough for his needs, he donated $500 from his own pocket in order to have the equipment he felt essential. [32]

The typical college year began at the end of February and extended through the following October. This would avoid the necessity of heating the college building during the winter and the students were given the opportunity to obtain teaching jobs in the secondary schools. They were thus able to accumulate funds to help pay their expenses during the following year. The daily schedule of the college afforded the student little time to meditate or even to read the few books which were available. Roberts reports a typical day at Iowa State:

The rising bell rang at 5:30 A.M.; breakfast was at 6 and inspection at 6:45 when students' rooms had to be in order or there was prompt reckoning. All unexcused students reported for work at 7 A.M. The officers of the day as well as others were obliged to make a daily written report to the President. The students were required and the faculty requested to meet at 4:30 P.M. in the Chapel where a short reading from the scriptures and prayer was followed by directions for the next day's work and by various notices. From 5 to 8 o'clock was given to supper and recreation. On Saturdays no duties except special details were required; on Sunday attendance at the morning service was treated the same as a class exercise.[33]

In the early college, of all the bare necessities among both faculty and students, probably courage and patience were the most essential. Such qualities would help them make the best of unfortunate conditions.

Dissatisfaction and Criticism

The period under consideration was a time of growing public interest in education of all types and at all levels. For the first time the economic as well as the social values of education were generally recognized. The possibilities of a utilitarian education became important to the working man who wanted his son or daughter to have a share in the growing American economy. Civic leaders recognized, too, that education could help to make better citizens out of the new and confused immigrants. Society had become sufficiently complex that it could no longer be called simple and agricultural. Men needed a broader understanding in order to find their place in a changing time. Thus the public developed an increasing interest in just what was going on in the new as well as the old colleges. In 1870 Yale's Noah Porter wrote:

The American Colleges have of late been somewhat formally challenged by what is called the American Public, to appear before its tribunal, and to give a satisfactory explanation and defense of their system of discipline and study, on penalty of being either condemned or "suffering a default." The challenge has been repeated too often, and from too many quarters, to be wholly neglected, however confident the friends and defenders of the college system may be of the goodness of their cause.[34]

In terms of the new colleges, the public had come to expect something really new. Their hopes had been built to the point of anticipating that the new education would solve all the old problems. They were somewhat astounded to discover how much of the old appeared in the new.

The criticism came from many quarters. Educators in the old colleges recognized the new as an incipient and threatening revolution. They spoke out boldly and frequently in opposition. There were both skepticism and fear of any type of vocational education at the college level. Those from the classical colleges considered that only abstract knowledge had a place in the halls of learning. It was traditional to train ministers, doctors, and lawyers because they were the traditional leaders, but farmers and mechanics had never shown themselves capable of performing any more than the necessary menial work. This strange inconsistency in thinking led to the charge that the new colleges were "prostituting the sacred cause of education to the business of making a living," and that agricultural studies "would convert a scientific institution into a cow pasture." In his volume, *The American Colleges and The American Public* published in 1870, Noah Porter commented:

The claim that the Scientific School [as he called the Land-Grant Colleges] proposes a better education for most men or even a more desirable or useful education for any man than the colleges, would seem to be premature to one who reflects how very short has been the experience of the oldest of these schools and how very discordant with one another are the theory and practice of those schools which have been organized the longest. The New Education, if it had been in operation long enough for its advocates to define or describe what it is, has not yet been proved by its fruits, and it would be the height of presumption and folly to pronounce it so far a success as to justify the abandonment of the old system which has at least a definite character and has produced some good results.[35]

Porter was not even ready to allow the land-grant institutions to be called "Colleges."

No less severe, but for different reasons, was the criticism of a majority of the farmers whom the new colleges were supposed to benefit the most. Roberts wrote that "it was as hard to get a respectful hearing among the farmers as to get a foothold in the universities; and it required infinite patience, perseverance and good temper." The dissatisfied farmers felt that they had been let down, that the new education had proven to be a dispensable and superfluous frill. They had been led to believe, probably because of the overemphasis on agriculture in the discussions of the Morrill bill, that the colleges would be devoted solely to farming. They were amazed to discover that the colleges offered other courses, other majors, and that even the farm students were expected to study other subjects. And so they greeted the efforts of the colleges with both suspicion and contempt.

The new education, according to the agricultural interests, should be farm-centered and not science-centered. If the students were schooled in the best of the existing practices, that was enough. Then send them back to the farms to practice. The opposition of the farm majority was to continue for some years. It would not be conquered until there was proof of the benefits of the merger of science and agriculture and until the organized farm interests were to take the lead in championing the colleges. In this respect, the organization of the National Grange in 1867 proved an important and fortunate event for the land-grant movement. But the Grange would not be ready or willing to offer its influential support for some years to come.

Because of the public interest in education, newspapers and journals of the day picked up the criticism and added their force to it. On top of all this came the censure of the churches. Now transferred from Iowa State to Cornell, Professor Roberts reported, "When the Press announced one fall that a large number . . . had entered the Freshman class, a leading denominational journal declared that 300 'fresh recruits for Satan' had entered this 'Godless college.' Another journal called it 'a school where hayseeds and greasy mechanics were taught to hoe potatoes, pitch manure and be dry nurses to steam engines.' " [36] The criticism was thus so severe and widespread that the struggling new educators were forced to spend an inordinate amount of time defending their practices before they knew sometimes what their practices were. As Roberts said, "These and many other things of the same sort were hard to bear, for at that time we were not sure that we should laugh last."

Presidents and faculties were bound to be confused and dis-couraged. In 1875 Dr. Kedzie of Michigan State lamented, "There is something wrong when the College, after 16 years of continuous work, is still denounced and decried in some of the most flourishing agricultural sections of our State." [37] Though they pleaded for a chance to prove themselves, their plea went unheard. White argued their case when he said, "The existing systems of education have had over 300 years for their perfection; the new system certainly then may ask for a decade of years." [38] They could take a little satisfaction in the fact that Congress was not moved to rescind what it had established. A House committee in 1874 investigated the organization, program, and finances of the colleges to determine whether or not they were fulfilling the law. Its affirmative report brought some comfort. But, despite Morrill's continuing interest and frequent efforts to gain more funds for the colleges (such as his defeated bill in 1872), Congress was not to act again in their behalf until 1887.

SOME SIGNS OF PROGRESS

The Laboratory Method

In terms of the future, all was not as dismal as it looked, although of course the colleges could not be aware of the importance and significance of much of their early struggle. Not the least among their accomplishments was their contribution to the development of the laboratory method. As early as 1835, the first chemical laboratory for student instruction had been started at the University of Pennsylvania. By 1868 the Massachusetts Institute of Technology offered the first laboratory work in physics. But up to 1872 only six colleges in the country taught either chemistry or physics by the laboratory method. The early use of the method, then, was scattered and purely experi-mental. It remained for the Land-Grant Colleges to assist in a de-velopment born of necessity rather than design.

Aside from these infrequent beginnings, the evolution received its first impetus when land-grant teachers, due to a lack of illustrative material, were forced to go into the fields. Professor Roberts describes how he started at Iowa State in 1869:

I began to tell the students what I knew about farming. It did not take me long to run short of material and then I began to consult the library.

I might as well have looked for cranberries on the Rocky Mountains as for material for teaching agriculture in that library. Thus, fortunately, I was driven to take the class to the field and farm, there to study plants, animals, and tillage at first hand. . . . I fell into the habit of taking the students to view good and poor farms; to see fine herds and scrub herds in the country round about, even though they had to travel in freight cars. I suppose I was the first teacher of agriculture to make use, in a large way, of the fields and stables of the countryside as laboratories. . . ." [39]

Excursions to nearby farms, such as those described by Roberts, and trips to agricultural shows and meetings frequently made up a large part of the classwork in the early days.

On the engineering side, the shop was rapidly becoming the laboratory. In 1874 the Report of the Department of Mechanic Arts at Cornell commented:

There are now closely connected with the lecture rooms in which the theoretical side of mechanics is presented, other rooms for the designing and manufacture of working models and machinery, fitted with power and appliances for working in wood and the metals, in which the practical side is presented.

The machine-shop is conducted wholly as a means of instruction, and each student in the department of mechanics is required to devote at least two hours per day to work in the shop, without pecuniary compensation for his labor, where he will not only obtain theory and practice combined, but will also have the opportunities to construct, as well as use, tools of the greatest accuracy.

Thus, despite its unpopularity, vocational education was to make a substantial contribution to all higher education by this emphasis on "learning by doing." The highly technical laboratories of the twentieth century began in part in the weed-patch and the machine-shop of the 1870s.

The trek to the fields was in keeping with the basis of the new education in the inductive system of learning. The student was encouraged to analyze and synthesize, to observe and compare. Not just the intellect but the senses were important in the process of gaining knowledge. He must be ready to smell, to taste, to feel, to watch, to measure, and to weigh. The new method was later to be illustrated by the frequently-quoted example: "Ask the grasshopper how many legs he has. Don't go to the book. The book may lie. Grasshopper will tell you the truth." The student in the classical college had relied on books and memory as his tools. The new student was to rely now on a great conglomeration of apparatus and machinery, from the test tube eventually to the atom-smasher, as his method of inquiry and determination. The professor would urge him not to depend upon the words of another but to verify and amplify for himself. Guidance replaced goading. In the beginning, the student watched the professor perform the experiment; finally the student conducted the experiment under the watchful eye of the professor. By adapting the evolving laboratory method to farming and shopwork, the Land-Grant Colleges were soon to find it a necessity in the teaching of a whole host of sciences.

The Beginnings of Research

The period under consideration saw a tremendous spurt in the development of scientific teaching and experimentation. The idea of experimentation had started early in the Land-Grant Colleges. Maryland had various agricultural experiments under way as early as 1858. Pugh in 1864 included investigation as one of the prime essentials of his ideal university. He stated that the institutions "must afford means of carrying on extensive investigations in order to settle many questions which are constantly being raised by men engaged in Industrial operations outside of them." As examples, he pointed to the desire of farmers to know how to maintain fertile soil, how to use manures economically, how to feed, keep and fatten stock, how to prevent disease in plants and avoid weeds and insects. On the industrial side, there was the question of changing or modifying the quality of metals. He concluded, "Each will have its appropriate question to propound to the teacher of an Industrial College, and his ability to answer will be dependent upon the closeness with which he can confine his attention and his investigations to the special subject to which his question relates." [40]

Scientific investigation was thus spurred on by the constant demand for practical application. The first efforts were the result of either accident or crude experiments. Without a body of proven knowledge available, each scientist was forced to make his own way, pending a more systematic approach. By 1873 Oregon State College was ready to list its first project in agricultural research. It consisted of an analysis of "white soil," with suggested treatment, and an analysis of "marl" from the Yaquina Bay District. California encouraged its faculty to conduct experiments to keep them occupied; there were too few agricultural students to fill their time. Similar work in engineering consisted mostly in the testing of materials.

Travel in Germany to observe the advanced universities of that country was at its height. The example of the investigations and publications of German scholars was to have a profound influence on all who saw its good work. Liebig had begun his important writing earlier in the century. It helped in the movement to establish at Mockern, Saxony, in 1851 the first regular experiment station supported by government funds. This station was followed by one at Halle in 1855. By 1880 the number in Germany had increased to more than fifty. Italy established her first station in 1870, Belgium and Denmark in 1872, France in 1875, and Holland in 1877. The spread was so rapid that stations in Canada and even in Java antedated those to come in the United States.

The German station idea became the goal of the struggling American agricultural scientists. One of the travelers to Europe, Wilbur O. Atwater, returned enthused and talkative. His energy and conviction led to the establishment of the first American station at his alma mater, Wesleyan University in Middletown, Connecticut, in 1875. It began with a grant of $2800 from state and private sources. Atwater became the first director of this first station and later the first director of the Federal Office of Experiment Stations, thus leaving his mark throughout his life on the new movement. The Station at Wesleyan was later moved to Sheffield at Yale and then, still later, became an entity of its own in New Haven.

California was next to organize its early experimentation work into a station-type program. North Carolina followed in 1877. The next decade would show an even greater number. The first stations concentrated on immediately practical problems, with fertilizer-control as a major part of the early work. In a report in 1875, the Connecticut station listed the following subjects of concern: analysis of fertilizers, analysis of feeding stuffs, experiments to determine agricultural value of fertilizers, seed testing, analysis of bogs and peats, analysis of different types of manures, poison tests, analysis of foods and of water. North Carolina, meanwhile, was beginning to organize and carry on the same kind of program in addition to studies of insects injurious to vegetation. Almost all of the states had begun by this time some type of organized experimentation work on the college farm, following the earliest example of Maryland.

The first agricultural experiment stations marked the start of the direct application of science to the problems of agriculture. The end of this period marked the beginning of a new and entirely different approach to agricultural instruction as well. The day was not long hence when graduate study would receive a place in the university world. While the experiment stations were starting in the late seventies, Johns Hopkins University, the forerunner of a new concept in advanced instruction, was being established in Baltimore under the inspiring leadership of its first president, Daniel Coit Gilman, who had earlier served as President of the land-grant University of California.

The Beginnings of Extension

The widespread and influential lyceum movement had declined after the Civil War. It was to be replaced by the Chautauqua system founded in 1874 in New York State as a ten-day Sunday School Assembly. The program included instruction, recreation, and entertainment. The movement gained strength until by 1878 the Chautauqua Literary and Scientific Circle had been organized on the principle of a four-year course in home reading. Its popularity was to spread until some sixty thousand persons were enrolled, many of whom received additional inspiration by attending the annual assemblies on New York's Chautauqua Lake. It was a sure sign of the revived interest in self-improvement among all classes and in all sections of the country. Across the Atlantic a system of "university extension" had begun in England and had spread to other countries.

The concept inherent in the founding of the Land-Grant Colleges had laid the groundwork for the direct, practical application of knowledge to the lives and interests of the people. The new colleges had brought learning out of the "Ivory Tower." It was only the organization which delayed extending it beyond the campus to the communities and farms of the people themselves. The record seems to indicate that the first "Farmers' Institute" had been held in Springfield, Massachusetts, in 1863 under the auspices of the Massachusetts State

Board of Agriculture. The Land-Grant Colleges were to give the institutes form and substance on a continuing basis. By 1875 Dr. Kedzie at Michigan State had proposed that the college conduct institutes for the farmers in Michigan's rural communities during the winter months to bring instruction to farmers who could not or would not come to college. On the evening of January 11, 1876, two teams of four professors each traveled to two Michigan communities, Armada and Allegan, to speak and conduct discussions on subjects of interest to the farmers. The sponsoring group provided a hall and half the program while the college trustees paid the professors' expenses and published the proceedings in their annual report. The institutes immediately met with favorable response and demands for annual sessions. The *Allegan Journal* reported that the farmers

. . . are thankful for the new light they received, and were agreeably surprised to find the agricultural college professors not a set of "starched up" book worms, but quite unpretending and very practical men, their hands without kid gloves, and their minds stored with the knowledge necessary for their position. Much more favorable views will henceforth be entertained of our State school of agriculture, and we will be surprised if in the future Allegan county is not more fully represented there.[41]

The colleges had found a direct way to gain the much-needed confidence of the farmers. It would serve them well in the immediate years ahead.

In the meantime, another method of reaching the farmers and of gaining their support had started in Ohio. In the winter of 1877–78, the University set up a noncredit, nonexamination course of four lectures a day for ten weeks open to all interested farmers who would come to the campus. The response was inadequate and so it was tailored in the following winter to four weeks duration. This lecture series met with success. It was the beginning of an effort to do "something for the farmers" on the campus itself.

Campus Informality and Equality

In their stark and isolated setting, the colleges were forced to become warm and communal on the inside to offset the exterior chill. Whereas there had been a wide gulf between the teacher and the student in the secure old colleges, the struggle in the new colleges was to bring the two closer together. The authoritarian attitude gave way to a consideration of the student as a responsible adult. The faculty became increasingly concerned with their students as individuals. As a result, the students were given far more authority for their own conduct and affairs than had been considered wise or possible heretofore. The campus became a family grouping in which, for the first time, all students were equal regardless of their economic status or social background. The circumstances and atmosphere made a contribution to the democratizing of higher education.

The Beginnings of Association

Thinking that there might be value in common discussion of common problems, Dr. J. M. Gregory, regent of the Illinois Industrial University, joined with a group of land-grant educators in issuing a call for a meeting of all those concerned and interested. It was held in Chicago on August 24 and 25, 1871, following the sessions of the Society for the Advancement of Science. Twenty-nine persons attended, including presidents or professors of Land-Grant Colleges. They exchanged ideas and experiences and discussed at length opposing views of the functions of the colleges. Dr. Gregory was chosen president and authorized to appoint a committee of one from each state to memorialize Congress and the state legislatures for the speedy establishment of experiment stations on the basis of the German examples. The group discussed, too, a possible permanent organization, but no action was taken.

On the following February 15th, the new United States Commissioner of Agriculture, Frederick Watts, called together in Washington a convention of delegates from state agricultural colleges, agricultural societies, and boards of agriculture. At this meeting thirty-two states and three territories were represented, including Senator Morrill from Vermont. Ross reports:

The committee on convention business recommended as topics for consideration the expediency of seeking further congressional land grants, the establishment of experiment stations, the modification of military instruction, and the best methods of cooperation between the colleges and the department. Committees on equalization of grants, military education, and experiment stations made their respective reports, and these were considered at length though without conclusive decision.[42]

Representatives of the colleges met again in Columbus, Ohio, in 1877 for a general discussion of problems, but no permanent organization was established until the latter half of the eighties. These, too, were the scattered beginnings of an association force which would serve well the Land-Grant Colleges in the formative years ahead.

THE PERIOD IN RETROSPECT

The obstacles had been enormous in relation to the size of the enterprise. The colleges had attempted virtually the impossible with a new purpose, subject matter, and method. They had met with the opposition of the classicists who resented the teaching of the farmer and the mechanic; of the farmer and the mechanic who resented the "book-men"; of many who felt that the experiment was inadvisable and even sacrilegious. The colleges had nothing to teach, and nothing to teach it with. Furthermore, they had no one to teach it. They found all of it unexpectedly expensive. They were confronted on all sides, including their own, with controversy, criticism, and disappointment. They were born in states rapidly becoming industrialized and states still fighting frontier battles. In New England, the textile industry had begun to boom. In Texas, the same session of the legislature establishing the new college offered an official reward of $4000 for the arrest of the notorious outlaw, John Wesley Harden, and the "delivery of his body, dead or alive, within the jail doors of Travis county."

All that saved the colleges was the commitment made by the states in exchange for funds which soon proved meager and inadequate. In spite of the implied pledge, the states were neither anxious nor willing to provide additional assistance. Fortunately, business, the dominant enterprise of the times, gave some support. And fortunately there were men like Clemson and Purdue and Cornell to catch the vision.

Before they would find a place in the changing nation, the colleges would have to find themselves. They would have to understand the size of the task they were called upon to perform. They would have to experience the dependence of a nation upon them. But a start had been made, and the struggle was soon to be over.

4

The Idea Takes Shape, 1880-1899

THE movements and changes which had marked the sixties and seventies of the nineteenth century were to continue, and some were to reach fulfillment in the century's final two decades. Economic and industrial expansion carried on unabated. Material wealth reached hitherto unthinkable proportions. The total value of farm property swelled to a new high of sixteen billion dollars in 1890 and, within another twenty years, jumped to forty-one billion. In the same period, the value of farm crops rose from two and a half billion to eight and a half. By 1889 manufactured products were valued at nine billion. Everywhere industry was producing magnifying results on the economy, and business and commerce responded to the stimulus. Population continued to increase until in 1890 the national total had reached sixty-three million and was on its way within the following ten years to seventy-six million. The exodus from the farms began in the late 1800's and changed substantially the proportion of urban to rural dwellers. Social as well as economic patterns had been transformed. Agriculture was to suffer a long depression from 1880 until approximately 1897, but still it remained in better condition than farmers had ever dreamed possible.

Partly due to the expanding nation and partly to the stimulus of another Morrill act in 1890, the number of Land-Grant Colleges increased substantially during these two decades. Twenty-four more were added to the list in somewhat the same pattern as in the previous thirty years.

Five state universities

Connecticut (replacing Sheffield at Yale as the land-grant recipient)
Arizona
Wyoming
Idaho
Rhode Island (replacing Brown)

Eight separate agricultural and mechanical colleges

Montana	North Carolina (as a separate col-
South Dakota	lege)
Utah	Washington
Clemson in South Carolina	Oklahoma
New Mexico	

Eleven Negro land-grant institutions

Virginia	Georgia
Tennessee	Florida
Princess Anne in Maryland	Southern in Louisiana
North Carolina	Delaware
West Virginia	South Carolina
Langston in Oklahoma	

The new colleges would struggle for their place as the old had before them. Many of the same problems were repeated, particularly in the Western states which were attempting to emulate the East without the facilities and funds. The first president of the University of Wyoming was listed in the original prospectus as professor or lecturer in history and social and political sciences, logic and metaphysics, psychology and moral philosophy, rhetoric and oratory, international law, didactics and history of education, history of mining and metallurgy and political science, theory and practice of agriculture and political economy, and history of commerce. In addition, he was attempting to fashion a respectable institution of higher education in the face of bleak prospects, "the one hall looming against the barren eastern hills, set in the midst of sagebrush without the relief of trees or other buildings." [1] The new era had arrived but not without throwbacks to the old.

This period was marked more than any other by a struggle within both old and new Land-Grant Colleges to maintain and, if possible, to raise standards. The chief difficulty remained the lack of preparatory education. As late as 1890 only 2526 public high schools were operating throughout the country. Even these, however, were concentrated in the larger cities and towns, leaving to the rural population the struggling district schools. The problem was particularly acute in the West where Wyoming was a typical example. In all the state there were but 39 school buildings of any kind in 1883, and no more than 130 by 1887. The schools were held in ranch houses, railroad section houses, and sheep wagons. Only 6 public high schools existed in 1890.

The colleges were forced to institute, or to enlarge where started, the preparatoty work. As late as 1896 the Report of the Section on Mechanic Arts of the new land-grant Association stated:

One college reports having endeavored to establish, by a great and radical change, a course that should be, in fact as well as in name, a college course. The experiment was tried, and the consequence was that they found themselves with depleted ranks and were forced to retreat to their former position. They found that the students coming to them had not the necessary preparation, and that the stand taken for a higher grade of work failed to bring about any noticeable improvement in the class of students coming to them for admission. . . . Acting on the assumption that "the colleges are made for the people," a number of the institutions report that, in order to afford such students an opportunity to acquire the needed preparation, they have introduced preparatory and subfreshman courses, which give a thorough preparation about on a level with a good high-school course.

Thus the institutions were attempting to fulfill their designated function but under conditions far from perfect. Oklahoma, organized in 1891, found itself with not a single student qualified to undertake college work. The consequent preparatory course enrolled forty-five students, with the number jumping to eighty by the end of the first year. Minnesota's experimental secondary school was widely hailed as an effective bridge between the gap of the elementary schools and the college. The institutions resigned themselves to continue work which they neither wanted nor liked to perform. In 1897 Professor Hilgard of California observed at a Land-Grant College meeting:

We may look forward to the time when we may dispense with the preparatory school, for the reason that the public school will do the work and do it adequately. But until that time comes (and I am afraid I am not enough of an optimist to see it in the very near future) it will be absolutely essential that we should continue our preparatory courses, and there is nothing legal in the way; it is simply a matter of propriety, or rather of expediency.

The "matter of expediency" forced the colleges to forego entrance requirements. A few required part of a high-school course before the student could enter "the college." Most admitted the students directly from the common schools. Some went as far as the University of Missouri, which in 1891 allowed any student to enter provided he made application and paid a fee. The situation was the result of conflicting desires. On the one hand, the colleges were determined to serve the people, which meant taking students at whatever level they could find them. On the other hand, the colleges wanted desperately to be "institutions of higher education" but they realized that this was impossible if they were to be true to their heritage of the democratic tradition. Entrance requirements were raised slowly, but it was not until approximately 1913 that a majority would require a full high-school course. In addition to the lack of high schools, the colleges found the work of the existing schools inadequate and often inferior. The level of college work varied widely. Some institutions maintained what would now be considered a technical high-school course of study. Others attempted strong four-year courses. It would be some years before standards had become uniform and interchange of students was possible.

In spite of these problems, the period witnessed a substantial increase in total student enrollment. The figures for the two decades are confusing because no effective method had been found nor any central bureau named to gather statistics. From a variety of sources some pattern is evident, however. The report of the Commissioner of Education for 1889, based on thirty-two Land-Grant Colleges, listed 10,000 students under the tutelage of 700 faculty members. The annual income of the colleges was said to be $1,500,000, with an endowment of $10 million. Grounds and buildings were valued at $6 million, and scientific equipment at nearly one million dollars. In the five years from 1884 to 1889, the number of students had increased 50 per cent and instructors 30 per cent. The totals sound impressive until one realizes that one of the oldest of the colleges, Michigan State, a third of a century after its revolutionary beginning, enrolled only 369 students in 1890. By 1896, the number of colleges listed had grown to 57, with some 14,000 students taught by over 1300 teachers. This was the start of an unprecedented expansion throughout all American higher education. The Land-Grant Colleges began assuming an increasingly larger share of the load.

THE CURRICULUM

The curriculum responded, sometimes slowly, sometimes immediately, to the growth of human knowledge. Until the twentieth century, institutions of higher education had only a small role to play in the expansion of this knowledge. It was assumed that their place was to be the conservative element in human affairs, to keep hold of the old until society had tested and found true the new. By the close of the nineteenth century, that concept had begun to change. As knowledge of the world and of the world's men increased, and as life became more complex, the college curriculum was forced to change. Devices were being fashioned to give to the colleges much of the future leadership in the expansion of knowledge.

Science had begun to come into its own in the eighties and the nineties. It now became academically respectable for a student to be concerned with the universe about him. By 1898 President Bryan of Washington State College could observe:

Slowly the notion was forming that the mind grows by what it feeds upon, and that it feeds upon the multitude of sensations which come flocking inward through the open windows of all the senses; that the blue-bird's wing and the silver sheen of the speckled trout meet with a corresponding somewhat [sic] in the human mind just as surely as does the epigram of Plato; that truth and beauty lie no more deeply concealed in every dull clod and crawling worm of this great cosmos about us than in the mysteries of this microcosm within us. And so it has come to be accepted that the mind may grow on chemistry as well as philosophy; that it may expand under the influence of science as perfectly as under the influence of poetry; that sociology is a not less comprehensive and useful instrument of higher education than mythology.[2]

The colleges were thus ready to follow society in its consuming interest in the world around it. The cause was due in part, no doubt, to the emphasis on "useful things," as well as to the dissatisfaction with the traditional. The combination of the two was to revolution-alize the curriculum in the same manner as collegiate objectives had been changed.

The curriculum virtually overflowed in its attempt to keep pace with expanding knowledge. In an attempt to solve the problem, the Land-Grant Colleges at first embraced the elective principle. By 1883 at Michigan State, the seniors were permitted for the first time to select three out of their five courses. And, as a curious but logical consequence, there came to the colleges a broadened concept of their function. No longer were they content to prepare the farmer's son for farming alone. In keeping with the freedom and possibilities of American life, the son should have the right to go his own way, and such a right "to adopt any vocation that his inclination and talent may lead to and his judgment approve, should not be abridged by an educational system designed to prejudge his future and train him for one vocation only." The farmer's son should not "measure his possibilities by his father's attainments. He may be farmer or physician, teacher or lawyer, merchant or mechanic, preacher or president." [3] The first break came by 1890 when the interest in agricultural education led to a demand for agricultural teachers. Thus began an increasing contribution of the Land-Grant Colleges to the preparation of teachers, a concern not envisaged in the original Mor-rill legislation. By 1899 the colleges were ready to become not just agricultural and mechanical institutions preparing farmers and me-chanics, but centers of learning and preparation for all areas of life. The colleges had begun the inevitable step toward becoming uni-versities.

Though these broad movements were apparent, there remained an amazing lack of uniformity and planning, particularly in agri-cultural instruction. The situation had been confounded by expansion and specialization in various fields, as well as the increase in the number of books available to give content to the teaching. Less than a hundred books on agriculture and related sciences had been written by Land-Grant College faculty members up to 1895, but nearly three hundred were issued in the period from 1895 to 1907. New subjects had been added because of the demand, and often in curious fashion. Roberts explains how poultry became a part of the curriculum at Cornell:

About 1888 a smiling young student approached me and asked me why we didn't have a poultry department? I replied rather sharply that I knew nothing about the chicken business; had no means to employ a man who did, if there was such a man; and that I had seen so many persons go through the chicken fever and come out looking like a moulting hen sitting on one egg, that I was in a critical frame of mind. Without being daunted in the least, he said that he knew something about the chicken business and would like to try his hand at it. He thought poultry culture ought to be taught at the college. . . . He finally got me interested and I told him to draw up plans for a poultry plant. . . . I proposed that with our own hands we should build the first chicken house out of a great pile of refuse lumber left from an old barn.[4]

Out of the growing wealth of material to teach came conflicting views regarding the end result of the teaching: should it be to train men to farm scientifically, or to train scientists and specialists to serve the farmer? Most colleges concluded that both were necessary and attemped to include both under one curriculum. Dissatisfaction with the compromise position was inevitable. Gradually, the handicraft gave way to the science. Where the University Farm was still maintained, it became a teaching aid rather than a center of instruction. It served the function of an experimental proving ground to test possibilities for which the ordinary farmer could take neither the time nor the trouble.

In agriculture the trend toward the elective system was to be short-lived. As specialties increased, so election narrowed. No longer was there one professor who taught "agriculture." By 1895 there were chairs in horticulture, botany, entomology, agricultural chemistry, dairy chemistry, agricultural physics, bacteriology, mycology, dairy husbandry, animal husbandry, as well as other variations peculiar to individual institutions. Soon the colleges would be faced again with the charge of being too practical, too technical, but in the meantime the practical and the technical had risen above the level of the handicraft. As numbers grew and funds increased and as science became respectable, laboratory equipment was considered essential. The equipment of even ten years previous which had been thought so magnificent was now regarded as "ludicrously inadequate." Standards were set for systematic organization and technique in the laboratories. Systematic classroom presentation followed.

The mechanic arts kept its lead over agriculture, not just in numbers but in more extended development, in better facilities, in increased recognition, and in standardization. By 1896 it was reported that "a glance at the schemes of study of the engineering courses will reveal a general similarity, indicating an approximately unanimous judgment of the teachers in these courses and of the framers of them." [5] The increasing specialization and subdivision of fields brought the charge, however, that engineering already was too specialized. H. C. White of Georgia, at the 1896 land-grant convention, pleaded:

Our colleges must give such good, genuine, broad education to their students as will equip them with the mentality requisite to cope successfully with their fellows in the intellectual struggles of life, or else they fail of their purposes, become a laughingstock of scholars, and a hurt rather than a blessing to the community. In no other way, in my judgment, can our colleges serve the great purpose for which they were founded—to make of the industrial pursuits intellectual occupations to be engaged in by educated men.[6]

But the increasing emphasis on utility was to take precedence. The colleges must turn out "a class of students who, when they graduate, shall know how to do something, something the world wants done." [7]

Typical of the period, too, was the increasingly close relationship between the instructor and the instructed. "A bridge of human sympathy" had spanned the gulf between the professor and student. As Silvester observed in 1898, "It is no longer necessary to overawe the scholar by a wise and vicious look in order that he may be respectful, obedient, and docile. The reign of the rod is no longer supreme in the hall of learning." [8]

Altogether, then, there were many changes taking place: the laboratory system strengthened, the libraries opened, physical exercise made systematic, studies made liberal and equal, the discovery of the individual, specialization leading sometimes to rivalry among departments, the commercial value of the college degree gaining new emphasis and importance, a change even in the teaching of the old liberal studies, and a continual evolution in subject-matter. In the words of Ross, the period marked "the transition from natural history and natural philosophy to the formalized basic sciences, from rule-of-thumb empiricism to scientific husbandry, and from elemental mensuration and mechanics to the emerging branches of engineering." [9] "Farming" was now "agricultural science" and the old "mechanic arts" had become once and for all "engineering."

Coeducation and Home Economics

The opening of college doors to women, begun earlier in the century and spread wider with the founding of the Land-Grant Colleges and state universities, became accepted nationally in this brief span of years. The number of women attending coeducational colleges increased sixfold, while the number of men grew only threefold. From this point on, few would question the wisdom or the benefits of coeducation as a permanent part of the college scheme.

With the increase in the number of women students came a concomitant increase in the colleges offering home economics. Whereas in 1890 only four Land-Grant Colleges had such departments (Kansas, Iowa, Oregon, and South Dakota), within the next fifteen years eighteen were organized. Again the West was to take the lead. With the exception of Connecticut and Tennessee, the eighteen colleges were all in the North Central and Western states. The interest in home economics had developed for a number of reasons, all of them a part of the changing times. The role of women had undergone substantial changes since the days when they had performed only the functions of mother, housekeeper, cook, and general handyman. With a change in function had come a rise in status. The evolving democratization of education also contributed. The rise of science and industry brought with it an increasing requirement for the services of women, not the least of which came through new emphasis on foods. Women were useful in many occupations, and utility was the doctrine of the times. With all these changes came, too, an increasing awareness of the value of college study of many of the same subjects pursued by men. Isabel Bevier described it well:

. . . much of woman's early work in chemistry was a more or less indefinite playing with test tubes in which one of three results was expected— a beautiful color, a bad odor, or an explosion. She was not long in discovering that her brother took chemistry and bacteriology . . . because he expected to use this knowledge later in his work with soil or in the dairy. . . . [Women] realized later that the laws of heat could be illustrated by the kitchen range quite as adequately as by the steam engine, that the life history of bacteria could be studied in many household processes, and that the chemistry of food was in many cases better suited to their needs. . . .[10]

Home economics had not yet reached the systematized pattern which would mark its later course. It, too, awaited the further development of the scientific method and of applied research. The first years of the new subject were not without human difficulties as well, and presumably not a few college administrators shied away from such offerings on this score as much as any other. Illinois' first professor of domestic economy around 1880 left the university to marry one of its regents, with the result that the professorship remained vacant for twenty years.

Veterinary Medicine

In the meantime, another specialized subject-matter field was making its way into the college curriculum. The Land-Grant Colleges were by no means the first to pioneer in the treatment of animals and diseases, but they were to transform the new field into a respectable scientific enterprise. As early as 1762, veterinary education had been offered in parts of Europe under state sponsorship. In the United States it began in private schools organized around 1857. The work centered almost entirely around the horse, an animal of great significance to both agriculture and transportation. The private schools had no research interest or function. They were purely business enterprises, subsisting on student fees. These schools, modeled on the English type since the founders were graduates of English schools, were amazingly primitive in both method and facilities. Before the turn of the century some twenty-seven schools had been operated at one time or another.

As the population and the accompanying food demand increased, the loss of meat-producing animals by disease assumed great economic significance. There were no doctors prepared to make well the ailing cattle, swine, and sheep. Furthermore, few had any notion what made the animals ill. To this already difficult situation came more problems, with the appearance in America of destructive diseases such as contagious pleuropneumonia in cattle and epizootics of foot-and-mouth disease. Whereas the proprietary schools had specialized in the horse, now came the demand for men trained to treat the food-producing animals. The private schools had neither the funds nor the interest to fill the need. The Land-Grant Colleges, ready to serve the farmer, stepped into the breach.

The development started in the new colleges with the teaching of animal husbandry in simple form as a requisite for any good farmer. In founding Cornell, for instance, President White obtained the services of the Scotch scientist, Dr. James Law, who was one of the pioneers in laying the foundations for the veterinary college to come. Most of the early veterinary colleges grew out of professorships such as this. In 1879 Iowa State College established a two-year course in veterinary medicine. Harvard followed in 1882, the University of Pennsylvania in 1884, Ohio State in 1885, Cornell in 1896, and Washington State in 1899. Harvard dropped its curriculum in 1901. The other six have continued to the present day and, with the exception of the University of Pennsylvania, all are constituent parts of Land-Grant Colleges. The private schools continued to flourish, with fourteen established between 1890 and 1900. They were all to disappear within the first three decades of the twentieth century. Again, additional land-grant schools were to fill the need.

Graduate Study

Graduate work was to develop slowly and only the beginnings are seen in this period. The first Doctor of Philosophy degree was awarded by Yale in 1861. By 1876 only forty-three more such degrees had been granted. Johns Hopkins, the institution later to be called the first truly American university, placed strong emphasis on graduate work and inspired other institutions to take it up. In the Land-Grant Colleges, graduate study originated from the recognition of the need for research. Credit is given to early scientists such as Bessey at Iowa State and Nebraska, Beale at Michigan, Bailey at Cornell, Hilgard at California, Hopkins at Illinois, Osborne at Ohio State, who inspired their students to go beyond the usual offerings. By themselves engaging in experimentation and exploration, the professors were to open new fields for conquest for the enterprising student.

The founding of the experiment stations as organized divisions of the colleges lent an even stronger stimulus to graduate work. The facilities and equipment for research provided the necessities for the developing graduate study. In this regard, agriculture can take some of the credit for stimulating graduate study in other fields in addition to its own. The start had been made; further development was yet to come.

Military Training

The teaching of military tactics remained in chaotic state throughout most of this period. Requirements and practices varied widely. Only six of the colleges made military instruction a four-year requirement. Five reduced it to three years, while fourteen colleges required two years only. The number of hours per week varied as widely. Until 1885 military instruction was unpopular with the students and faculty. The colleges attempted to reduce the requirement to a minimum necessary to comply with the vague law. Then there came a period of increasing interest, partly due to national events. By 1898 about 75,000 young men, during the previous ten years, received at least one year's instruction and practical training in military science and tactics in the Land-Grant Colleges.

With the revival of interest, even though spasmodic and half-hearted, the colleges did attempt to lift military tactics by its bootstraps. In 1889 the War Department finally moved to bring closer cooperation between itself and the colleges. The Adjutant-General proposed measures which included faculty status for the professor of military science and tactics "with all the rights, privileges, and authority of other heads of departments or professors." A suitable uniform for the students to wear when engaged in military instruction was suggested for prescription by the colleges. For the first time a proposal was made that "all undergraduate students capable of performing military duty should be required to attend the prescribed military exercises." In that year a report of the Commissioner of Education showed that 54 per cent of the students were receiving military instruction, and the president of the land-grant Association was led to observe that this was "a gratifying result, furnishing evidence that the trust is executed in accordance with its requirements," even though no one knew for certain what the requirements were. As the colleges developed in size, the military commandant became less influential and lost the original status as a disciplinary officer he had enjoyed in some institutions. The military instruction took its place as one of many different departments, except in several institutions such as Clemson and Texas A. and M. where the military emphasis continued to recent times. By 1898 forty-two colleges had fully organized military departments with 572 student officers and 1456 noncommissioned student cadets supervising the work of 7000 "privates."

Conditions were far from perfect, however. Beyond the detail of army officers, to act as professors and the allowance of a small quota of antiquated arms, Congress had done nothing to indicate an interest. The War Department had started some measure of regular inspection in 1887, but refused to recognize the military graduates with any standing except "the empty honor of enrollment in the Army Register." No opportunity for a military career was open to the graduates either in national or state military organizations. The first genuine but small recognition came during the Spanish-American War when President McKinley appointed a few graduates to the Regular Army. It would take a major war before the military work of the Land-Grant Colleges received just recognition.

THE EXPERIMENT STATIONS

Experimental work in the Land-Grant Colleges had begun almost with the organization of instruction. As the subject-matter became more formalized, the faculty found many questions without answers. The professor's own dilemma was compounded by the number of requests from farmers who wanted additional answers to complex questions. The attempt to find the answers led to explorations of great significance. Each answer raised more questions until it was evident how little everyone, including both professor and intelligent farmer, really knew. To this situation were added the serious national problems of soil exhaustion and abandoned farms. To answer the questions, the states followed the lead of the pioneers of the seventies in organizing during the early eighties a number of new experiment stations. By 1887, additional stations had been established in Alabama, Indiana, Kentucky, Louisiana, Maine, Massachusetts, Minnesota, Nebraska, New Hampshire, New Jersey, New York at Cornell, North Carolina, Ohio, Tennessee, Vermont, and Wisconsin. Field experiments and increased experimental work on the college farm were a part of the informal or organized effort in nearly every state. By the time Federal assistance came, at least twenty-eight states were carrying on experimental work in a formal pattern.

The early stations were beset with many difficulties. Few trained workers were available. The demands for answers were so great that a smattering of effort resulted rather than a concentration on thorough answers in a few well-chosen fields. The public often did not understand why there were no ready answers to questions. Station work was little known and even less appreciated. Nevertheless, the colleges and the states were attempting to do something—and to do it on their own. The basic pattern of state support was established in those early years before the Federal government made funds available. It was a pattern which would serve agricultural research well in the years to follow because it meant that the stations were free to concentrate their attention on problems of purely local and regional significance. With their attention so focused, few would question eventually the desirability of increased state support.

The early stations, unlike the colleges, could look to Europe for concrete examples to follow. The Rothamstead Station had set an almost ideal pattern for what the American scientist hoped he could accomplish. The American work became in time even more practical, responding to the principal concern of the farmer over varieties and breeds. The farmer wanted to know what was best and most profitable in wheat, corn, and livestock. He wanted to know how to control disease in plants and animals, how to feed both plants and animals to obtain better returns. The concern over disease and insect destruction led to a rapid development of entomology. Horticulture, too, became increasingly important, as did agronomy. The stations were too hard pressed to find immediate answers and too understaffed to delve into more fundamental problems. Generalizations would come from a multitude of individual experiences, and from these generalizations would stem principles to be explored and proven. But in the early years the emphasis was on today's best action, not tomorrow's lasting solution.

The beginning work emphasized even more the tremendous need for more scientific research in the problems of agriculture. Help was needed not just for the sake of the individual farmer but for the nation whose food supply and economy rested in large part on the farmer's efforts. This concern provided, therefore, a substantial reason for the Land-Grant College representatives to assemble once more. In January of 1882 and again in 1883, a convention of representatives met in Washington on the call of the Commissioner of Agriculture. The most important item of business was the need for federal aid to agricultural experiment stations because of their national significance. Legislation was prepared in 1882 by a group of those associated with the Land-Grant Colleges. It was introduced in Congress but failed to win support. One educator observed, "Our ideas were crude and we ourselves hardly knew what we wanted, but we all knew that we needed something more than was within our reach." [11]

Soon farmers and their organizations as well as agricultural officials and teachers were to lend their support. The newly inaugurated Grover Cleveland made a strategic appointment for the Land-Grant Colleges in naming as Commissioner of Agriculture an old friend of the colleges, Norman J. Colman. By 1885, at the first meeting with Colman, Professor Knapp of Iowa was able to comment, "I think all thoughtful men have long since agreed upon two questions: First, the necessity of accurate experimentation, in charge of trained men, to determine the important agricultural problems that now confront the people of this great producing country; and, secondly, that it is impossible that that investigation should be carried on by private means." [12] The advocates of federal support recognized that the benefits of investigation would not fall just to the farmer but to all who consumed his produce—and that meant the entire population. Furthermore, farming was subdivided into many activities and operating under such varied conditions that it would be virtually impossible to organize self-supporting research, as well as impossible to control its findings by patents. The farmer's work is not a big business, they argued, and he needs the assistance of the government where business and commerce do not.

A number of Congressional bills establishing various forms of experiment stations were introduced in the years from 1882 to 1887. Finally, an important and influential Congressman, Representative William H. Hatch of Missouri, took up the cause and gave his name to a measure introduced in the House. Senator J. Z. George of Mississippi presented the same bill in the Senate. Hatch was not only

Chairman of the House Committee on Agriculture but an able and skillful parliamentarian. His interest was so great and his arguments so persuasive that the bill passed easily in 1887, and to it has been attached his name in recognition of his leadership.

The Hatch Act provided for a department to be known and designated as an "agricultural experiment station" in each of the colleges established under the Morrill Act of 1862, or subsequent legislation, "in order to aid in acquiring and diffusing among the people of the United States useful and practical information on subjects connected with agriculture, and to promote scientific investigation and experiment respecting the principles and applications of agricultural science." The work specified by the act was a catch-all for the concerns of all the regions and could not fail to interest farming of all types.

The legislation gave the United States Commissioner of Agriculture authority to supervise the program, to furnish forms for the tabulation of results, and "to indicate, from time to time, such lines of inquiry as to him shall seem most important," as well as "to furnish such advice and assistance as will best promote the purposes of this act." An annual report from the stations was also required. Of particular significance was the provision for the dissemination of the results of research so that all might benefit. The stations were required to publish periodic bulletins or reports of progress and to make them available to each newspaper in the state as well as to "such individuals actually engaged in farming as may request the same." The government franking privilege was added to help encourage a wide distribution. A sum of fifteen thousand dollars was appropriated to each state accepting the provisions of the act through legislative assent. The funds were provided "for the purpose of paying the necessary expenses of conducting investigations and experiments and printing and distributing the results." The amount was not large but it served eventually to stimulate the states to provide at least matching or greater sums from the state treasuries.

Twenty-five years after the passage of the act establishing the colleges, the Federal government had finally recognized the value of their work. With the Hatch Act, the Federal government entered into a systematic and cooperative relationship with the colleges, though the institutions were to remain distinctly state organized and sponsored. Local initiative was maintained but national interests were recognized by the direct concern and coordination of the Commissioner of Agriculture. It was a "unique example of national administration in which influence rather than coercion" was the policy. Mumford called the act "a recognition of a national faith in science as an instrumentality for solving the practical problems and difficulties confronting the farmer." [13]

The passage of the Hatch Act immediately stimulated the growth of the experiment stations. Where there were none before, the states established them. Those already in existence were expanded. The number of staff members employed for experiment station work doubled within ten years, so that by 1897 at least 628 were reported on the rolls. In the period from 1887 to 1903, the stations published a total of 6143 bulletins, circulars, and reports. For a number of years the investigations remained relatively simple, along the same lines as those earlier undertaken. The Eastern stations, for the most part, continued and expanded their inspection work. By 1899, a report listed as articles under inspection "commercial fertilizers and feeding stuffs, seeds, human foods, water supplies, Paris green, creamery glassware and apparatus, nursery stock, and cattle." The experiment station personnel felt a strong obligation, in accord with the provisions of the Hatch Act, to bring results of investigations to the personal attention of the farmers. Distribution of printed matter would not suffice. Director J. S. Newman of the Alabama Station told the 1889 meeting:

We find that if men who are working in the line of scientific agriculture, as teachers of farmers, so to speak, understand how to talk to them and to project their own thoughts into them, there is nothing more effectual than personal contact in assemblies of farmers, through lectures, through farmers' institutes, through conventions of every kind, through the Grange, the Alliance, or the Club. If we can spare the time or afford the expense of sending the proper men out as missionaries—it is well to use plain language—much good will be done. There is a vast deal of missionary work to be done before we can accomplish what we are seeking to do in the advancement of agriculture through the instruction and elevation of those engaged in it. [14]

With the emphasis thus on practical problems and direct lines of communication to the farmer on the farm, fundamental research would have to await the more complete recognition of its need. Such a time was not far off. It would come as soon as farmers were accepting without question the wisdom of applying science to daily work in the pasture and in the hayloft.

Relations between the state experiment stations and the United States Department of Agriculture were cordial from the start. Fortunately each appreciated the other, and all were impressed by the magnitude of the task entrusted to both. Even before the passage of the Hatch Act, the colleges suggested that the Department act as a central agency to compile and distribute the information on experiments from the several states. At the convention in 1885 and again in 1887, the new Association urged Congress to create and finance a central office. Finally, Congress did insert a clause in its 1888 appropriations bill to establish the Office of Experiment Stations within the Department. In 1894, for the first time, the Office began a thorough annual review of the work of each station. Its prerogatives and control were to increase as Federal funds increased.

During this period the states left to the Federal government most of the financial responsibility for the operation of the stations. As late as 1903, over half of the stations received no direct state aid, six received less than $1000 a year, while eight were reported to have a state income equal to or in excess of the Hatch money. In not a few states, therefore, in the early days the stations were apt to be called "Hatch Experiment Stations" rather than state stations. Without state funds and their often concomitant controls, and without definite Federal restrictions, the stations grew under a tradition of free inquiry. The Board of Regents of Wisconsin in 1894 set forth a policy followed by most trustee bodies: "We cannot . . . believe that knowledge has reached its final goal, or that the present condition of society is perfect. . . . In all lines of academic investigation it is of the utmost importance. that the investigator should be absolutely free to follow the indications of truth wherever they may lead. . . ."

Under the stimulus of Federal money and without Federal or state controls, the stations were ready to forge ahead in many areas of concern to agriculture. Not the least of their early accomplishments was the perfection of new scientific techniques such as the manufacture of vaccines and serums, inoculating materials for legumes, laboratory services in lime determinations for fertilizing purposes, and the diagnosis of plant and animal diseases. Atwater's work at Connecticut in human metabolism was an exceptional contribution to understanding the function of food in the body. Probably the most famous of the early discoveries was the invention of the revolutionary butterfat test by Professor Stephen M. Babcock at Wisconsin in 1890. As a result of the station work, the farmers had gradually but decidedly become science-minded while the scientist was becoming farmer-minded.

The work of the experiment stations had changed the character of the colleges as well. For the first time organized research became an organic part of the college structure. Faculty were dividing their time, both to the profit of agriculture and of the student, between class-work and research effort. Slowly a sound body of scientific knowledge was evolving and with it came far better and more thorough tests and treatises. For the first time the farmer found that the work of the "book-men" at the state college actually could and did affect the farm income and daily labor to the farmer's great advantage. There would be little hesitancy now on the part of the farmer to support what had become *his* college.

With all the bustle of activity in agriculture, engineering was not to be left behind. By the late eighties many colleges had taken the natural step of fashioning an experimental laboratory, particularly in testing, out of the old shop. Experiments in mechanical and electrical engineering were fairly common. Where such laboratories did not exist, the colleges showed increasing interest in their establishment. The first engineering bulletin appears to have been issued by the University of Wisconsin in 1894. By 1896, with the agricultural stations now firmly entrenched, the proposal had been made for an Engineering Experiment Station in each state or territory. A bill was prepared and introduced in Congress to establish such stations. At the end of the year the new Association's Executive Committee was forced to report sadly that the legislation failed to emerge from committee. After ten years the effort would be made again. In the meantime, the colleges developed what they could along experimental lines without formal organization. But industry was prospering sufficiently so that no national demand would result. In addition, unlike the farmer and his soil, there were no individual engineers confronted by an exhausted supply of metal.

The Morrill Act of 1890

Throughout the struggling years of the new colleges, their great champion—now Senator Justin Morrill—had been struggling, too, but in vain, to get them more help. Ten years after the first Morrill Act had passed in 1862, the Senator introduced a bill to provide for their further endowment. It was defeated in 1873. Morrill was not easily discouraged. In the eighteen years between 1872 and 1890 there were but six years when Congress did not have before it a Morrill proposal to grant further aid. His persistence was not only admirable but amazing. In his eightieth year of life his efforts on behalf of "his colleges" finally ended in success.

This time, however, he would be bolstered by two forces which had been denied him in previous efforts: the colleges themselves, and the increasingly strong national farm organizations. The proceedings of the youthful college association contain many references to the work of its executive committee in helping to frame the 1890 bill as well as guide it through the Congressional halls. The bill was introduced on April 30, 1890, in the first session of the 51st Congress. Four months later it was signed by President Harrison, but not until it had been subjected to strong arguments against both the measure and the colleges it sought to benefit. Its opponents claimed that the farmers themselves were not in favor of the act, that there was not yet a distinctive agricultural college emanating from the 1862 grant. One representative stated that "the trouble is that in some of the States there is very little difference between an agricultural college and a literary college." Politics, too, entered the picture once more. The support of the organized agricultural groups was highly significant in combating the criticism. It was sufficiently influential, too, to provide curricular restrictions within the bill. The National Grange was fearful that funds intended to aid agricultural instruction would be diverted to other pursuits, as the Grange contended they had in the past. In the opinion of this powerful farm group, to offer more funds without restrictions would be to continue an already unfortunate practice. Thus the amendment which would restrict teaching areas was prepared by the Association's Executive Committee to satisfy the Grange and secure its powerful support.

The act conferred upon existing Land-Grant Colleges (or those to be organized subsequently under the terms of the 1862 legislation) an additional endowment, derived from the sales of public lands, of $15,000 for each state or territory. To this basic sum would be added annually $1000 a year until the annual payment amounted to $25,000. The money was to be applied "only to instruction in agriculture, the mechanic arts, the English language and the various branches of mathematical, physical, natural and economic science, with special reference to their applications in the industries of life, and to the facilities for such instruction." The states must enact legislative assent as well as guarantee against the loss of funds through mishandling. Once again the funds could not be used for "the purchase, erection, preservation, or repair of any building or buildings." On this point the House report observed:

The theory of this provision (which is repeated in the present bill) evidently was that the States should furnish the material plant required for the proposed institutions, while the fund contributed by the United States was intended to make adequate provision for the actual cost of instruction. . . . The States have done their part well . . . your committee believes it to be a matter of the soundest public policy, and even of good faith with the States, that Congress should increase the provision for the annual maintenance of these institutions somewhat in proportion to the growing demands on them.[15]

For the first time provision was made for Federal administration and more centralized Federal jurisdiction over the colleges themselves. The president of each college was required to submit an annual report to the Secretaries of Agriculture and of the Interior, the latter to ascertain and certify whether the college is entitled to receive its share of the annual appropriation.

Probably the most significant feature of the new act was a guarantee that the Negroes would benefit from its provisions. The states maintaining separate colleges for white and colored students must propose and report "a just and equitable division of the fund to be received under this act between one college for white students and one institution for colored students." Thereafter, the institution for colored students would be entitled to the benefits of the act and subject to its provisions. The states which had used the 1862 funds entirely for the education of white students were now forced either to open their facilities to the Negro or to provide separate facilities. Here is one of the few instances in Federal legislation in which there is both an injunction against discrimination and a specification that "separate but equal" satisfies the mandate. The Second Morrill Act thus inspired and encouraged the establishment of a number of Negro Land-Grant Colleges throughout the South. At least seven of the colleges had their beginnings prior to 1890 but only three had offered agricultural instruction before 1890. The states took various means to meet the new provisions. Five named the existing state-supported Negro institution as the Negro Land-Grant College. Six established new colleges under state control, whereas six others either designated existing private colleges as the Negro land-grant institution or took over such existing colleges. The results were far from satisfactory. Because the conditions under which the Negro colleges were to operate were so different from those of other institutions, we shall review their development in a separate chapter.

The 1890 bill was amended by the House to limit funds to the teaching of specific fields. For the first time provision was made for instruction in some of the arts and all of the sciences. The institutions were to interpret the restriction as an obligation to offer work in the arts and the sciences. This widely-held view contributed to their development as universities rather than colleges limited to agriculture and the mechanic arts. In effect, it accomplished what the Grange had attempted to prevent.

In many ways the colleges truly came into their own under the stimulus of the 1890 act. State support had been meager throughout the sixties, seventies, and eighties. The states had felt under no obligation to help the colleges, which the states regarded as "national institutions" because of their national origin. The land-grant income was considered sufficient except for a few necessary buildings which were provided only because Federal money could not thus be used. Following 1890, however, the states assumed an increasing share of the burden of expansion. With better definition of their role, with wider appreciation of their work, and with increased interest and support on the part of the people, the colleges came to be regarded more as state than national institutions. As a result, Federal funds decreased in importance. By 1907 the states were carrying more than 85 per cent of the increased expenditure. Tuition and fees had not yet become an important source of income for many colleges.

The passage of the Second Morrill Act serves as an important milestone in the history of the Land-Grant Colleges. The institutions which had struggled to survive were now ready, with this additional

Federal aid, to become permanent and progressive segments of American higher education.

EXTENSION EXPANDS

"Farmers' Institutes" were the occasional first steps in extending the boundaries of the campus. Early efforts were given impetus by the growth of the experiment stations, leading to a further extension of campus lines. Though no formal name was given to the work, experiment station staffs from the beginning accepted as part of their duty making the information of the laboratory and experimental field available to anyone who desired it or could use it. Correspondence as well as personal contact were frequent devices. By 1885 the Wisconsin Legislature had passed a bill appropriating $5000 annually to the conduct of Farmers' Institutes. By 1893 the appropriation had risen to $12,000 annually and the institutes were under the management of a superintendent with faculty status. The decade of the eighties saw the expansion of institutes or equivalent public meetings in some twenty-six states on a more or less permanent basis. By 1903 all but six of the fifty-two states and territories had well-established institute programs.

Many of the colleges were beginning to organize formal extension departments, Rutgers probably being the first in 1891. In New Jersey short courses were offered in seven different towns on the subjects of soil and crops, feeding plants, and animal nutrition. The movement was so widespread and accepted that by 1891 special state appropriations had been made for institute work in 14 states. In the fall of 1895 and the winter of 1896, Michigan State College sponsored seventy institutes, one in each county of the state. A special section for women was included as a part of the whole program. Cornell expanded its extension program in 1896 to include local experiments as a means of teaching, expository bulletins, itinerant horticultural schools, elementary instruction in nature study in rural schools, and instruction by correspondence and reading courses. In the following year the state legislature increased the extension appropriation to $25,000. Among the figures reported were 200 local experiments with various crops; 10,000 teachers reached through visits to schools, lectures at teachers' institutes, and distribution of nature-study leaflets; 15,000 pupils enrolled for nature study; and 1,600 young farmers taking correspondence courses. It was apparent then that all forms of extension work, including demonstration on the farm, were a part of the extension program before the turn of the century. The later and more organized extension developments were not as new and as revolutionary as many would have us believe.

The national agricultural depression which had begun in the eighties and extended almost through the nineties led to a demand for expanded extension efforts. A college report in 1897, almost joyful over the plight of the poor farmer and what his misfortune meant to the college, observed, "Fortunately we have been greatly aided by the hard times and the multitudes of bugs and special difficulties. These things have driven people to thinking and to asking for information. The agricultural communities are thoroughly aroused, and now is the time to teach." [16] By 1899 the figures showed all but three states conducting farmers' institutes, with an approximate national total of $170,000 spent on the program. The estimate was made that some 2000 institutes had been held that year with more than a half million farmers in attendance.

The popularity of extension worked hardships on the already hard-pressed college faculties. Many of those working in the experiment stations were carrying class loads as well. Now they were asked to travel throughout the state, to conduct voluminous correspondence, to compile bulletins and reports, and to write articles for newspapers and journals, as well as to attend frequent farmers' meetings. Here was emerging the tri-part function of the Land-Grant Colleges—instruction, research, and extension—only in those days it was combined in the life and work of a few men, rather than through a well-developed college organization and staff.

The programs of the institutes were at first largely inspirational. The change was made gradually to the scientific as more information became available. By 1900 women speakers were taking part in institute programs in a number of states. In 1890 cooking schools had become connected with institutes in Minnesota. In 1895 in Michigan a separate section for women had been organized. By 1898 in Illinois the women had formed a "domestic science association" in several counties in order to work with the men in planning and carrying out the institutes.

The benefits to the farmers of the various phases of early extension were immediately recognized. Some claimed that the extension program had helped turn the tide of the extended agricultural depression. As early as 1893 James wrote with enthusiasm:

The improvement of the agricultural condition of the state effected by the University in thus extending its activity is remarkable. Many cases can be noted in which the industries of communities have been changed from unprofitable grain raising to horticulture, dairy farming, etc., with accompanying prosperity and a raise in land values. It is not too much to say that the rapid progress made by the State in the direction of dairying, horticulture, and improved stock raising, is in no small degree owing to the work of the Institutes. The farmers are becoming more intelligent and more prosperous. They participate more freely in the discussion, they learn self-help and cooperation at the same time, and become interested in public concerns.[17]

The further development of extension in agriculture and home economics was not so much a matter of ideas and form as of time. The far-seeing Isaac Roberts rose in a national land-grant meeting to comment, "So far am I convinced that the minds of the masses have become receptive, that I predict that the question in the near future will be not how we may reach the farmer, but how we may satisfy his demands."

The early lyceum movement and the subsequent Chautauqua system were to form the foundation stones for another type of extension work in the Land-Grant Colleges. It was known as "University Extension" in England before it became transplanted in this country. This second form is, therefore, designated "University Extension" in some colleges while other institutions call it "General Extension." University extension as a formal movement began in 1887 when a speaker before the American Library Association meeting aroused the enthusiasm of his audience by describing the benefits of home study work. It grew out of a desire to compensate many people for their lack of formal education.

The possibilities of carrying education to the people through reading circles, evening classes, lecture series, and correspondence courses seemed immense. University Extension differed from its agricultural counterpart because it did not pretend to solve special problems related to occupation. It further differed by its attempt to transfer the work of the classroom into the home and community, whereas agricultural extension sought to make available the results of research and new methods. University Extension emphasized culture and advanced education. It was not, therefore, limited to the Land-Grant Colleges, although they played an important role in its subsequent development. After passing through its first wave of popularity, it fell into a period of questioning and sometimes disrepute. There were those who felt that "taking education to the masses" would lower institutional standards. Others thought it could be nothing but superficial and inferior. University Extension developed particularly in the state universities rather than the separate Land-Grant Colleges. Its methods, however, were profoundly influenced by the accompanying development of agricultural and home economics extension. The two movements grew up together.

"Short Courses"

The offering of "short courses" in agriculture grew in the same period and out of the same impulses and needs. When the colleges discovered that the four-year course did not serve adequately the needs of all the farmers, they attempted various patterns of courses lasting from two or three days to two years. As it became evident that less than a majority of the four-year graduates would enter farming directly, the colleges devised a way to offer work in the limited occupation of farming originally envisaged in the Morrill Act. In a sense, this was an admission that the four-year curriculum was not always feasible for all who wished only to do farming.

The short course work began at Wisconsin in 1885. In 1894 Professor Clinton D. Smith at Michigan State "fitted up a small room in the basement of the agricultural laboratory and here . . . the first short-course classes of twenty-seven students were held for six weeks in January and February." [18] Minnesota started a school in 1888 for women students who lacked a high school education. The course was primarily for training in homemaking and lasted for six months each year for three years. In some institutions short courses took the form of work over a brief period for farmers and homemakers who could come to the campus; in others, it provided a purely practical education for students lacking the necessary preparation to enter the four-year course or wanting only intensive work in farming methods. Many felt that it might be the solution to the vexing problem of how to offer higher uniform collegiate work. By 1895 the New Hampshire Legislature had authorized the establishment of a two-year course in agriculture for those unprepared or financially unable to enter the four-year curriculum.

The short course served as an effective agent in helping to solve many of the problems of the growing colleges. It counteracted the criticism directed against a lack of practical farming in the curriculum. It left the colleges free to train teachers and scientists as well as the more able practical farmers. It gave an opportunity to offer to farmers and their wives more extensive training and more scientific training than was possible in the sometimes superficial institutes. Here, too, was the beginning of a part of the college scheme which would continue into the present day. It was another indication of the desire of the colleges to serve the people as adequately and as thoroughly as possible, regardless of the consequent break with traditional methods.

The New Association

The Land-Grant Colleges, from the beginning, had never fostered nor enjoyed competition among themselves. They were bound together in a common purpose by one legislative act which had promoted all. Their common problems were new and unique. The criticism leveled at one institution was equally true of most others. It was natural, then, from the very start that they would cling together. Out of their early "clinging" came a force of tremendous later significance.

In the first two decades of their existence, the colleges frequently exchanged ideas and plans on an individual basis. This unorganized counsel was not sufficient, however. The colleges felt the need for definition of common program and increased stature. Some thought that a national organization would not only benefit the individual constituent units but would call attention to the important work accomplished by all. In 1882 and 1883 representatives from the institutions gathered in Washington to discuss problems and policies. The first genuine convention, however, came in 1885 at the call of the United States Commissioner of Agriculture. In May of that year he sent out a circular letter calling attention to the benefits of such a meeting not only to the colleges but to his department and to all agriculture. The letter was signed by Norman J. Colman, an old friend of the colleges. It attracted the attention of the colleges undoubtedly because of the wide interest in the possibility of Federal aid for the experiment stations.

Seventy-eight people met in Washington on July 8, 1885, in response to the call. They represented the Federal Department, boards of agriculture, the agricultural press, representatives of foreign agricultural interests, the colleges, the experiment stations then organized, and individual delegates. They resolved to meet again within the organization of a formal association. The Proceedings of the meeting are the first record, aside from individual recollections, of discussions taking place at the early land-grant national assemblies. The first annual convention of the new body met in Washington in October, 1887. The cooperative campaign for the Hatch Act, waged by the colleges and their friends, had taught them that further common effort might produce equally significant results. The delegates adopted the name "Association of American Agricultural Colleges and Experiment Stations." The Treasurer was later to lament that he had been informed by a number of college treasurers that "there would be no difficulty in getting dues if our name were shortened." It would eventually become even longer.

In the beginning years the work and problems of the experiment stations constituted the principal items of concern. The Preliminary Circular for the second organized meeting in January, 1889, commented, "Existing circumstances seem to make it important that the . . . meeting should consider experiment station matters rather than college affairs, except as the latter involve the former. It is therefore suggested to the several institutions interested that the delegates to this convention should particularly include directors and staff workers of experiment stations." In that same year, two permanent sections were proposed and subsequently adopted: one for college work and one for experiment station work, for "the discussion of such matters relating to the work of the colleges or stations as from their technical nature are unsuited to the general meetings of the Association." By 1892 five sections had been organized: College Work, Agriculture and Chemistry, Horticulture and Botany, Entomology, and Mechanic Arts. Engineering, however, was to play an insignificant part in the meetings and the administration of the Association. Mechanic Arts was dropped in 1903 and was not represented again for at least ten years. The Association was preoccupied with agriculture. Engineering depended on some of its own professional societies for exchange of information.

In 1890 the Association adopted the practice, continued ever since, of meeting during alternate years in Washington. By 1891 the representation at the annual sessions had grown considerably. The Proceedings recorded 124 delegates and attending representatives from 38 states and territories and from 42 stations and 38 colleges. The Association immediately grew strong from the leadership of a number of great figures of the early land-grant movement. Among them were President Henry E. Alvord of Maryland and Oklahoma, President George W. Atherton of Pennsylvania, Director Wilbur O. Atwater, President Henry H. Goodell of Massachusetts, and President Henry C. White of Georgia. From the start the delegates determined to exercise no authority over the individual institutions which constituted the membership. It was a cooperative body but not one to meddle in each other's private affairs. Every college, regardless of size or standards, was represented equally and participated equally in all of the activities and deliberations. Aside from the opportunity to exchange views and exert united pressure, the Association gave the members an excellent means of continual self-examination.

The agenda was at first largely scientific. Administrative problems were incidental until scientific national organizations provided the forum, leaving the Association free to concentrate on methods and policies. As one president was later to observe, "Imagine the university presidents of today listening, as did their predecessors of the nineties, to six lectures on soil nitrogen (1891), to five on horticulture (1892), or to the development of the role of alkali salts in soils and the whys and wherefores of the formation of pinholes in cheese (1895)." [19] Other topics of less extended concern were "How to Induce Young Men to Study Agriculture" (a subject discussed continually from the first meeting to the present day), admission requirements, course offerings, and degrees.

From its first meetings in the early eighties the collective land-grant group was active in promoting Federal legislation in behalf of the colleges. The 1882 session adopted a resolution asking Congress to appropriate funds for experiment stations. The first station bill, introduced in the House by Representative C. C. Carpenter of Iowa in 1882, was drafted principally by Professor Seaman A. Knapp of Iowa, one of those who attended the meeting. The meeting in 1883 approved a plan for the establishment of stations by a Federal act carrying supporting appropriations. At the 1885 session a committee was appointed to work with Commissioner Colman on the many experiment station measures before Congress. After its successful efforts in behalf of the Hatch Act, the Association officers worked assiduously to make sure that Congress would appropriate the funds for which the act called. In 1890 the Executive Committee reported its persistent and ultimately successful efforts in behalf of the Second Morrill Act, "It is safe to assert . . . that this new measure is now operative law, and the colleges generally are now in receipt of the new income because this Association exists and because of its action during the last six months. . . ."

These were obviously no feeble beginnings. Within a few months after its inception, the new Association had become a power to be reckoned with. It has continued as a force both educationally and legislatively beneficial. To this united effort of the colleges can be attributed much of the stature of the Land-Grant Colleges as a system of education recognized in its collective form. In later years President Day of Cornell was led to comment, "No educational organization in this country carries greater prestige than the Association. . . . None has wielded greater power or rendered greater service."

THE PERIOD IN RETROSPECT

While the nation had been expanding economically and socially during the last decades of the nineteenth century, the new colleges expanded in size and function. There is an obvious parallel relationship between the developing nation and a growing national system of higher education. As the population increased, enrollment reached new heights. As national interests broadened, the curriculum widened. As the methods and benefits of science became the basis of industry, agriculture, and commerce, science provided the colleges with the long-sought body of truth. As life became specialized and systematic, subject-matter became technical and methodical. As the general level of education rose, academic standards followed. As men sought education, education began seeking men, wherever they might be. As the Federal government became the central power, measures were taken to tie in more closely its collegiate stepchildren. As society became more complex, the colleges lost their singleness of purpose and became universities serving all interests. At the turn of the century, the Land-Grant College idea had finally taken shape. The colleges had grown in concert with the age of their childhood. Now they were far stronger, and prepared more to lead than to follow.

5

Form and Substance, 1900-1914

WITH the dawn of the new century much had
changed in American society. The emphasis on practicality was given
strong impetus by the unprecedented expansion in all things "useful." The pioneer was no longer identified with the frontiers of geography but of technology. This was a different pattern of life. The
power was in industry and in its exploitation of inventions and
mineral resources. Mechanized farming slowly made available hundreds of thousands of men and women who previously had been tied
to the land. Living standards rose, and America became a rich and
powerful nation.

The trends of the previous decades continued unabated. In 1850
the total population stood at 23 million of whom 20 million lived on
farms or in rural communities. The figure stood at 105 million in
1920 with over half now living in cities or incorporated towns. Despite the drop in rural population, the number and size of farms expanded. Between 1889 and 1914, the value of manufactured products
rose from nine to twenty-four billion dollars. Not all, however, were
happy with this age of materialism. Writing in 1906, Thwing
lamented, "The altar fires of the creative imagination are burned out,
and in their place are the fires of the steamship boiler and of the
mogul locomotive." [1]

The years stretching from the opening of the century to the First
World War were prosperous for American agriculture. With rising
prices came expansion and diversification. Reck describes well the
changes in the life of the farmer:

Farmers were not only making more money, they were emerging from

113

frontier isolation. Mail was now coming to them by rural free delivery. The crank telephone, hanging on the hallway wall, was becoming more and more common. Electric interurbans, here and there, were bringing farmers closer to the city, picking up their milk and delivering their mail orders. The years following 1900 marked the beginning of the horseless carriage age and the great campaign to pull rural America out of the mud.

All of these factors aroused in farm people a growing discontent. They began to dream of some better fate than a lonely, unrewarding life of hard work. Comparing themselves to city folks, they too wanted better clothes, plumbing, home decorations, proper diets for their children, and a host of other things that improved communications brought into their orbit.[2]

The general prosperity and the breakdown of isolation contributed to a demand for greater service from educational institutions. The farmers were to ask for such extended and continual help that the colleges and the Federal government would be forced to create new divisions to meet the requests.

Higher education followed the nation in this period. Colleges expanded in size and function to keep up with a rapidly changing nation. In 1897 the total income of the Land-Grant Colleges amounted to $5,178,580. By 1907 the figure had risen to $14,560,537, and by 1912 to $25,967,130. Once more in 1907 the colleges received additional assistance from the Federal government. In an amendment to the appropriations bill for the Department of Agriculture, Senator Knute Nelson of Minnesota proposed an additional and annual sum of $25,000 for the colleges, starting with $5000 and increasing each year for five years to the $25,000 figure. In its only change from the Second Morrill Act, this amendment gave the colleges the right to use "a portion of this money for providing courses for the special preparation of instructors for teaching the elements of agriculture and the mechanic arts."

In this period, in the midst of the expansion of funds and interest, the Land-Grant Colleges would settle on the form and find the substance for their educational contribution to the nation. The idea had begun to take shape in earlier years, but now it had become sufficiently clear so that college spokesmen were commenting, as did Wisconsin's President Charles Van Hise in 1904, "I shall never rest content until the beneficent influences of the University . . . shall be made available in every home of the state." Aristocratic education had found a powerful rival in the attempt of the Land-Grant Colleges and state universities to reach all of the people. The Association's Committee on College Organization and Policy reported in 1911 that "it is not inconsistent with high scholarship and scientific research for an institution to be actively engaged in popular teaching and demonstrations." The Committee concluded, "It is undoubtedly the duty of our institutions to render service to industrial needs in every possible way." The nation seemed to agree. As early as 1901, President William McKinley commented, "Although I am a graduate of one of the greatest institutions founded upon another basis, the institutions represented in your Association are more nearly in accordance with the genius of the growing development of the American people than any other branch of higher education." [3]

The people responded to the new philosophy and work of the institutions. The University of Wyoming, as an example, could report that it "has at length been recognized as something more than a local school. People feel that it belongs to all Wyoming." [4] Such recognition brought the Land-Grant Colleges out of an era of relative obscurity into a period of great demand. In 1911 Dean Eugene Davenport commented, "Now we work in the lime light, which is perilous to the judgment as well as to the vision, and questions come to us in multitudes. . . ." "The inventive genius" in the expansion of industry and agriculture brought great demand for land-grant graduates. Engineers and scientists were sought in unprecedented numbers. The colleges which once had to plead for a place for their graduates now became concerned over their quick success. The new age demanded useful men in useful occupations. The colleges finally emerged self-confident after fifty years of struggle for status. The "new education" was no longer new. It had found its place in the expanding nation so that by the end of this period the Secretary of Agriculture could call the Land-Grant Colleges "the most systematic and gigantic attempt ever made to help the laboring man and woman, to better their processes and enlarge the scope of their thinking." [5]

In terms of achievement, this period is best marked by the emerging philosophy of the Land-Grant College system. The growing self-confidence helped each institution to think more clearly of its function. The first conclusion was that the colleges must not limit themselves to the narrow role of training men and women only at the collegiate level. The colleges had a function to fill as social agencies devoted to finding solutions to any and all human problems. This would mean the perfection of a unique internal organization. By 1904, Kenyon L. Butterfield, who would serve as president of three Land-Grant Colleges, was ready to recommend that each college

should develop as rapidly as possible a definite tripartite organization that will reveal the college in its three-fold function—as an organ of research, as an educator of students, and as a distributor of information to those who cannot come to the college. These are really coordinate functions and should be so recognized. The colleges should unify them into one comprehensive scheme. The principle of such unity is perfectly clear: We have in research, the quest for truth; in the education of students, the incarnation of truth; and in extension work, the democratization of truth.[6]

The growth of the colleges affected all segments of American education. Secondary education was stimulated by the expansion of opportunity at the college level. Even the traditional colleges had come to accept much of the new approach. Chemical, physical, biological and engineering laboratories had become common in institutions of higher education. The classical and the scientific existed side by side in the same institution, equally respected at last. By no means could all of this change be attributed to the Land-Grant Colleges, but they must be given a large share of the credit for persevering in unpopular days.

As the Land-Grant Colleges had helped to stimulate the growth of public schools, so in turn the increase in number and character of the high schools affected the colleges. The percentage of the total population attending high school tripled in the first two decades of the new century. As the high schools expanded and improved, the colleges found it possible to drop their preparatory courses. The growth of the schools and the increase in per capita income made it possible for more students to attend college. The total enrollment for all higher education in 1890 had been 156,756. In 1910 the figure stood at 355,215. The total Land-Grant College enrollment increased in the fifteen years from 1895 to 1910 from 22,565 to 73,536. Davenport reported in 1912 a distinct and somewhat amazing change from the days not long past, ". . . most of the better colleges are overflowing with students, and many of them are discussing the best methods of limiting attendance—all within ten years from the time when all of us were going out into the byways and hedges for students and 'compelling them to come in' on almost any terms." [7] Under these conditions it was natural for the colleges to gain the confidence necessary for their expansion in scope and character.

A good example of the change is found in the substantial development of Land-Grant College libraries beginning around 1900. In the early years, the libraries had grown more slowly than the colleges themselves. They consisted almost entirely of standard reference works, and suffered the three dangers of dust, fire, and mice. As the fields taught in the colleges expanded, more volumes were written and acquired. In the first two decades of the twentieth century the libraries, like the curriculum, became complex and authoritative.

The Land-Grant Colleges in their first thirty years had never been certain of their place on the educational ladder. Some thought themselves purely trade schools; others attempted, often unsuccessfully, to emulate the standards of the older institutions then regarded as at the top academically. By the early twentieth century, the necessity for quality was widely recognized. In his inaugural address in 1904, President Tisdel of Wyoming stated what many land-grant educators were then repeating: "The value of an institution of learning depends not so much upon the number of its students as upon their scholarship and character." The colleges could not, of course, be transformed overnight. An example of the continuing misunderstanding over their purpose and function was highlighted by the Carnegie Foundation report at the end of the first decade of the new century. The report was highly critical of the work of the institutions and particularly of their motives both in establishing curricula and setting standards. They were accused of responding too readily to popular demand. The report caused extensive self-examination and may well have served a most useful purpose.

THE CURRICULUM

Among the curricular concepts emerging in the new century was the belief that a varied civilization, as America certainly had become, demanded a variety of tastes and of educational processes. What once fitted all men for life in a less complex society could no longer be the pattern. In 1907, Liberty Hyde Bailey pointed up the new thinking, "It was an old idea that education in some way should be 'adapted to' the needs of life. We now have taken a somewhat different point of view, feeling that education should develop out of the needs of life and be fundamentally native and indigenous. It is one thing merely to apply education, it is quite another to develop it out of the very affairs of life." [8] The curriculum began to reflect society and society's needs in a much greater fashion than ever before. The Social Sciences became more accepted as necessary to the training of the whole man. Preparation for citizenship became an important element in curricular planning. President William Oxley Thompson of Ohio State noted in 1903, "We believe in education not only for the sake of the individual but for the sake of the Nation." This emphasis would serve the Land-Grant Colleges well. The early radical notions finally had been accepted within the prevailing educational philosophy.

The growth of teacher education was rapid in the new century. The University of Minnesota in 1906 was one of the first institutions in the nation to create a separate College of Education. Departments specializing in particular areas of education, such as vocational, agricultural, home economics, and industrial, grew steadily. The movement was well under way before the Smith Hughes Act of 1917 made Federal funds available.

The increasing diversification of the curriculum inevitably led to intra-institutional rivalries. R. W. Silvester in 1897 pointed to circumstances which continue down to the present day, "How often have we seen the narrow, incomplete products of our handiwork in our faculties; in men decrying the usefulness of other departments save their own; in the schedules insisting upon time out of proportion for the reason that this department or that department is not so important in the general make-up of the product out of the raw materials in hand." [9] Not only was the curriculum diverse but also expectations of the individual faculty member. It became increasingly obvious that each department, at least in the agricultural divisions, had a trifold function. The demand arose for specialists in particular lines to relieve the individual of the tendency to do all things and none well. By 1905 President Thompson sighed in public, "Students are now less of a problem than faculties are."

The question of curricular balance was a subject of early debate. As science became more extensive in scope, it became more intensive within a particular area. The Land-Grant Colleges had been among the first to break from the traditional education and to concentrate on the technical. But as the technical became more intensive and complex, the pendulum would swing back by degrees. The new century saw consideration given to a possible middle course. Bailey commented, "If we can not teach everything, neither can we afford to break with experience, and the question is how much of the new we shall combine with something of the old." The view was held that specialism by itself was not adequate for the varied civilization. It must be integrated with the totality of which it is a part. J. E. Stubbs of Nevada called attention to the vocational necessity for the humanities as a part of the curricular picture, "The scientific method and the philosophic spirit, the practical aim and the cultural life, ought to be kept in union at every stage of education. To divorce them is to miss, in a measurable degree, the true aim of education." [10] Thus with the new century came a new problem for the colleges. It was not one to be solved easily. Probably the question of balance couldn't be answered to the satisfaction of everyone. As time would show, it wasn't.

Agriculture

As American agriculture became more diversified and mechanized, the demand for men trained in agricultural science increased. For the first time, agricultural courses became "popular." With the public now on the side of the colleges and with their handiwork in demand, the colleges were more free to break from their own brief traditions. They were at last able to admit in public that their primary purpose was not the training of farmers for farming. True, this training continued to be a part of the collegiate picture, but the colleges were now more free to concentrate on training for agricultural occupations such as teaching, research, and specialists to serve agricultural industries. There remained, however, early in this period, little agreement over topics to be taught and methods of presentation. The lecture system continued out of the past, even with the strong curricular emphasis on science. Laboratory work was still not well-planned or executed.

The course-offerings became remarkably diverse. Too much worthwhile knowledge had accumulated, and the faculty was not yet prepared to sort the necessary from the desirable. Cornell University offered 3 subjects in the field of agriculture in 1890. Ten years later the number had increased to 37, and, within another ten years, jumped to 169. By 1910, Kansas was offering 112 courses; Iowa, 170; Oregon, 123; Michigan, 80; and Illinois, 142. A. B. Storms of Iowa reported in 1905:

Instead of a general course called an agricultural course . . . which contained a little general agriculture, with one professor giving such instruction as was given in the whole field of agriculture, we now have in agronomy proper nineteen distinct courses of study; in dairying, thirty; animal husbandry, twelve; horticulture, seventeen; agricultural chemistry, twelve; botany, with special reference to agriculture, nineteen.[11]

The emphasis continued to be on the productive side of agriculture, despite the increasing intensity of the sciences. It was thought that among the great contributions of the Land-Grant Colleges could be teaching the people how to raise the standards of production. The theory of "more and better crops" influenced the curriculum to such an extent that little place was given either to the humanities or to business and economic insight, social conditions, and citizenship training. Little by little educational leaders began talking about treating agriculture as an art as well as a science.

The introduction of agricultural subjects in the secondary schools led to a demand for teacher-training in agricultural education. The Nelson Amendment in 1907 stimulated what had already begun. Massachusetts introduced a Department of Agricultural Education in 1907, and by 1909 the colleges were beginning to consider the value of graduate work in the teaching field. The Report of the Committee on Instruction in Agriculture in 1912 indicated the rapid development of this specialized area within the course of ten years:

From the best available sources of information it appears that 40 of the agricultural colleges for white students are offering courses designed to train high school teachers of agriculture. . . . The dignity to which agriculture has arisen in recent years as a subject of study in public schools is indicated by the fact that 20 of the agricultural colleges now offer courses in agricultural pedagogy, or as it is sometimes called "industrial pedagogy," in which special attention is given to methods of teaching this new high school subject. Fifteen of the agricultural colleges have outlined four-year courses for teachers of agriculture, the work of which in many cases is largely prescribed.

The gradual mechanization of agriculture brought curricular emphasis on "rural engineering." A committee report in 1903 stated the belief that "the greatest opportunities for students and for the improvement of the general agricultural practice of this country will be found in the systematic study of the manufacture and use of agricultural machinery." Departments of irrigation engineering were started in Colorado and California, and the first curriculum leading to a degree in agricultural engineering was established in 1904.

By this time, the so-called "Short Courses," designed to "improve those who are at work" or those who want just intensive farming, were offered in practically all of the Land-Grant Colleges. The time involved varied from a "corn school" for practicing farmers, lasting five days, to a regularly organized two-year course leading to some form of certificate of completion. In the brief sessions, the standards were as low as the ability of the "students" involved happened to be. In the two-year courses the standards sometimes were identical to those of the degree curriculum, and the same students attended some of the same classes.

Engineering

The engineering curriculum, meanwhile, had been developing even more rapidly than agriculture. In many respects, land-grant engineering had been left to make its own way. Many of the Land-Grant Colleges separated from state universities were called "agricultural," and the Association continued to place its deliberative emphasis on the problems of instruction and research in agriculture. While agriculture could chart its own course in terms of curriculum, engineering was forced to take cognizance of the pattern being set by non-land-grant engineering schools. In the early days the colleges had begged industry to give the graduates an opportunity to prove themselves. This industry had done begrudgingly at the pay rate of 7½ to 10 cents per hour. Now the supply could not keep step with the demand. Faculty members, too, were lured away by industry and commerce. No longer was there any doubt about the wisdom or place of engineering education at the college level.

The engineering curriculum was highly specialized and technical. The popularity of the graduates tended to lull engineering educators into a feeling of satisfaction over their product. A few raised voices of concern, such as President Butterfield in 1904, "[The engineering student] secures in college little incentive and less training for intelligent performance of his duty as citizen and as a member of society. . . . A democratic society must insist that all its educated men shall be leaders in solving society's problems. But even the educated men can not lead unless they have first been taught." [12] But the engineering educators were too busy keeping up with developments in industry and commerce to concern themselves with the social problems their students might face. It would take a war and a depression before the problems of people became objects of concern in proportion to the problems of machinery. The definition of "mechanic arts" adopted by the Land-Grant College Engineering Association in 1914 still gave no indication of the curricular thinking later to be debated so intensely: "Mechanic arts is a broad educational term, which includes engineering education as its higher or professional phase, trade school and short course instruction as its collateral and extension phase, and experimental and other technical investigations as its research phase. Engineering is the professional phase of mechanic arts."

Home Economics

The most dramatic expansion in this period was in home economics. In 1890 only four Land-Grant Colleges had departments of domestic science. By 1900 nine institutions, including those in Iowa, Kansas, South Dakota, Oregon, Utah, Colorado, Michigan, Ohio, and Montana, were offering courses in "domestic economy." By 1905 the number had grown to eighteen; by 1928, to forty-two.

Though the expansion was great, the determination of curriculum proceeded more slowly. The questions of content and sequence were ones "about which no two persons have the same opinion," a speaker in 1905 reported. There were those who questioned whether it was justified to offer a college course leading to a degree in this subject. The speaker asked his audience, "It is pertinent to inquire if at the present time such a course is feasible, justifiable, or educationally wise." He concluded, however, that ". . . there will follow in due time a legitimate course of study of collegiate character, in which cooking, sewing, laundering, etc., will have no place, but in which there will be thorough study of the natural sciences, with a generous allowance for the liberal arts, and for which the degree of bachelor of science may consistently be given." [13] By the end of the first decade, an Association committee had been appointed to prepare a four-year curriculum in home economics. Its effort led to success and the curriculum was subsequently adopted by many of the colleges. At the same time all were urged to follow a uniform practice of designating the course work as "Home Economics." The accompanying development in extension work and the formation of the American Home Economics Association both helped to give the subject-matter a place and a purpose. The curricular emphasis on "fancy cookery" and "fancy stitches" changed slowly to courses in the natural, physical, biological, and social sciences and in the humanities.

Veterinary Medicine

Developments in veterinary medicine were less spectacular, although there was a steady growth in the number of Land-Grant Colleges offering the new subject. Georgia and Arkansas organized schools which later closed, but five others—Alabama, Colorado, Kansas, Michigan, and Texas—continued on a permanent basis. As late as 1910, twelve proprietary institutions taught a majority of the 2717 students enrolled nationally in veterinary course work. In the following year 706 graduated, with 487 receiving degrees from the private schools and 219 from the state-supported.

Military Instruction

Little change was evident in military instruction during this period. Conditions remained poor both academically and in the degree of support by the War Department. Military tactics continued to have no established or respected place as a part of the college plan. There were a few who attempted to justify it on the basis of the value to the individual student, but no one paid much attention to such rationalization. The colleges had struggled to provide a place for military tactics and finally, without Federal encouragement, admitted defeat, letting it ride along as an auxiliary but not particularly respectable part of the institution. The attitude would change only after a war forced Federal authorities to recognize its value.

Agriculture

By the turn of the century the Agricultural Experiment Stations were well established and on their way toward an eventual accumulation of a vast body of valuable and essential information. More than any other factor, the stations had helped farm people to accept the methods of science in their thinking and planning. This achievement within a relatively few years is all the more significant when one considers that rural population is traditionally among the most conservative elements of society.

The stations had attempted at first to concern themselves with the immediately pressing problems of the state or region in which they were located. The factor of economic utility was an important one in the practical answers given to the practical questions of the farmers. It soon became evident, however, that fundamental research was not only desirable but necessary if station workers were to provide answers to any question, no matter how practical. As farm economy changed from the depression days of the end of the nineteenth century to the prosperity of the twentieth century, station workers were more free to concentrate on original research. By 1905, J. M. Hamilton of Montana, in a paper on the "Relative Amounts of Pure and Applied Science in the Land-Grant Colleges," was ready to offer a definition: "Scientific research that is carried on for the acquisition of truth only and the mere sake of extending the boundaries of knowledge is pure science. Scientific experiment conducted with the immediate end in view of utilizing the results in an economic problem is applied science." [14]

Station leaders, recognizing the necessity for pure science in some of their work, became concerned over the continual pressure for practical results. They enlisted the aid of Representative Henry Cullen Adams of Wisconsin who introduced a bill in 1904 to provide further aid for the experiment stations. Early in 1906 the bill was passed and then signed by President Theodore Roosevelt. The Adams Act called for an appropriation of $5000 for each station, to be increased annually by $2000 until the maximum of $15,000 had been reached. The funds could be "applied only to paying the necessary expenses of conducting original researches or experiments bearing directly on the agricultural industry of the United States, having due regard to the varying conditions and needs of the respective States or territories."

The plans and policies subsequently adopted for the administration of the Adams Act gave the Federal government more authority over the type of work to be pursued than had resulted from any previous legislation. The act directed the Secretary of Agriculture to "ascertain and certify . . . whether [each station] is complying with the provisions . . . and is entitled to receive its share of the annual appropriations." As a result, the Secretary of Agriculture called the attention of the stations "to the necessity of outlining the work to be supported by the Adams funds in the form of specific projects for approval by the [Federal] Office of Experiment Stations in advance of making expenditures on them." For the first time in Land-Grant College history a Federal department had been given direct authority over state units. The selection of topics and the plans for investigation were left to the states but their ultimate suitability had to be passed upon in Washington. Key comments on the significance of this new provision:

By the [advance] review of plans and budgets outlining proposed programs of action, the federal agency may assure itself that the contemplated work is in accordance with the policies of the federal act. This is the primary utility of the method, but it has collateral values. It may compel a planning attitude and a periodic re-examination of state programs. It permits federal technical advice and assistance to be offered at a time when it may exert the greatest influence.[15]

It was the beginning of frequent disagreement, often friendly but sometimes bitter, between the Department and the colleges. The complaint was made by the stations that the Department was encroaching upon their exclusive territory. The stations felt that the Department should be concerned with national questions, leaving to the states matters of local concern. By the end of the first decade, the Department was conducting a full scale research program of its own. Dean Davenport in 1913 spoke for many of the colleges in rebellion against being forced to cooperate:

. . . "cooperation" has become the slogan everywhere. Cooperation in what and how? In purely local matters clearly within the realm of the state institutions but according to projects outlined by the Department.

In this way the Department has changed its form of procedure without changing in the slightest its fundamental policy of engaging in local activities whenever and wherever it pleases. Thus it has thrown upon the state institutions declining to cooperate the appearance-of being disagreeable. . . .

[The Department] pushes straight ahead in its plan for doing anything anywhere, justifying the procedure by inviting the state institutions to cooperate. In plain terms, it has substituted by main strength its principle of cooperation for the sounder and more acceptable principle of division of labor which has been repeatedly laid down.[16]

The problem of relationships was not easily solved. It would rise again and again throughout the years to come. Despite its frequency, however, the stations would be given relative autonomy in a period when highly centralized and authoritarian Federal control was the trend. Over the years the relationship proved productive and cooperative despite occasional friction.

In addition to increased Federal control, the Adams Act proved important to the stations in two other ways. For the first time the "project" system in investigation became systematized. No longer would research be purely a matter of "hit or miss." Of even greater importance was the provision for fundamental research in the stations. The stations had the funds and were now both obliged and free to proceed with the discovery of essential scientific principles which could lead to the permanent solution of the more difficult practical problems of agriculture. This emphasis led to a rapid development of graduate work in agriculture in the Land-Grant Colleges.

The stations were soon to accomplish much of great economic significance to the nation. As an example, Sudan grass introduced by the Texas station in 1909 is now a forage crop said to be worth $15,000,000 annually to the State of Texas alone. Other examples of early achievements of station research were listed by Andrew M. Soule. He included among them:

Agronomy: Of the 47 varieties of native cotton now grown in the South, 35 were bred at the college and experiment stations located in that section of the country or developed by men trained within their walls.

Animal Industries: As early as 1884, Sanborn of the Missouri Agricultural College started research studies in the feeding of pigs which have exercised a most pronounced influence on both rural and urban life. From this small beginning has been developed most of our knowledge of animal and human nutrition in the United States. Early in the beginning of the present century, many research workers found that proteins, carbohydrates, fats, and minerals are not all that is necessary to afford a satisfactory ration . . .

Horticulture: The discovery of sprays and spray compounds, the invention of spray machinery, and the development of modern, scientific methods of disease and insect control have all come from the impetus given these enterprises in the beginning through the medium of our horticultural divisions . . .

Veterinarian: Following the discovery of the true cause of hog cholera and the production of the anti-hog cholera serum, these institutions manufactured this serum for distribution to swine growers at cost . . . At an average value of $10 per head, the losses from hog cholera were cut from $63,043,200 to $29,593,220 in a period of three years. At the same average price per head, the value of the country's hog crop increased $83,200,-000 in the same period, largely owing to the greater surety of maturing the hogs because of the decreased danger of losses. . . .[17]

Thus the stations were already saving the American farmer millions of dollars. By helping the farmer, they were assisting the consumer as well. Within a short period of time, they had become essential and integral parts of the Land-Grant College system.

Engineering

In the meantime, engineering research was lagging. Most of the reasons were identical to those which had prevented the extension of the principle of Federal support to engineering investigation. Engineering Experiment Stations suffered from a lack of a well-knit social group to lend support, such as agriculture had in the farmers. Furthermore, industry was inclined to develop its own research facilities. Discoveries meant private profit and could be patented for exclusive use. The research effort was concentrated in big industries, such as the General Electric Company which began investigations on its own as early as 1900. It would be difficult, if not impossible, to justify the use of state or Federal funds for appropriations to support research of direct commercial value. This situation was to be altered substantially only after national interests became involved. In addition, professional engineering societies were providing means for publishing papers as an effective substitute for station bulletins. There was no agency in the Federal government for centralizing engineering research work or for backing a movement for Federal funds in the same manner as the United States Department of Agriculture had done so successfully for the Agricultural Experiment Stations. An important contributing factor, too, was the lack of an association among the land-grant engineering colleges. As we have noted, mechanic arts was dropped almost entirely from the new "agricultural" association. It was not until 1913 that the engineers formed their own unit, later to merge with the other land-grant interests.

In spite of all these drawbacks, the colleges did move haltingly toward productive research in engineering fields. Faculty members were doing some experimental work under inadequate conditions. In 1903 the University of Illinois became the first land-grant institution to organize a separate and distinct Engineering Experiment Station. The Trustees acted "in recognition of the need for more accurate knowledge of the materials and processes of engineering and the conservation of those resources upon which engineering industries depend." It was hoped that all engineering education would thus be stimulated by the study of problems of special importance to professional engineers and to industrial interests. Provision was made for the publication of results through bulletins and circulars. The first such bulletin appeared in 1904. In the following twelve years, eight other land-grant institutions followed Illinois' early example. Iowa was next in 1904, Pennsylvania in 1908, Missouri in 1909, Kansas in 1910, Ohio in 1913, Texas and Wisconsin in 1914, and Maine in 1915. To a large extent, they were all patterned after the flourishing agricultural stations.

Funds were not immediately forthcoming. In Pennsylvania no provision was made for the employment of a staff and the Station restricted its activities to the publication of bulletins prepared by teaching faculty members. Standards were set up for machines and materials, methods of testing devised, and reference material accumulated. The period from 1910 to 1915 saw the extension of research laboratory work on a sufficiently strong basis to lead other institutions to establish organized stations in the years to follow.

Efforts had been made during this period to obtain action on legislation for Federal funds to support the engineering stations. Because it concerned the Land-Grant Colleges and because the colleges were popularly interpreted as "agricultural," the bill introduced in 1907 by

Representative McKinley of Illinois (at the instance of the University of Illinois) was referred to the House Committee on Agriculture. No opportunity for consideration was forthcoming. In addition, "difficulties arose in adjusting the interests of State universities having engineering departments in States in which the land-grant college is separate from the State University," according to the report of the Association's Executive Committee in 1908. This contention was to haunt the effort for Federal funds for a number of years. By the time either side was ready to compromise, the time had passed when effective Congressional action could be taken. Other means of promoting industrial research had come to the fore.

AGRICULTURAL AND HOME ECONOMICS EXTENSION

The last two decades of the nineteenth century witnessed the slow but steady growth of the extension idea. The early colleges had started on the premise only of helping the farmer's son. Now they recognized a responsibility to help the farmer help himself. This obligation stemmed from the increasing frequency of contact with the farmers through the experiment stations. An effective agency had to be devised to carry the results of the work to the farmers. The first decade of the new century found the creation of many new devices and the strengthening of old. By the time fifteen years had passed, the effective agency would be created, Federally sponsored, and ready to serve the nation in peace and war.

Extension work in the colleges by 1900 was expanding rapidly. It consisted largely of institutes, correspondence schools, and reading courses in agriculture. The President's Report of Cornell University in 1900–01 pointed with pride to the 25,000 farmers and 5000 farmers' wives reached through reading classes; to 11,500 teachers of nature-study passing along information to 21,000 children; to 2,770,000 pages of printed matter made available annually for their use; and to 4,240,-000 pages of bulletin material printed by the Experiment Station. Other land-grant institutions had similar programs, partly designed to provide for the deficiency in rural schooling. In 1905 Liberty Hyde Bailey observed that "this whole land-grant enterprise has been seized with the missionary spirit, it has been thoroughly democratized, and the effort is being made to carry it to the homes of the people by means of extension propaganda." [18] The enthusiasm spread throughout the country. Illinois had organized an extension staff in 1901, and Ohio State appointed the first permanent director in 1905. By 1910 thirty-five institutions had organized extension work. The appointment of a separate staff to carry on extension work had started with a concern on the part of station workers that their efforts were being spread too thin. With the passage of the Adams Act, they were anxious to concentrate on genuine research and to leave to another agency, more distinctly educational, the institute, lecture, distribution, and demonstration work. In 1904 President Kenyon Butterfield had taken a look into the future and urged the creation of a separate extension division:

To carry out the function of the agricultural college we need, finally, a vast enlargement of extension work among farmers. This work will not only be dignified by a standing in the college coordinate with research and the teaching of students, but it will rank as a distinct department, with a faculty of men whose chief business is to teach the people who cannot come to the college. . . .

Such a department will be prepared to incorporate into its work the economic, governmental, and social problems of agriculture. It will give the farmers light upon taxation as well as upon tree pruning. The rural school will have as much attention as corn breeding. The subject of the market . . . will be given as much discussion as the subjects bearing upon production. We shall find here a most fertile field for work. The farmers are ready for this step.[19]

Butterfield's comments were remarkably foresighted. The Association appointed him as chairman of a new committee on extension. In 1906 the Committee found "the need of concentrating, systematizing, coordinating, and developing the more important aspects of extension teaching" and recommended ". . . that each college represented in the association organize as soon as possible a department of extension teaching in agriculture, coordinate with other departments or divisions of the agricultural work, with a competent director in charge and if possible with a corps of men at his disposal." In 1908 the Committee recommended that extension work be placed on the broadest basis with full recognition of the economic and social phases of agriculture as well as the productive. It urged expansion into "the great untouched field for educational work—home life on the farm." The heart of the rural problem will never be reached, the Committee concluded, "until we at the land-grant colleges . . . are prepared to be of assistance to the farmers and their families along the higher reaches of their own lives."

So much was taking place that it is impossible to report it chronologically. We shall examine first some of the highlights in the work of the colleges, and then the efforts of the Federal Department.

Efforts of the Colleges

Until the formal establishment of cooperative extension work between the colleges and the Federal government in 1914, Farmers' Institutes continued to play an important part in the college extension program. In 1902, 820,000 farmers and their wives attended 2772 institutes costing $163,124 from state, college, and other funds. Beginning with prizes offered for exhibits by young people, some states were developing local fairs with many exhibits by farmers, wives, and children, held in connection with the institutes. Special emphasis was put upon subjects that would touch the interests of women and give them new inspiration for study and improvement. Bread-judging contests and exhibits of sewing and cooking were included, as well as exhibits and lectures on the rural school. By 1914 the institutes were held in every state and territory, with 8861 sessions attended by 3,050,150 people at a total cost of $449,882. At the same time the colleges were beginning to bring the farmers and their wives to the campus for an annual Farmers' Week, consisting again of lectures and exhibits.

Among the general results reported were more intelligent efforts of farmers to improve their farms; inculcating in young people a respect for agriculture as a profession; reaching illiterate farmers; the organization of farmers' clubs, cooperative associations, cow testing and breeding groups; improvement of roads, homes, schools, and school buildings; and the development of a number of capable agricultural teachers and lecturers. Groups of women had begun to meet in an effort to achieve a more beautiful and serviceable home as the center for raising the family. Shortly after 1900, the pioneer head of home economics, Cornell's Martha Van Rensselaer, sent out from "her makeshift office" the first bulletin for homemakers, entitled *Saving Steps*. It was reported that, soon after, she received a letter from a farmer's wife asking for additional help and suggesting that she meet with a newly-organized group of wives. The wife, upon reading Miss Van Rensselaer's bulletin, had driven "in one direction while her husband drove in the other to invite the women within a ten-mile radius to come to her house . . . [to] read the bulletin together and discuss it." [20]

In the meantime, the colleges had found another device for reaching both the men and the women. In 1904 Professor Perry G. Holden of Iowa State had enlisted the help of two railroads to run special trains through the farming area for the promotion of better seed corn. The train would stop at each community where lecturers would address the assembled farm group, displaying charts, specimens, books, and demonstration material. The train was filled with exhibits as well. In 1904 and 1905 the "Seed Corn Gospel Trains" in Iowa traveled a total of 10,000 miles, stopping 1235 times to reach 145,363 people. The newspapers were quick to support this unique and colorful way of reaching the farm population. The train device reached its peak in 1911 when 71 trains were run in 28 states, and 995,220 people stopped to listen and inspect.

The efforts of the colleges in this brief period had proven the wisdom of carrying information directly to the people. The institutes and trains would be dropped as other methods became more effective, but they had shown dramatically the importance and popularity of extension work. The colleges would soon be ready to undertake a more formal and systematic method of helping the farmer to help himself.

Efforts of the Federal Department

During this same period the Federal government had begun efforts on its own to reach the farmer. The movement began apart from the Land-Grant Colleges but, before long, would be merged in one larger program. While the colleges were promoting the idea of "demonstration farms" as a method to prove to the farmer the wisdom of better practices, representatives of the Department of Agriculture had started "demonstration work" with individual farmers. The claim is often made that extension began with the efforts of one man in one particular locality. As we have seen, extension in various forms was well under way by the time Seaman Knapp reached Texas, although credit must be given to Knapp for his enthusiasm and wisdom. His was not the first demonstration, but to those who wish a milestone in extension history, it served as the impetus to extended further endeavor.

The cotton boll weevil had made a disastrous descent on Louisiana and Texas in the early years of the century. In 1903 the Secretary of Agriculture recommended a plan of relief and employed Dr. Seaman A. Knapp of Lake Charles, Louisiana, a former president of Iowa State College, as special agent to direct the field work. Knowing of the resistance of farmers to trying anything new until its value had been proven, Knapp conceived the idea of conducting demonstrations on the farmer's own land rather than using a government-owned farm to which the farmer must travel. At a mass meeting in Terrell, Texas, on February 25, 1903, Knapp proposed to the farmers and citizens of the surrounding area that the community sponsor a demonstration of better practices devised by the Department on a suitable farm to be selected by the community. He suggested that the businessmen and farmers, all of whom were deeply affected by the boll weevil ravages, raise an indemnity fund of $1000 to cover any loss to the farmer who agreed to grow cotton under Knapp's direction. The fund was raised, and Walter C. Porter volunteered his farm as the site. The object would be to show what might be done with various varieties of planting, cultivation, and fertilizing. Seventy acres of land were used, divided between cotton and corn. According to True, although "there was much damage to the cotton by the bollworm and to the corn by wind and hail, the crops gave Mr. Porter a profit of $700 more that he probably would have obtained if the methods commonly used in that region had been followed" [21] The demonstration was a success. Knapp's philosophy had involved showing instead of telling and had stressed the need of local test and demonstration. His most famous remark which summarized his method now appears on a marker at the Porter farm: "What a man hears, he may doubt; what he sees, he may possibly doubt; what he does himself, he cannot doubt."

This method of demonstration work spread rapidly in Southern states. In the following year Knapp was given $40,000 by the Bureau of Plant Industry to extend the demonstrations. Headquarters were established in Houston, Texas, and by the close of 1904, more than seven thousand farmers were participating under the direction of twenty-four agents. The work was a Federal enterprise, not involving the colleges. Since the government had funds only to counteract the boll weevil, other financial sources had to be found. At this time the General Education Board, established by John D. Rockefeller from Standard Oil Company funds, was attempting to raise the level of education in the South. The Board agreed to finance the new "Farmers' Cooperative Demonstration Work" and gave to it sums ranging from $87,000 in 1906 to $187,500 in 1913 and 1914. Through the Seed Improvement Committee of the Council of North American Grain Exchanges, Julius Rosenwald in the North offered one thousand dollars each to one hundred counties to organize and employ a county agricultural agent for crop demonstration work.

In the meantime, the first county agent, W. C. Stallings, had been employed in Smith County, Texas, in 1906. Farmers had asked for more local demonstrations and information than the Federal regional agents under Knapp could supply. The loss from the boll weevil had been particularly severe in that year, and businessmen were concerned over the number giving up farming. At the same time the first Negro agent was appointed by the Department of Agriculture in cooperation with the Tuskegee Institute in Alabama. Within a month of his employment, another agent was appointed in cooperation with the Hampton Institute in Virginia. By 1914 there were 230 agents in 27 northern and western states. Farmers, business men, and bankers had helped to support the work of the "adviser" or "expert" who came to be known popularly as "agent."

Canada, meanwhile, had started to plan for an agent in each county. The first discussion of such a possibility under the direction of American colleges was evidently held in 1911. In that year the Association's Committee on Extension Work reported:

The extension departments will soon be obliged to recognize the necessity of keeping one or more men in the field substantially all of the time, as traveling or resident advisors. Probably the greatest efficiency will come from an assignment of a given area or district to one man, in order that he may become thoroughly acquainted with the conditions of agriculture and country life, learn to know the people intimately, and thus have an opportunity to gain their complete confidence.[22]

The colleges had recognized that their own or government-sponsored "demonstration farms" would no longer suffice. Men in the field were needed to learn the territory and work directly with the individual farmer. The college representative must be available at all times to help the farmer help himself. Before we examine more closely the movement which led to systematized Federal support of extension, we shall have to turn back the clock and scan another device which had arisen in the meantime.

Youth Work

Scattered instances of work with rural boys and girls can be found throughout the Land-Grant College history. It was not until the new century, however, that the effort reached substantial proportions. It stemmed from the trend toward vocational education at the public school level, with the dissatisfaction with rural schools, and with the desire on the part of farmers and their families to raise their standards. Some were concerned over the exodus of youth from the farm. They felt that young people would be more satisfied with their rural lot if they could become more enthusiastic over its possibilities. As a result, in this period youth work had a more spectacular growth than perhaps any other form of extension.

It started with simple contests and led to the organization of clubs. It was not confined to one state or one area. Professor Perry Holden was at work in Iowa, and others like him took an interest in young people in their communities and states. By 1904 the Department of Agriculture Yearbook reported some twelve boys' clubs organized in Illinois with a state membership of at least two thousand. The boys were encouraged to grow a perfect ear of corn on their own time and effort. Prizes were offered for the winner, and the results were displayed in exhibits. By the time farm demonstration work was under way, contests were held on the basis of acre-yields rather than one perfect ear.

The first Federally-sponsored corn club for boys was organized by William Hall Smith in Mississippi in 1907. He became the first Federal agent for club work with rural boys and girls. In 1908 Dr. Knapp, aided by funds from the General Education Board, was attempting to promote an expansion of the work. Its purposes were stated to be:

To place before the boy, the family and the community in general an example of crop production under modern scientific methods.

To prove to the boy, his father, and the community generally that there is more in the soil than the farmer has ever gotten out of it; to inspire the boy with the love of the land by showing him how he can get wealth out of it by tilling it in a better way and keeping an expense account of his undertaking.

To give the boys definite, worthy purposes at an important period of their lives and to stimulate a friendly rivalry among them.

To furnish an actual field example in crop production that will be useful to rural school teachers in vitalizing the work of the school and correlating the teaching of agriculture with actual practice.[23]

On July 1, 1909 the North Carolina State College signed the first of many "Memoranda of Understanding" to come, leading to co-operative work with the Department of Agriculture for "aiding, encouraging, and extending practical farm demonstration throughout the State." The memorandum provided for the appointment of a club expert whose salary and travel would be paid by the Federal government and whose work would consist of planning and conducting demonstrations in schools and on farms and among organized boys' clubs. By 1912 nine colleges had agreed to such an arrangement, and the first Federal club agent was employed for the North and West.

The work with girls began with a "canning club" in Aiken County, South Carolina, in 1910. The boys' clubs had become sufficiently popular for the girls to want to join the work. In 1911 instructions were sent from Washington to the club membership on such subjects as the preparation of seed bed and fertilizing; hot bed, cold frame, and raising tomato plants; transplanting; staking, pruning, and cultivation; treatment of diseases and insects; marketing of fresh vegetables, crating and grading; membership cooperation; canning of surplus products in both tin and glass; labeling and grading. In the same year the objectives of girls' club work were listed:

To provide some means by which the girls may earn a little money in their rural homes.

To help furnish the home with a constant supply of vegetables, both fresh and canned.

To encourage all rural families to live better and at a lower cost than under the present conditions.

To make the home and the farm more interesting and helpful to all members of the family.

To make mother and daughter partners with father and son in the more efficient farm and home life.[24]

A four-leaf clover was adopted by the clubs in 1911 to symbolize their work—head, heart, hand, and health. The names of most clubs were thereafter changed to "4-H" to go with the emblem. Contests and prizes continued as a part of the program, in addition to fairs, institutes, and expositions. Trips were made to the state college and to county and state fairs. The clubs had begun originally within the framework of the public schools, often with the teacher as adviser. As they expanded, the tendency was to cut off from the school and to develop an organization of their own, usually on a county and state basis. With this development came an expansion of program emphasis to include recreation, dramatics, music, and other more social events.

In 1909, the Richmond, Virginia, *Times-Dispatch* printed Dr. J. D. Eggleston's "unique recipe for agricultural uplift" which symbolized the work and goals of demonstration work with youth:

FORMULA FOR A SUPERINTENDENT

From one parent willing to give his boy a chance, extract one acre of land.

To that boy add one demonstrator who will supply expert knowledge.

Use one teacher, sympathetic with this work and capable of guiding and encouraging the boy, to stir into the boy from time to time bulletins and circulars on corn raising.

Mix the boy and the acre of land regularly.

At the end of the year state the results in terms of social chemistry.[25]

Early Cooperative Work

With countrywide activity and interest flourishing, the thinking inevitably led to a desire for greater Federal support and participation. In the past when the Land-Grant Colleges had needed assistance in launching a new type of program on secure footing, they had turned to Congress for financial backing. Once again the movement started to ask the Federal government to underwrite what the colleges and the Department had already begun. Bills were introduced in Congress in 1909, 1910, 1912, and 1914. While Congress first postponed and then deliberated, the colleges set to work to perfect what they and the Department had started. Association Committee recommendations included the appointment of full-time state directors of extension with substantial funds at their disposal. The directors should be assigned the work of dissemination of information carried on by the stations. The extension staff members should have close connections with the teaching departments. Finally, the public must be convinced of the true nature of extension work.

In 1908 President Theodore Roosevelt had appointed a Commission on Country Life with Cornell's Agricultural Dean Liberty Hyde Bailey as Chairman and President Kenyon L. Butterfield of Massachusetts Agricultural College as one of the Commission's five other members. The Commission was asked to recommend legislation to correct what the President called a barrier to the nation's "permanent greatness" in the lack of well-being of the farmer class, "for it is upon their welfare, material and moral, that the welfare of the rest of the nation ultimately rests." In his letter of appointment he concluded that "the social economic institutions of the open country are not keeping pace with the development of the country as a whole." A year later, in 1909, the Commission submitted its report. It recommended strongly the establishment of "a nation-wide extension work," based no doubt on the firm conviction of President Butterfield who had served for some years as chairman of the Association's extension committee. The Commission's report is said to have made a strong impression on the country and helped speed the day when Congress would act favorably on Federal aid. The Commission concluded:

The first, or original work of the agricultural branches of the land-grant colleges was academic in the old sense; later there was added the great field of experiment and research; there now should be added the third coordinate branch, comprising extension work, without which no college of agriculture can adequately serve its State. It is to the extension department of these colleges, if properly conducted, that we must now look for the most effective rousing of the people on the land.[26]

Help would come, too, from the old and the new farm organizations. The National Grange continued to support the colleges. In 1911 the first organization with the name "Farm Bureau" had been started in Broome County, New York, by the cooperative effort of the Binghamton Chamber of Commerce and some leading farmers, with the purpose of employing a farm adviser or agent. Although this movement was still in its infancy, it was indicative of the growing group interest of farmers and their friends.

In 1912 Clemson College entered into a joint agreement with the Department of Agriculture for supervision of the work of a state agricultural agent stationed at the college. The same cooperative agreement was reached soon with a number of other Southern Land-Grant Colleges. By this time the Association's Committee on Extension Work could report a great variety of form and method:

A. Systematic instruction
   1. The extension school
   2. The demonstration farm
   3. The correspondence course
   4. The lecture and reading course
   5. The study club
   6. Boys' and girls' clubs

B. Informal Teaching
   1. The convention and lecture
      a. The farmers' institute
      b. Farmers' week
      c. The conference
      d. The occasional lecture
   2. The object lesson
      a. The demonstration
      b. The railway "special"
      c. The exhibit
      d. The educational excursion
   3. Publications
      a. The press bulletin
      b. The leaflet and periodical
      c. The monograph
      d. The traveling library
   4. Advisory work
      a. Correspondence
      b. The traveling agent or expert
      c. The district field agent.

C. Organization
   1. The rural conference
   2. The campaign
   3. Organization, co-operation, and federation.[27]

Statistics for the year 1911-12 revealed that 333 members of the college or extension staff in 37 states were active in some form of extension work. In 21 states it was estimated that 36,340 registered students and 49,643 others attended 175 "movable or extension schools." Some 2 million people in all were reached through the extension program, and 1,949 special pieces of literature were printed for distribution. The total funds for 1913 came to $990,504, of which $663,310 were from state appropriation, $160,404 from local contributions, and the remainder from miscellaneous sources. Thus extension was already a sizable and respected enterprise before Federal aid was sought. As yet, in spite of the widespread activity, the efforts had not proven adequate to meet the need or demand. The colleges, the Department, and their friends turned to Congress.

The Smith-Lever Act

The history of Congressional effort in behalf of extension is long and confused. Between 1909 and the end of 1913, at least thirty-two different bills were introduced in the House or the Senate to provide aid in some form. The act finally adopted was itself a combination of two measures. Sixteen bills were pending at the same time. The Land-Grant College Association Executive Committee and its Extension Committee, which had been guided for almost a decade by President Butterfield, prepared a modified form of a bill which had been introduced in the House by Representative Asbury F. Lever of South Carolina on June 12, 1911. The modification was introduced in the Senate by Senator Hoke Smith of Georgia on July 16, 1912. Its wording was the result of study by both the colleges and the Department. The bill, together with many other similar measures, was discussed and criticized at length in both branches of Congress. Finally, the Smith-Lever Act was passed and signed by the President on May 8, 1914.

The act was a part of the pattern of previous Land-Grant College legislation. It extended the benefits of Federal aid to those colleges established under the Acts of 1862 and 1890. Its purpose was to inaugurate in connection with these colleges "agricultural extension work . . . in order to aid in diffusing among the people of the United States useful and practical information on subjects relating to agriculture and home economics, and to encourage the application of the same." Pending the development, neither the farm management work nor the farmers' cooperative demonstration work of the Department were to be discontinued. The work to be carried on was defined in Section 2:

. . . cooperative agricultural extension work shall consist of the giving of instruction and practical demonstrations in agriculture and home economics to persons not attending or resident in said colleges in the several communities, and imparting to such persons information on said subjects through field demonstrations, publications, and otherwise; and this work shall be carried on in such manner as may be mutually agreed upon by the Secretary of Agriculture and the State agricultural college or colleges receiving the benefits of this Act.

To finance the work, the sum of $480,000 was appropriated for each year, $10,000 of which would be paid annually to each state accepting by legislative assent the provisions of the act. In addition, the sum of $600,000 was appropriated in the second year, and for seven years thereafter an additional sum of $500,000 each year, until the annual appropriation reached the figure of $4,100,000 in excess of the $480,-000 first provided. The states would receive the larger appropriation "in the proportion which the rural population of each State bears to the total rural population of all the States." Then there followed for the first time in Congressional legislation a new "matching principle" set down in these words: "That no payment out of the additional appropriation herein provided shall be made in any year to any State until an equal sum has been appropriated for that year by the legislature of such State, or provided by State, county, college, local authority, or individual contributions from within the State . . ." None of the money could be used for land or buildings or "in college-course teaching, lectures in colleges, promoting agricultural trains, or any other purpose not specified in this Act, and not more than five per centum of each annual contribution shall be applied to the printing and distribution of publications." Plans for work in each year must be submitted to and approved by the Secretary of Agriculture.

The heart of the work contemplated would be the personal contact between the extension service and the farmer. Some were thoroughly skeptical. One agriculturist commented that "if this thing were undertaken at no distant day the shores of the agricultural ocean would be strewn with the wrecks of county agents." Senator Smith felt, however, that "this agricultural extension movement is likely to prove the greatest work [the colleges] have ever done. It opens the doors . . . to the majority of your fellow citizens." [23] The act had been

designed in part to eliminate much of the duplication in extension effort among the colleges, the Department, and other government
agencies. It set up one distinct service combining all interests. No
longer should there be the overlapping and working at cross purposes.

In one respect the act had greater significance legislatively than
educationally. It was the first of many measures to require financial
participation by the states on a matching basis. Eugene Davenport
later made a wry comment on the importance to extension of this
principle, "It is a queer kink in human nature, and a fortunate one
for us, that any state is willing to put up two dollars for the sake of
getting one from the federal treasury." [29] As the years passed, a
majority of the states came to provide state and local sums in an increasingly greater ratio to Federal funds.

The required pre-audit approval and certification for payment by
the Secretary of Agriculture led to far closer relations between the
colleges and Federal authorities working in the same field. The Department, soon after the passage of the act, reorganized its administrative structure dealing with the Land-Grant Colleges and established
a "States Relations Service," uniting in one bureau extension, experiment station work, agricultural instruction, home economics, institutes, and farmers' cooperative demonstration work. The emphasis in
the act was on cooperation, and so it was to be. It started at the local
level with farmers, officials, and organizations in each community and
county evolving plans to solve their own problems with the help of
extension workers assigned to the area and local voluntary cooperators
and demonstrators. The state extension organization would offer help
as needed and would deal with statewide matters. The Federal bureau
assisted the states and dealt with matters of national concern. As
much as possible, conflict in organization and supervision would be
avoided. Within ten years, C. B. Smith was able to report:

The result has been that the farmers themselves and their wives have been
made partners with their government—national, state, and county—in
organizing, developing, and carrying on extension work in their respective
communities. This is one of the most significant and outstanding things
in the development of extension work during the past ten years, that the
people concerned actually sit down in common council with the agents
of government and, working thus together, develop plans for promoting

more effective farming in the community, better homes, and a greatly enlarged and more significant home, community, and social life.[30]

The Smith-Lever Act did not create extension, but it gave nationwide recognition as well as a firm financial basis to a work already valued and widespread. It served as a vote of national confidence in a tried and proven effort of the colleges and the Department. The decades since the first Farmers' Institute had offered sufficient experience so that no delay would be suffered in following up the act. The Department had already entered into a Memorandum of Understanding with several states for club and county work. Within six months after the passage of the Smith-Lever legislation, the Land-Grant Association's Executive Committee and the Department had drawn up a new memorandum to fit the new conditions.

The Memorandum provided that the college should "organize and maintain a definite and distinct administrative division for the management and conduct of extension work in agriculture and home economics, with a responsible leader selected by the [college] satisfactory to the Department." Further, any and all funds received for extension from whatever source should be administered through this division. The college agreed to cooperate with the Department in all extension work conducted in the state. For its part, the Department agreed to organize and maintain a central administrative unit for handling all such work and to do so in cooperation with the college. The two parties mutually agreed to joint supervision and planning of all Federally-financed extension work within the state. All agents receiving funds from direct Congressional appropriations would be joint representatives of the college and the Department. The cooperative effort would be so designated on all publications and printed matter. In addition, plans for the use of the Smith-Lever fund would be made by the Extension Division within the college, but subject to the approval of the Secretary of Agriculture. Thus was provided a close alliance in the conduct of the work. Its immediate effect was to change the type of work undertaken by both the colleges and the Department. The Federal authorities discouraged the use of funds for Farmers' Institutes, and, in their place, the colleges began organizing a permanent system of county agents. The two great national forces for agricultural betterment now were merged into one system.

The colleges at last had found an appropriate and well-financed method for direct public service. It was a long step forward in the democratization of education. The people, through their governments, had created institutions to expand knowledge. Now the institutions were under an obligation to return to the people the benefits of the knowledge thus expanded. The program would be built around the problems and needs of the people who would learn as they worked. The sum of agricultural progress would depend, then, ultimately on the intelligence and resourcefulness of the people themselves. The college had broken with tradition, had extended the boundaries of the campus proper, and would be firmly entrenched in the local community. In this unique way the college would benefit in equal proportion to the people. It could no longer separate itself from human life and human problems. It was now inextricably intertwined with society.

Extension would have to endure years of trial and error before it could perfect its new system of education. Those years are still not ended. Part of the difficulty would stem from the fact that many of the "students" were adults, governed by their own experience and bias, resistant frequently to new ideas and to the process of learning. The teacher would have to depend upon voluntary cooperation. He could not force the student to come to class. He must, therefore, offer in "the class" instruction which the student would recognize as helpful and valuable. The "classroom" would not be confined within four walls but within state lines and would include eventually every section of the state. The teaching would have to be adapted to many different conditions. It must be flexible and informal, designed for the many and not the few. No matter how dogmatic, the teacher's conclusions would not be accepted by virtue of their espousal. The subject-matter would have to prove itself. Nevertheless, this was education—of a new type and at a new level.

ENGINEERING AND UNIVERSITY EXTENSION

In marked contrast throughout this same period, little progress was made on mechanic arts extension activities. Pennsylvania State College, under Louis E. Reber, was one of the few institutions to have organized industrial extension, beginning in 1907. Industrial concerns were not particularly sensitive to the need of education among employees. Further activities would have to await a realization by the industries that on-the-job training was insufficient. The initial efforts would be made without the cooperation of industrial leaders. Penn State organized its first evening extension class at Williamsport in 1910 in cooperation with the training department of the local high school. Dunaway reports that other efforts followed and that practically all the work was offered in connection with shop or local organizations.[34]

Some of the lag may have been due to a lack of organization among the engineering educators, the type of organization which had served the agriculturists so well through their powerful Association. It was not until 1913 that engineering deans formally discussed engineering extension. In that year Dean E. B. Norris of Wisconsin spoke of the extension obligation of the colleges at the second annual meeting of the newly organized Land-Grant College Engineering Association. He emphasized the importance of short, practical, and carefully planned engineering extension courses, and concluded that the obligations of the engineering colleges "include every element of our industrial structure, from the broad foundation of unskilled industrial workers to the narrow pinnacle of professional engineers and captains of industry." Further developments hinged upon the cooperation of industry as well as coming national emergencies.

In the meantime, some of the land-grant institutions, particularly Wisconsin, were developing programs as well as departments of university extension. Wisconsin, after starting its work as early as 1892, had established a full-scale department in 1906 and was ready to offer university extension work on a much broader scale. Between 1906 and 1913 at least twenty-seven other institutions were engaging in organized university extension. The work included extramural courses, correspondence study, institutes, lectures, reading courses, and publications for adult study in a wide variety of fields. It was obvious that university extension was not confined to the state universities and that even the separated Land-Grant Colleges had become active in extending to the general public the benefits of the arts and sciences.

THE ASSOCIATION

The period was further marked by a strengthening of the Association. As the colleges grew in stature and as their work became more complex, the change was reflected in the structure and the discussions of the Association. By 1902 the presidents of the colleges and the experiment station directors had ended, in favor of the presidents, a long and bitter wrangle over control within the Association. It was concluded that "final responsibility for action on public and administrative matters should be lodged with [the Presidents] and that the danger of their being outnumbered or out-voted should be obviated." With the Association thus in the hands of the top administrators, they were called to its leadership. Among the giants of the times were William Oxley Thompson, President of Ohio State University for more than twenty years who served as Association President and as Chairman of its Executive Committee for ten years; Whitman Howard Jordan, who had attended the organization meeting in 1885 and who was a member of the Executive Committee for sixteen years, in addition to serving as President for a term; Kenyon L. Butterfield, sometime president of several Land-Grant Colleges and prime mover of extension organization; and A. C. True, eventually and for many years the grand old man of the Department of Agriculture who served as the Association's official bibliographer for twenty-four years.

The progress of the extension movement could be measured by the activity in its behalf within the Association. A standing committee on extension had been created in 1905, and by 1909 the Constitution had been amended to create a section on extension work composed of directors, superintendents, or representatives of extension departments within member institutions. The Association was an important force behind the eventual passage of the Smith-Lever legislation. It took active leadership in establishing graduate work in agriculture as well. In 1902 it helped to sponsor a graduate summer school at Ohio State University with Dr. True as dean. The school was next held at the University of Illinois in 1905 where it was termed an unqualified success. The sponsorship by the Association of summer graduate programs at various centers convinced the individual institutions of the need and desirability of such work on a permanent and formal basis. The development of graduate study in agriculture can be traced directly to the experiment station work and to these early Association beginnings.

With the Association dominated by agriculture, the engineering representatives had gradually slipped away until only the presidents were present to represent engineering interests. In 1912 the deans of engineering gathered together and organized a separate Land-Grant College Engineering Association. In 1913 they suggested section membership in the over-all body, but no action was taken. In 1915 the two organizations met jointly. The engineers moved back slowly into the parent association but it was not until 1920 that they were given final status with a change in the name of the body to the Association of Land-Grant Colleges.

Three new Land-Grant Colleges had been founded during the decade and a half we have been examining: The Universities of Puerto Rico and Hawaii, and the Tennessee Agricultural and Industrial State College (for Negroes). The list would be complete by 1922 with the addition of the University of Alaska.

THE PERIOD IN RETROSPECT

The Land-Grant Colleges had emerged by 1914 stronger and far more secure after another period of quick growth. Their property value had soared over one hundred million dollars. Their annual income was well over one-fourth of this figure. They had received Federal votes of confidence and additional funds for instruction, for research, and for extension. They were now institutions of genuine size and stature. Kuhn depicts well what had happened to Michigan State College, for example, in the years between 1896 and 1915. There were four times as many students and five times as many teachers. The number of extension workers and county agents in 1915 equaled the teaching staff alone of 1896. The admission standards had been raised from an eighth grade certificate to a high school diploma. The inventory had trebled, and the equivalent of nine major buildings had been added to the campus. In 1896–97 the Legislature had appropriated $16,000 for support of the college and its activities; the figure was $560,000 in 1915–16.[32]

Perhaps most significant of all was the emergence in all the institutions of a unique philosophy of service—to youth, to farmers, to homemakers, to industry, to agriculture, to the entire nation. The substance was the combination of liberal and practical education. The form was the tripod of instruction, research, and extension. The colleges would no longer be allowed to grow at their own pace. From this time forward their history would reflect a nation in periodic peril from forces external and internal.

6

The Response to Crises, 1915-1937

THE next period in the life of the Land-Grant Colleges demonstrated even more clearly how much of a part of the pattern of American life the colleges had become. In the twenty-two years stretching from 1915 to 1937, American industry continued to expand, population increased, and the nation became a unit as never before. The colleges took their place within this unit but, curiously enough, their ultimate value to American society was proven finally not in a time of peace and prosperity but of war and depression. In the last analysis, the national character of the colleges became evident in their response to national crises.

This twenty-two year period was marked by emergency and turmoil. It began with American intervention in the European war, extended into the twenties with the farm depression, followed by the deep and severe depression of the thirties. With the outbreak of war in Europe, all of the trends of industrial expansion during the first decades of the century suddenly were accelerated. Almost as suddenly the crash came, and business fell into a period of chaotic disorganization.

Agriculture had become almost as mechanized as industry. The farmer of 1920 was using 26 per cent more horse power, had 46 per cent more capital invested in machinery, and was producing 15 per cent more than the farmer of 1910, in spite of the fact that the number of farmers in the same period had decreased 16 per cent. Farming was no longer a question of individual self-sufficiency, with the family surplus being sold in nearby local communities. The farmer was now producing mainly for market, and the market might be located in any part of the world. What happened in Washington, or in a foreign capital thousands of miles away, became almost as important to the farmer as what happened in his back pasture. He realized for the first time that he could help influence the forces affecting his welfare. This realization led to a tremendous surge in the number and size of farm organizations.

The Land-Grant Colleges became enmeshed in the happenings of the times. They could not remain apart and still serve farm and industry, as well as all society. They, too, would be forced to change as the nation changed. The first major crisis was World War I. As soon as President Woodrow Wilson had declared that a state of war existed with the Imperial Government of Germany, the colleges began to mobilize their staffs, their military departments, stations, shops, laboratories, and students. In the relatively brief period of actual conflict, several trends of importance to the colleges could be noted. Since war inevitably brings centralization of power in the national government, manpower, food, money, and transportation were directed from the national capitol. Though there had been a previous tendency in this direction, the First World War set the pattern for national power continuing to the present day. The war, too, stimulated scientific and technical research as never before. And extension, both agricultural and industrial, was called upon to help in a manner not previously contemplated.

With the end of World War I, foreign markets disappeared. Industry and the farm discovered that sources for consumption were drastically limited. The farmer was the first to be affected. He had been producing both for an expanding nation and for the industrial nations of Europe. The goal had been maximum food production, with token regard for conservation. With markets vanishing, the farmers were hit in the early twenties by a depression beyond their comprehension. The colleges could not remain immune. The charge was made frequently that their efforts had stimulated overproduction and thus caused low prices. The farmers, the colleges, and the government set to work to find answers and remedies, but quick solutions were not uncovered easily.

There was no doubt that the farmer was a producer of unprecedented magnitude in the history of agriculture, but his greatest handicap was a lack of understanding of the economic and social forces affecting his production. The Land-Grant Colleges, unfortunately, were not entirely blaméless. They, too, had concentrated on production without adequate recognition of other factors affecting agriculture. Beginning, therefore, with this farm depression of the twenties, the colleges turned from helping only the individual farmer to the much larger economic and social arena. Funds and personnel were devoted for the first time in large amounts to research, teaching, and extension work in marketing, as well as the social sciences. In 1927 a speaker at an Association convention outlined the four general ways in which the colleges could serve agriculture:

1. To help agriculture view itself historically.
2. To assist farm people to reevaluate agriculture as a way of living.
3. To encourage agriculture to shift from the basis of individual competition to group action.
4. To exhort agriculture to raise its standard of living as a means of getting its share of the national income.

Within a few years, however, the moderate recovery achieved after the depression of the twenties was wiped out by the severe national economic crisis of the thirties. Looking back, the farmers would see that their problems of the former decade were minor compared to the collapse facing them in the thirties.

The depression extending throughout most of the thirties hit all segments of the national economy. In recalling later its severity, President Milton S. Eisenhower commented, "Our economic self-containment disappeared. Suddenly we saw farmers who were efficient and blessed with abundant rainfall go broke because of difficulties in our own national economy, or because Italy raised the tariff on wheat, or because other nations devalued their currency or suffered economic depressions." [1] Once again the colleges were criticized for having taught the farmer to produce too much. As public institutions, they were on the defensive in more than one way. The depression found the institutions with decreasing revenue, and their graduates without employment. A complete reexamination of the functions of research and extension appeared necessary.

The Land-Grant Colleges did not remain on the defensive long, however. As the Federal government sought solutions, it turned almost immediately to the colleges for assistance. The creation of many new agencies by the "New Deal" and their subsequent programs in the states thrust upon the colleges an action role which they had neither played before nor were sure they wanted to play now. They were asked to provide advice and guidance and to serve as a clearinghouse. The dangers were great, but in the final analysis the colleges had no other choice. They became agents for public policy because the government found education to be a useful tool in the solution of many pressing problems.

The Land-Grant Colleges came of age under the stimulus of these crises. An examination of the Proceedings of the Association shows rather clearly that, until the 1920's, the colleges had no clearly defined concept of their place in American society. The decades of the twenties and the thirties witness a remarkable growth in self-assurance, concept of place, and recognition of a mission for the future. It was as if the colleges suddenly discovered that they were a force of great importance and were determined to help the nation by capitalizing on their discovery. The result was growth, enthusiasm, and achievement. The slow but steady shaping of the pattern in prior years had been fortunate because it laid a firm foundation for the sudden awakening. The major topics discussed at annual conventions disclosed institutional awareness of a new and important place and function: national agricultural policy and its relation to the colleges, improvement of teaching, development of research to fit the needs of the nation, survey of education, conservation, the relation of water resources to land use, and the placing of extension personnel on a sound professional basis.

In the first ten years alone, from 1916 to 1926, the colleges showed their growing strength. The following figures are illustrative of their expansion:

	1916–17	1926
Number of professors and instructors	10,344	23,979
Number of students	133,405	388,636
First degrees conferred	11,361	21,095
Advanced degrees conferred	1,313	3,163
Volumes in libraries	3,982,816	7,060,502
State aid (69 institutions)	$ 21,378,962	$ 57,463,142
Funds for instruction and administration	$ 37,841,260	$107,265,332
Grand total receipts	$ 46,769,397	$136,680,675

Total value of assets for 69 institutions
(round figures) $193,000,000 $400,000,000

In this period, too, other changes were to become apparent. The
two partners of the land-grant movement, agriculture and engineering, developed together. With their growth, both were to realize
that the emphasis on "useful things" was no longer sufficient. The
human element was equally important if not more so. Social environment could no longer be ignored. Man as well as science must
have a place in the curriculum and in research. Only in this way
would the colleges be preparing the true leaders.

The basic resources of the colleges—the students—were arriving
in larger and larger numbers. By 1935–36, the Land-Grant Colleges
were enrolling 17 per cent of the college students in the country, and
graduating 21 per cent. In 1882 the total land-grant enrollment had
been 2243. By 1928, over 100,000 were enrolled in nondegree courses,
in addition to 32,297 in short courses of less than one semester. The
national proportion of rural to urban residents already had changed
the background of land-grant students. In 1928, 34.34 per cent of the
graduates had been farm reared, while 34.75 per cent had been raised
in communities of more than 10,000 population. Other factors were
becoming evident in the expanding colleges. More and more women
students were arriving on the campus, and home economics enrollment increased some 2209 per cent in the period from 1910 to 1928.
By that latter year, too, the Land-Grant Colleges were training
almost 50 per cent of all engineering students in the country.

National agricultural conditions determined to some extent the
number pursuing that subject. The numbers increased in times of
prosperity and dropped suddenly in times of depression. Despite the
fluctuations in agriculture, the colleges were serving in increasing
numbers their constituencies. The University of Minnesota was a
typical example. In 1910 there was one student for every 309 residents
of the state; by 1928 the figure had risen to one student for every 106
residents. As national economic conditions made educational opportunity more restricted, the students turned to part-time employment
to help themselves. In the midst of the depression of the thirties, the
national government established the National Youth Administration

as a separate division of the Works Progress Administration, designed in part to offer Federal aid for the first time to college students.

State Support and State Relationships

The period witnessed also a substantial increase in state support of Land-Grant Colleges. In the four years from 1920–1924, the average increase in state support reported by thirty-two institutions was 55.4 per cent. In the next four years another increase of 40.6 per cent was reported by forty institutions. The ratio of Federal to state funds changed substantially, too. At the end of the first decade of the twentieth century, land-grant institutions were receiving approximately one-third of their total income from Federal sources. By 1932 only 10 per cent came from the Federal government. In 1935 Congress enacted the Bankhead-Jones Act which carried additional sums for each of the three phases of land-grant education. Under this act, the eventual total sum for resident instruction was $2,480,000; for research, $3,000,000; for extension, $12,000,000. The distribution for resident instruction was based on total population; for research, rural population; and for extension, farm population.

Within the states, the colleges found themselves increasingly in competition with other state agencies for the state tax dollar. During the depression years of the early thirties, the colleges suffered particularly; practically every college received a substantial cut in state revenue. Salaries and equipment funds suffered the most. Within a few years the colleges found themselves with their highest enrollment on record, but without a complete restoration of funds. By 1935 some had been fortunate enough to secure full or partial restoration of salary cuts and general reductions; but losses of as much as 30 per cent were still reported. It was not until the end of the thirties that most colleges found themselves in adequate financial condition to operate satisfactorily, although increasing enrollments continued to bring problems which, in many states, have not been solved to this day.

With an increase in state funds came an increasing interest in state control. The colleges had argued from the beginning that they were not a part of state government as such. Dean Eugene Davenport, for instance, claimed that the college "is an extra-governmental and highly technical enterprise needing its own special machinery and dependent upon the legislative rather than the administrative branch for direction and support." Despite this view, the colleges recognized as early as 1922 the seriousness of the problem. In that year the Association discussed the feasibility of a thorough study of administrative relationships with respect to centralized financial control. Again in 1925 it was reported that "some states are being seriously hampered by policies determined for them at the state capital." In 1930 the United States Office of Education published an extensive two-volume study of the Land-Grant Colleges. Its conclusions summarized the increasing difficulty: "Recent reorganizations of State governments, the creation of State budgets, and the extension of the power of State agencies over the finances and the internal affairs of the Land-Grant Colleges have in many instances tended to supersede the authority of institutional governing boards and institutional administrative officers." [2] The shortage of state funds in the depression of the thirties made the situation even more serious. Uniform state policies restricted the institutions. The economy-minded state officers did not trust entirely the alleged unbusinesslike notions of educators. In many states no effective solution would be reached. The problem would rise again and plague the colleges to the present day.

The Curriculum Responds to the Times

In increasing measure, the curriculum responded to national changes. One of the most obvious concerns stemming from the particular times was an emphasis on citizenship and training for national service. As national and state institutions, the Land-Grant Colleges came to feel a special responsibility for the development of American citizens. In the view of one president, the colleges were "based entirely and exclusively on the idea of social provision through governmental activity for social needs." As a result, the institution "has its philosophy in devotion to human welfare, and it must exemplify that philosophy in the building up of citizenship or it has no basis for existence."

Vocational education had become both respectable and necessary, not only in terms of its benefits to the individual but to the community of which he was a part. Wars and depressions convinced the public of the economic and national benefits of vocational education which trained men for making a living as well as rendering public service through a particular occupation. The social emphasis in terms of citizenship plus increasing specialization led to a reexamination of the curriculum. The number of courses had expanded so greatly that by 1931 it was said that a student in a university could spend a lifetime carrying a full load of undergraduate subjects, without repeating a course. Factors outside of the college contributed, too, to a reexamination within the college. The progressive delay in the age when youth entered employment, plus the general commitment to the idea that educational opportunity should be open to all, made higher education more feasible in the minds of many who previously had not considered it possible.

In the beginning, the method of satisfying the need for citizenship, or "general," education took its form in two ways, according to the pattern of the individual institution. In those Land-Grant Colleges which were also state universities, the offering to agricultural and engineering students of so-called "service courses" by the existing division of liberal arts was strengthened. In purely agricultural and mechanical colleges, new divisions were established to fill cultural needs. The latter further led to the emergence of the separated colleges as true universities. The new divisions came to fill the need for education in a variety of previously neglected occupations. At Michigan State, for instance, between 1915 and 1928, new divisions of applied science and liberal arts were created, graduate study revived, a music school founded, and curricula developed in medical biology, physical education, business administration, and hotel management. At Penn State the liberal arts division had at first been little more than a service unit. In this period it grew rapidly to become the largest division within the college. This was a common development.

Even the liberal arts divisions were not immune, however, from specialization. The 1930 Office of Education study reported on the multiplication of courses in the arts and sciences and the concomitant specialization. In the twenty-five years following 1903, it reported an increase in courses in economics of 240 per cent in Land-Grant Universities and of 766 per cent in separate Land-Grant Colleges. The number of English courses increased in the universities by 92 per cent and in the separate colleges by 266 per cent.

To meet the need for basic and cultural training, some institutions undertook survey and orientation courses; a few in this period pioneered by establishing a separate division similar to the fast-growing junior college. Wisconsin in 1927 set up a short-lived Experimental College emphasizing synthesis and unity. In 1932 the University of Minnesota established a General College for an "overview" of human learning, designed to fit "the individual abilities, interests, and potentialities of a very considerable number of young people whose needs were not being met elsewhere in the University," in the words of President Lotus D. Coffman. It was a protest against stereotyped methods long in use, and was designed to develop new methods of learning. A few years later, in 1935, the University of Florida established another General College, designed as a basic division for all freshman and sophomore work. Again it emphasized the broad approach to all human learning.

In the meantime, the depression had accelerated reexamination of purpose and function in almost all institutions. The Association's Committee on College Organization and Policy in 1934 reported that "a number of the institutions are making curricula studies to determine the needs of their states, to define objectives, to eliminate duplication, and to improve the efficiency of teaching." Various new methods of teaching were devised and old ones revamped to achieve better integration and more individualized instruction. Experiments were made with the problem method, the case method, the project method, seminars, discussions, "socialized recitation," and special types of examinations. Guidance work, unit housing, and tutorial schemes occupied the minds of a considerable number of land-grant educators. The thirties became a decade for fancy experiments, some of which proved sufficiently valuable to become accepted parts of the curricular pattern.

Agriculture

In agriculture, each passing year brought new and different problems to the colleges. Practical farming had given way to "book farming," then to science as the only answer. Finally, in this period, agriculture came to be regarded as a profession of its own, as complex and varied as any other. Reasonable uniformity among all the colleges was established in both entrance and curricular requirements. The student was expected to gain a knowledge of the basic sciences, some cultural training, and intensive specialization in one or more fields. The colleges were preparing master farmers, research scientists, extension workers, agricultural business specialists, teachers, and government workers. As a recognized and essential industry, agriculture was sufficiently related to all other life interests that its graduates could no longer limit themselves to the subjects related to "farming" as such. A single curriculum was insufficient for the needs of the students. A speaker in 1929 reported that "a multitude of 'branches of learning' are clamoring for admission to the category of agricultural science. Several new agricultural sciences are christened every time a new . . . catalogue goes to the press." Dean Carl E. Ladd observed that "the period from 1915 to 1932 has probably seen the development of more new agricultural science than was developed from the passage of the Morrill Act up until 1915." As specialization increased, so graduate study grew. The Summer School of Agriculture, founded by the Association after it had abandoned plans for a national graduate school, had served its purpose of encouraging individual institutions to offer graduate work. It was discontinued in 1919.

The agricultural depression of the twenties sent shock waves through the agricultural curriculum. Educators recognized that the curriculum offered little assistance in the solution of the vast economic and social problems affecting the individual farmer as well as all agricultural industries. Agricultural economics was given a far more important place in the curricular scheme. Rural sociology was recognized as a subject of great importance. In 1925, President William Oxley Thompson observed, "Where the college of agriculture tried to make two blades of grass grow where one grew before, it does not care much about whether grass grows at all now. . . . The outcome of all this is that we have had to modify our idea of what a college of agriculture is and what it ought to be." The students were no longer regarded as "mere producers of food," but as potential leaders in an industry crying for leadership.

The combination of the new emphasis on economics and sociology together with the impact of the times in terms of human welfare caused the agricultural educators to wonder, along with the rest, if their curriculum, too, had not become overspecialized. There was great fear in the thirties that the research scientist might never glance up from his microscope to see the hungry face watching him through the window. The path of learning must not be so narrow as to exclude consideration of the history, culture, and psychology of mankind. In the thirties, then, the agricultural colleges began opening the door slowly to the humanities. Methods did not change as fast as subject-matter, however. In 1929 H. H. Whetzel issued a complaint which makes sense today:

The procedure in presenting laboratory courses in biological subjects . . . is, with rare exceptions, that introduced half a century ago; one or more laboratory exercises per week in which all of the students study the same subject and the same material under the solicitous guidance of immature instructors; a lecture or two by the professor; a mass recitation conducted by one of these same instructors or rarely by the professor himself and a voluminous weekly report which is usually only a slovenly and inaccurate misalliance of poorly digested laboratory pickings.[3]

The Smith-Hughes Act of 1917 had stimulated the preparation of teachers for secondary-level instruction in agriculture, industry, and home economics. By 1928 the Land-Grant Colleges in some thirty-six states had been chosen to conduct the work. The consequent expansion in vocational classes in high schools can be seen from an enrollment increase of 164,200 in 1917 to 1,500,000 in 1936. With opportunity available in the home community, farmers and their sons no longer needed the existing short course work at the college. In addition, the increased number of county agents lessened the demand. As a result, the character of short courses changed. The brief sessions lasting from several days to a week became specialized units of work in a particular field. The Smith-Hughes Act, on the other hand, strengthened the two-year non-degree course, so that by 1933 nineteen land-grant institutions were offering this practical training. Some were reported to have large enrollments. Agricultural instruction at all levels had thus been modified and changed in tune with the changing times.

Engineering

Engineering followed a similar course. The Land-Grant Colleges were ready to look upon engineering as the more specialized and professional phase of "mechanic arts." In forty-two of the institutions during the years between 1910 and 1920, the number of four-year engineering students increased 65.1 per cent. The gross enrollment, including baccalaureate, graduate, special, and non-degree students, increased 75.5 per cent, while the number of faculty giving engineering instruction increased 47.5 per cent. In spite of the relative youth of the larger number of recent graduates, it could be claimed in 1931 that 43 per cent of the engineers listed in *Who's Who in Engineering in America* were land-grant graduates. The Office of Education study in 1930 noted that "engineering teachers of these institutions are responsible for a large portion [nearly two-thirds] of the textbooks and reference books used in colleges and by the engineering profession."

The Land-Grant Engineering Colleges were largely responsible for setting the example in engineering education. They became also the chief bone of contention with separate state universities. Both types claimed right to the disposition of work in engineering. As early as 1916, S. P. Capen reported, "Neither has been willing to concede the claims of the other. The resulting rivalry has led to intolerable mutual jealousies, and antagonisms, to factional strife between alumni and faculty bodies, to waste of high-class men and equipment, to the infusion of politics into higher educational affairs." [4] Bitterness would prevail and probably will continue until each is so overwhelmed with the immensity of its task that it can do no more than perfect its own. In some states where rivalries aroused the public to the need for drastic action, consolidated boards and state-initiated reorganization have resulted.

In the first years of this period, engineering education was undergoing many changes. Some were similar to those occurring simultaneously in other subject-fields. Others were distinct. In one way or another, however, engineering followed the changing collegiate pattern. The war and the depressions forced the engineers also to take a long look at themselves. They had been concentrating for many years on building up a special field of knowledge. The multiplying technical subjects had forced out of the curriculum most of the liberal studies. A gradually increasing number of engineering educators became concerned over the high degree of specialization. The state of society in the twenties and thirties was making new social and economic demands on the engineers who had been trained primarily to deal with material problems. Some observed that engineers could run machines but not business and industry, that they were deficient in an understanding of human problems as well as knowing how to express what human concerns they might have. For a while the criticisms fell on deaf ears. Then in the year 1930, under the sponsorship of the Society for the Promotion of Engineering Education, the famous "Wickenden Report" was issued. It was the first of a number of reports to call attention to the gradually decreasing cultural emphasis in engineering education and the need for broader trained men with skill both in technical and human understanding. Some years would pass before the colleges came to grips with the problem. In the meantime, they concentrated on the expansion of education in new fields such as aviation, typical of the modern times.

Increasing technical demands and increasing curricular specialization led to the necessity of expanded graduate study in engineering. The four-year baccalaureate curriculum was no longer sufficient for advanced scientific training. Industry recognized the desirability of graduate study and offered higher salaries to men so trained. The colleges responded by developing to a greater degree than ever before the offerings leading to Master's and Doctor's degrees.

Home Economics

The Smith-Hughes Act, promoting vocational education in the high schools, had its most profound effect at the collegiate level on the home economics curriculum. The high schools took over much of what had been taught in collegiate home economics, leaving college faculties free to develop higher and more specialized instruction. Much of the training of women for the profession of home-making as such could be accomplished at the high school level. As a consequence, the college courses emphasized home economics as a gainful profession. Its character changed from liberal-vocational to liberal-professional within a few years. The change was accelerated in large part by the new demand for trained home economics teachers to accomplish the Smith-Hughes work in the schools. In the college curriculum, specific skills and subject information, such as sewing and cooking, were rapidly eliminated in favor of scientifically-based study, such as textiles and chemistry of foods. As the science of home economics developed, home economics educators adapted for themselves the laboratory method. As their field became more specialized, they, too, recognized the desirability and need of graduate work. By 1932 the proper direction and standards of graduate work were items of great concern in the colleges and in Association meetings.

Because its professional status came late, home economics did not suffer as much as other fields the dangers of overspecialization. Its curricular objectives were still evolving at a time when agriculture and engineering, for instance, were being forced back to reexamine what had become established. There had always been a mixture of the liberal and the practical in home economics. As the new subject of child development grew, for instance, it could not be treated as a science alone; its primary concern was with human beings. In 1935 the report of an Association subcommittee on instruction in home economics listed the following objectives of a possible core curriculum:

I. The establishment of attitudes essential to rich and significant living.

II. The acceptance of standards of enjoyment and ideals of living, satisfactory to the individual and profitable to society.

III. The development of that questioning scientific attitude of mind which enables the individual to solve problems intelligently and independently.

IV. Mastery of an adequate body of functioning subject matter that will give to the individual factual basis for and facility in meeting those responsibilities that are essentially woman's for the continuance of life, its care and protection, its enrichment and fulfillment.

Home economics was no longer home-making. It included preparation for such diverse occupations as teaching, dietetics, extension work, institutional management, journalism, merchandising, and research. It was now a combination of scientific and social education of a highly professional nature.

Veterinary Medicine

The effect of the changing times is seen most dramatically in the changing character during this period of veterinary medical education. The automobile replaced the horse, cutting sharply into the business of the private veterinary colleges which had been located almost entirely in cities. The advent of science, with all its accompanying equipment and apparatus, made it virtually impossible for the proprietary school to subsist on the basis of student fees alone. Rising educational standards found the private school inadequate and backward. With all these changes following World War I, the private veterinary college all but faded from the scene, leaving the field open to publicly-supported colleges. The last of the private schools closed in 1927. The number of public colleges was reduced by one in 1933 when Georgia ceased operating. The ten that were left, only one of which was not in a Land-Grant College or University, graduated between 1933 and 1949 all of the new practicing doctors in the United States with the exception of a few who came from other countries.

During the twenties and early thirties veterinary enrollment was low. In 1930 only 106 doctors emerged from all of the existing schools. Then the number rose steadily until it had reached 823 graduates for the year 1953. The demands for service by veterinary doctors changed in character. Their work became far more scientific and specialized. The colleges responded by raising admission standards and revising the curriculum. By 1936 all required at least one year of general college preparatory work, and by 1949 the requirement had been raised to two years. Basic sciences and general subjects such as English were included in the preveterinary college training so that the veterinary curriculum could consist largely of strictly professional subjects. The new subjects taking the place of the basic courses were those previously lacking or inadequately treated, such as virology, pharmacology, roentgenology, food hygiene, genetics, and nutrition.

With the public veterinary colleges now well established and scientifically based, it was possible for them to carry on some measure of research in connection with their teaching. In addition, veterinary extension work began in the latter half of this period. It followed the pattern of agricultural extension but without assigned county agents. Short courses for veterinary doctors were conducted at the colleges, and the faculty frequently visited about the state, bringing to the practitioners the latest developments of the laboratory and clinic. The college served as a continuing informational center for new problems arising in the field. By correspondence, lectures, and courses, it helped to raise the level of the work of practicing doctors at the same time that it was preparing for practice the new supply.

Military Instruction

Prior to the beginning of World War I, military instruction in the Land-Grant Colleges had reached its lowest ebb since the earliest days of the colleges. The institutions continued to blame the War Department for its refusal to cooperate and its reluctance to provide the basic incentives for student enrollees. A perfunctory annual inspection and a few appointments of graduates to the regular army were the only indications that the War Department was aware of the existence of military work on the college campus. The situation changed suddenly when war broke out in Europe. In September 1916, Congress passed the National Defense Act, reorganizing the Army and creating for the first time a system of military training in civilian schools and colleges. The legislation in its final form embodied much of what the Executive Committee of the Association had suggested. This was the birth of the Reserve Officers' Training Corps, later to be known popularly by its initials ROTC. The Land-Grant Colleges were to be headquarters for units of the national corps. With the exception of preliminary organization in some states, the final establishment of the new system had to await the Armistice in 1918.

In the meantime, the colleges were to serve in another way. The Students' Army Training Corps, established by presidential directive, utilized the student manpower and the campuses for selection and training of officer candidates and technical experts so urgently needed. Many students in the Land-Grant Colleges, however, did not wait for the military to come to the campus. With the outbreak of the war, they entered service voluntarily. It was later estimated that at least 100,000 graduates and former students were in military or naval service. More than 30,000 were officers. More than a thousand received military honor awards. Thirty-nine of the land-grant institutions later recorded a total of 1759 graduate and student fatalities during the official war period.

Some of the provisions of the 1916 act were changed or strengthened by a second National Defense Act in 1920. The two pieces of legislation were responsible for establishing the ROTC on a sound basis. The college military program was divided into two periods—the basic training for students in the first two years, and advanced work for selected upperclassmen. The basic course, required of all able-bodied men, was presumed to fill the original requirements of the Morrill Act of 1862. Students showing "leadership, initiative, and powers of command" were selected for enrollment in the advanced course during the last two years of college. The intent was "to keep on the reserve list an adequate number who have had advanced training to officer all branches of the service in case the utmost strength of the nation is required." With the establishment of ROTC in the Land-Grant Colleges, the institutions were given more personnel, better equipment, and a formalized curriculum. The War Department attempted to make the course educational as well as practical. In addition to regular drill, the practical military arts would be emphasized strongly in the required summer camps for advanced course students. Within a few years, twelve different branches of service were operating on the college campus. These included infantry, cavalry, field artillery, engineers corps, coast artillery, signal corps, ordnance, medical, dental, veterinary, air corps, and chemical warfare. The War Department fixed the curriculum for each branch and revised it according to experience. Though the intent was to make the ROTC academically respectable, it would take at least two decades and another major war before the colleges recognized it as comparable to academic departments.

The national reaction against war in any form and thus against military training was soon to be felt on the college campus. During the twenties and thirties numerous attempts were made by individuals and organized groups to do away with the compulsory features of ROTC. The state legislatures and the colleges, in addition to the Congress, were recipients of frequent petitions against military education in any form but particularly the basic ROTC requirement. For some sixty years since the enactment of the original Morrill legislation, the Land-Grant Colleges had attempted to live by the act's vague military specifications. In one form or another, military drill had been offered. Now that the War Department was finally offering some degree of interest and cooperation, the majority of colleges resolved not to change the pattern. The first break occurred in Wisconsin in 1923 when the legislature made participation optional. Students were allowed a choice of military science, physical training, or band practice. In 1933 the Maryland Court of Appeals in the case of Coale vs. the University of Maryland ruled that the colleges had the autonomy to fix the requirement or to waive it. In 1934 the Department of the Interior, charged with administering land-grant funds, ruled that Wisconsin had the right to make military science optional without losing Federal funds. A highlight of the period was an historic decision of the United States Supreme Court which upheld the right of the trustees of a public university (California) to require military training of all students, providing it was compulsory for all students in a certain class or category, i.e., in this instance, all male students.

Despite this defined freedom, however, most of the Land-Grant Colleges favored requirement. The Association passed a number of resolutions backing up the stand of the great majority of the membership. In the mid-thirties, the University of Minnesota and the North Dakota Agricultural College followed the lead of Wisconsin and also dropped the required feature. Later, by the end of World War II, Wisconsin and North Dakota reinstated it but Minnesota did not and has not. In addition, Texas A. and M. College more recently has eliminated the requirement. Virginia Polytechnic Institute, although retaining the provision officially, grants liberal excuses.

The establishment of ROTC, together with this freedom of choice, did not solve all the problems. The colleges were badgered again by inadequate military staffing during the thirties. Once more they became aware of Federal indifference to the program. In 1936, in a sharply worded report, the Association's Committee on Military Organization and Policy observed that "no expense, explanations or alibis can persuade anyone that the Army is not indifferent toward R.O.T.C. if, with the all-time high appropriations in peace times, there is no evidence of sincere and vigorous effort to provide for R.O.T.C." No response was forthcoming, and the colleges continued to press for recognition and provision. The Committee concluded in 1937 that "only by these repeated and insistent presentations of needs . . . to the Congress, which has always shown itself friendly to them, and to the War Department, which is indifferent, can we expect to secure any progress toward better things." As we have noted, "progress toward better things" finally came after the nation realized it would have been virtually helpless without the graduates trained by land-grant ROTC.

RESEARCH RESPONDS TO THE TIMES

Agriculture

During this period the agricultural experiment stations continued to expand and to change in form and character in response to the increasing demands made upon them. By 1920 the "project method" had become the standard procedure for investigation. The stations formulated definite outlines of each proposed study, including its scope, method, and purpose. The Federal Office approved the project, and the stations proceeded in its undertaking. In 1920 a total of 4750 projects were reported. The stations were not yet free from control and regulatory activities. They were restive under such functions. A president of the Association commented that "the mass of routine duties that naturally devolve upon service institutions that must see that the laws are enforced develops an atmosphere that, if not antagonistic to, at least hampers and often smothers research." Finally the Association made an agreement with the National Association of State Departments and Commissioners of Agriculture providing that "State Departments now handling various forms of education and extension work are to transfer the same [to the Land-Grant Colleges] as soon as circumstances permit; likewise, Experiment Stations are to transfer [to the state departments] regulatory functions now located with them." [5] Some years would pass before this arrangement would become fully effective. Even in some states today, the college performs certain regulatory and inspection functions normally handled by state departments of agriculture.

One illustration of the expansion of the stations during the early twenties may be found in the increase in funds available for research. The aggregate income rose some 60 per cent in the five years from 1921 to 1926 while direct state support nearly doubled. With the development of extension, the responsibility for dissemination of the knowledge acquired in the stations was transferred to the county agents and extension specialists. Only the printing of bulletins and circulars remained a duty of the stations. The research worker now was far more free to concentrate on investigation. As a result, the stations developed intensive specialists in certain fields of research. Some station directors, as well as college administrators, became concerned over the possibility of the research worker losing touch with those whom he should be serving. To a degree, the First World War helped to remedy such a condition by making the station worker more aware of the value of the extension specialist who, as he carried forth information, might also return to the station with new problems and results of experience.

The agricultural depression of the twenties soon made the station workers aware of serious deficiencies in their program. Little had been done to this point on economic and social research. Suddenly the problem of marketing and of rural social conditions became of greater importance than production. Once again the colleges turned to the Congress for assistance. Representatives of the Association drafted a measure for increased specific aid to the stations, and it was first introduced in the House in 1921 by Representative F. S. Purnell of Indiana. Except for a change in the amount of appropriation appearing in the original bill, the legislation was finally enacted in 1925 after the Association had enlisted the active support of a number of national farm organizations. The Purnell Act authorized increases in annual grants to the stations of $20,000 for the first year for each state and territory, to be increased by $10,000 annually until the maximum of $60,000 had been reached. Together with funds from the Hatch and Adams Acts, the total Federal appropriation would then amount to $90,000 for each state station. In Connecticut only was there a division of funds between the station at New Haven and the station founded in Storrs as a part of the University of Connecticut. The usual provisions were added, including administrative responsibility by the Secretary of Agriculture.

The type of research was expanded to include economic and social investigations, thus broadening the scope to meet the needs of a declining agriculture. The expansion was interpreted to include questions of farm management, grading and standardization, transportation, storage, marketing of farm products, financing agricultural enterprises, home economics, and social problems of country life. The act was intended to stimulate and extend investigations already somewhat under way in the states. Fundamental research in problems of agricultural economics, rural sociology and home economics would thus take precedence over problems of production. In effect, this was the first time the Congress had encouraged specifically problems of strong national interest as against state and regional concerns. With the passage of the Purnell Act, the colleges began moving toward the accumulation of data which would make easier their efforts in the formulation of public policies.

The new Federal funds under the Purnell Act made possible an increase in permanent station personnel, better facilities, and more prompt publication of research results. Soon after the passage of the act, the stations agreed with the Federal Department to undertake cooperative study in the following fields:

In agricultural economics:
  Distribution and marketing of farm products
  Problems of surpluses of farm products
In home economics:
  Vitamin contents of food in relation to human nutrition
  Rural home management studies
In rural sociology:
  Rural social organization and agencies essential to a permanent and
    effective agriculture
In the field of production:
  Factors influencing the production and quality of meats.

The depression of the thirties found the stations again aware of deficiencies and dissatisfied with their efforts. The call went out for a more comprehensive program of research, and for projects selected not on the basis of idle curiosity but of importance to human welfare. The already apparent trend away from production research was accelerated by the depression need for study of farm incomes, standards of living, and consumption. Since this depression affected urban dwellers as well, the stations became more aware of the relation of agriculture to the total economy and total society. Marketing was no longer a matter of getting the produce from the farm to the store but into the stomachs of the consumers as well.

The two depressions focused attention on the regional and national significance of research. Until 1920 research had been largely on a state basis. Some efforts had been made, partly as a result of Purnell stimulus, to evolve a cooperative approach. One of the first results and one of the lasting significance to agriculture was the work on hybrid corn begun cooperatively in 1925. A joint committee of the Department and the Association had been established in 1913 to promote the correlation of research efforts. Its initial work began to bear fruit in the late twenties and throughout the thirties. By 1930 the Committee reported that 1196 of the 7000 active projects were being conducted by stations or groups of stations and the Federal Department. The result was a more comprehensive, more thorough, and better coordinated research program. In New England the station directors set the example for other regions by meeting together periodically to exchange information and agree on joint sponsorship of particular projects. With the expansion of effort, internal friction became almost inevitable. As early as 1931 the colleges had complained that the Department was interested only in cooperating on those projects originating in the Department. The program was moving steadily forward, however, despite this occasional friction and jealousy.

By 1935, with the effects of the depression keenly felt throughout the country, the Federal government was ready to add more funds to the research work. In that year Congress passed the Bankhead-Jones Act which authorized one million dollars additional research money for each year until the maximum of five million dollars had been reached. Forty per cent of the funds went to Department-sponsored research projects, and the remaining 60 per cent to the stations, allocated on the basis of rural population. The states, however, were required for the first time to match the amount. The research provisions applied to "laws and principles underlying basic problems of agriculture in its broadest aspects." Several new features appeared in the Bankhead-Jones legislation. For the first time in land-grant enactments, a portion of the funds was given over directly to the Department with the expenditure directly under the control of the Secretary. In addition, the Secretary was empowered, and in effect directed, to establish separate regional laboratories in major agricultural areas. Emphasis on research was given to new and improved methods and markets. The authority given the Secretary for the direction of station research was broadened considerably over previous experiment station legislation. For the first time, too, funds could be used by the states for buildings and land. Soon after its passage, the Secretary of Agriculture, Henry A. Wallace, interpreted the legislation to mean fundamental research largely on a cooperative basis.

By the mid-thirties, the stations together had received the following amounts in Federal funds:

Hatch Act	1888–1936	$34,106,185
Adams Act	1906–1936	20,113,413
Purnell Act	1926–1936	23,988,801
Bankhead-Jones Act	1936 only	600,000
Total (up to and including 1936)		$78,808,399

The national investment in the agricultural experiment stations brought rich returns to many agricultural areas. In a great many instances, the projects begun on a local level with the end view of solving a local or regional problem turned out to have profound national and world-wide significance. By the thirties the number of requests for the results of research coming from foreign nations greatly accelerated. Long before the days of foreign technical aid, the Land-Grant Colleges were extending help to the people of foreign lands.

Examining the benefits of research from its beginning to 1928, the Office of Education estimated that the economic value to the agricultural industry of the contributions by the stations amounted in the year 1928 alone to $841,470,000. From this point on, it would be virtually impossible to find a comparable annual figure. The results are better measured perhaps in their meaning to states and regions. Across the country vast areas of land, perennially disregarded as unproductive, were opened through research in soils and crops. New varieties of existing crops were developed to the great benefit of many regions. In Louisiana, for instance, the introduction of new varieties of sugar cane saved the industry from extensive losses caused by the mosaic disease affecting the old variety. In Texas, feterita became a fodder crop valued annually at $16 million. Minnesota perfected Grimm alfalfa for hardy and adaptable use in all the major alfalfa-producing areas of the nation. The soy-bean brought to Missouri an industry conservatively estimated to be worth $15 million a year for that one state alone. Control of the cotton boll weevil, the corn borer, and the fruit fly saved from ruin cotton, corn, and citrus fruits throughout the nation. The poultry industry was revolutionized by new methods of breeding perfected in Oregon, the trapnest devised in Maine, and the day-old-chick enterprise begun in New Jersey. Numerous other examples could be cited. Suffice it to say that by the mid-thirties agricultural research in the Land-Grant Colleges had helped immeasurably to save a nation in distress.

Home Economics Research

There were a number of cogent reasons why home economics research had not progressed as fast as its agricultural counterpart. The subject-matter in home economics was not yet fixed and certainly far from standardized. The home economists had been busy discovering what they might teach effectively before they were in a position to extend the boundaries of knowledge. They were uncertain as well of the best way to undertake research. Few had been trained for such efforts; few had been sufficiently interested; and funds had been lacking.

The crises of the times changed all of this, however. The necessity for food conservation and preservation during the First World War brought home economists up sharply in the realization of how little they actually knew about food and nutritive values. Their first problem was to learn how to preserve and store food to be sent overseas, and then how to make less edible food more attractive and useful at home. With the shortage of food both overseas and at home, the home economist became concerned over the effect on growth and development of missing food essentials. With all of this there was a necessity to devise labor-saving methods and machines which would make available more manpower.

The efforts of home economists during the war had brought greater respect and dignity to the field. Teachers were in demand, and the whole new area of dietetics and institutional management had been opened. Home economics was no longer an "art" or a "how to do" technique. The art had become a profession, and the "ways of doing" were scientifically based. More than anything else, the Purnell Act of 1925 stimulated home economics research. Its provision for "studies relating to the rural home" was interpreted to mean home economics in all of its phases. By 1931 some 95 per cent of the home economics research program was supported by Purnell funds. Research was divided roughly into three types: physical, economic, and sociological. The prevailing method of study was experimental, or, as Thatcher defined it, "the assembly of observations and facts under conditions which permit a cause and effect interpretation and deductions therefrom of principles which form the basis of knowledge." [6] The central unit of study was the home and its problems. With this emphasis, home economics research workers, busily occupied with Purnell funds, found again during the depression of the thirties how little they really knew about the home. The depression stimulated research into a number of new areas such as time and money management, housing, household equipment, rural organization, methods in adult education, and especially nutritional conditions in rural areas.

Engineering Research

The further development of engineering research was controlled by many factors outside of the colleges. The period witnessed a tremendous expansion in corporate industrial research, with the number of industrial laboratories jumping from 300 in 1918 to 2300 in 1940. The research workers on the payrolls of large corporations numbered 1200 in 1918 and rose to 27,000 in 1940.[7] In 1920 the expenditure for industrial research was approximately $40 million per year. In 1950 it was estimated to be in excess of $600 million. As an example of the growth of industrial research in comparison with university research, the National Resources Planning Board estimated that chemical industries in the single year of 1940 budgeted $50 million for research, a sum equal to the amount spent in that year by all universities for all research purposes.[8] Though industrial research in the Land-Grant Colleges grew steadily, engineering would still have to depend heavily on industry for much of its basic information.

In increasing numbers, the Land-Grant Colleges established engineering experiment stations following the early lead of Illinois and Iowa. Whereas five stations existed in 1910, the number rose to twenty-six by 1925 and to forty-six by 1946. Many of the early stations seemed to exist in form only, however. The Office of Education study in 1930 estimated that "fewer than 10 of the land-grant college engineering experiment stations are receiving support from any source sufficient to develop research in engineering." Despite the meager funds and inadequate equipment, some progress was made. As early as 1916, bulletins were published on such subjects as tests of timber, reinforced concrete beams and columns; the holding power of railroad spikes; smokeless consumption of coal; tests of boilers and locomotives, of local sand, stone, and gravel; sewage disposal; protection of buildings from lightning; road legislation and administration; and dredging by hydraulic method.

Attempts were made again to obtain Federal support. Each measure met with the opposition of some of the separate state universities which resisted the allocation of funds only to the Land-Grant Colleges. When legislation was introduced leaving to the individual states the decision for placing the funds within the state borders, the Land-Grant Colleges opposed the measure. Interinstitutional rivalry continued to block Federal aid in any form. With this highly important stimulus missing, the colleges and their Association attempted as best they could to promote engineering research. In 1920 a standing committee on engineering experiment stations was established within the Association framework, and a quarterly "Engineering Experiment Station Record" was authorized for publication. It made its first appearance in 1921 as a mimeographed bulletin. The statistics for 1921 estimated that at least 53 men were employed full-time in engineering research in the colleges, with another 324 devoting part-time. The total funds available from all sources were listed as $318,760. Two years later the total amount was said to be $590,680, and the claim was made that the colleges now "constitute by far the most important organized public agency for engineering research in the United States, if not in the world." The efforts included commercial testing, cooperation with individuals, firms, associations, and corporations, publication and distribution of bulletins, training men in the methods of research, and furnishing answers to specific inquiries. At least 808 bulletins had been published by all of the stations up to 1928. The ratio of expenditures for agricultural research against engineering research continued to drop, although the funds for engineering research were still meager. In 1910 the ratio was 50 to 1; in 1920 it was 30 to 1; by 1925 it had changed to 21 to 1. In increasing fashion, the work of the engineering stations was being tied into graduate study. Advanced research appeared to have little application to undergraduate teaching but could be used to great advantage in the training of graduate students.

As the years passed, the stations and industries began to work together. As early as 1914, the Illinois station had undertaken a cooperative project on Stresses in Railroad Tracks with the American Society of Civil Engineers and the American Railway Engineering Association. The number of such projects increased until industry recognized the value of the stations by lending financial support to their operation. During the five year period from 1923 to 1928, industry contributed some one and one-third million dollars for engineering research in the Land-Grant Colleges. This contact with industry would lead to increasingly larger sums donated for teaching and extension, as well as gifts of equipment not obtainable otherwise.

Though the amount of work seemed minor in comparison to the industrial research program, the results were still significant. Industries profited substantially from standardized tests developed for sewer pipes, drain tiles, and culvert design, and from new types of utilization as well as disposal of industrial wastes. Station research and tests led to the modern carburetor and to new theories of heat transfer. Long distance transmission of electric power resulted from research on high voltage. As W. J. Kerr observed, "Land-grant institutions have been the chief factors in standardizing coal grades at the mine, lessening the smoke nuisance, reducing domestic heating to a science, and placing farm electrification on a rational basis." [9]

The engineering experiment stations were growing in strength and in contribution, in spite of the handicap of limited funds and personnel. To understand why their role was not as significant as the agricultural stations, one needs only to compare the personnel and resources. In the year 1936, for instance, the total staff engaged in agricultural research numbered 3,818 and total funds available amounted to $16,425,489. For engineering research the staff numbered 960 and the funds $1,303,923.

EXTENSION RESPONDS TO THE TIMES

Agriculture

During this period of successive crises, cooperative extension in agriculture and home economics appeared to undergo "phases" of development. Each phase was closely tied in with national changes. For the few years following the enactment of the Smith-Lever legislation in 1914, cooperative extension was involved principally in the creation of its own internal organization and in establishing procedure with the Department of Agriculture. In response to needs during the First World War, the extension program and personnel expanded tremendously. Following the war, emergency funds were withdrawn, and extension was forced to reorganize and readjust to a peacetime program. Soon afterward, however, came the agricultural depression of the twenties and the demand for a new and different kind of service. The depression taught the extension workers that emphasis on more than production was necessary. As a different type of program emerged, the nation was plunged into the economic depression of the thirties. Cooperative extension was forced to respond by dropping much of its purely educational activity in favor of "action programs" in cooperation with Federal agencies.

Despite these sudden changes, a measure of stability came to extension development throughout the years of crisis. A philosophy of approach and a set of objectives slowly emerged. Cooperative extension recognized itself as primarily an educational movement. Its definite relationship as a part of the Land-Grant Colleges gave it an educational emphasis which might otherwise have been lacking had it been merely a government program. Extension was clearly a part of the college framework with the sole purpose of carrying knowledge to the people who, by virtue of their occupation and often their age, could not come to the traditional campus to learn. The Smith-Lever Act had assigned the function of extension education to the colleges as the recognized agency of the state and Federal governments. Until the depression of the thirties brought direct action programs of the national government into the states, the colleges were assumed to be the smallest units through which the Federal authorities should attempt to reach the people.

As extension grew, it took as its fundamental purpose the development of people. It regarded the citizen as the sovereign unit in a democracy and his home as the fundamental unit of civilization. It considered the family as the first training group of the human race, and looked upon the farm as endowed with great resources and possibilities. In the words of Martha Van Rensselaer, one of the pioneers in home economics and home demonstration work, "It is the purpose of extension to stir in men and women the desire to take the next step and then to give them help in taking it."

The ultimate aim was the development of people. The first method chosen to reach this aim was improvement in home and farm practices. By intelligent, cooperative effort, the end result might be better men and women. Often it would appear that the goal of cooperative extension was increased farm income rather than a higher standard of living, more and better crops rather than abundant life, efficiency rather than richness. But extension leaders seemed to feel that increased income, better crops, and greater efficiency were only means to the end. With these achieved, a higher standard of living, and abundant life and richness in attitude would come naturally. As C. B. Smith observed, "We put [increased income] first in significance because culture and education and spiritual advancement usually come only after a man has provided for himself a living and has some leisure to observe, read, study and associate in cultural activities with his fellow man." Extension work thus seemed to recognize from the start that America was a materialistic civilization with "advancement" tied closely to income and with richness dependent on riches.

To reach the goal, various methods of education would be used. "Participation" and "cooperation" were the words most frequently in use. "Trials" and "demonstrations" were devised to meet different interests and needs. The county agent and the specialist were expected to use every means at their command to reach the farmers and their wives and children. Sometimes they would be accused of more activity than achievement. The high ideals of abundant living would not always be consistent with material interests. Yet the strange mixture somehow seemed to work over the years, and out of it came almost universal acceptance of this new form of land-grant education.

During this period cooperative extension changed from the limited and often fumbling efforts of the few to the large and highly professional staff of many. The number of workers in the states and territories practically tripled in the twenty-year stretch from 1920 to 1940. The emphasis on local demonstrations, locally sponsored (there were some 800,000 of them recorded for the year 1927 alone), increased informed participation to such an extent that the agents found it possible to lean heavily on local leadership. This trend was accelerated during the depression of the twenties when county agents could not handle all the necessary work, and volunteer labor was used to supplement their efforts. With insufficient funds to employ salaried agents, the extension service called on volunteers in the individual communities to undertake sufficient specific training so that they could then share with their neighbors the specialized knowledge. The subsequent development of rural leadership is regarded by many as one of the major contributions and accomplishments of cooperative extension.

This active participation by the farmer in his own program helped to keep the extension program at the level of the farmer and in harmony with local conditions. Time and again it was pointed out that the development of people hinged largely on the extent of their active participation. Group effort became the accepted process of the extension method. The local programs should be locally determined and locally managed with the college acting only to suggest, guide, and standardize. In turn, it was felt that the county agent was actually much more a part of the local community than of the college. He was regarded by some as a "community builder." This concept did not always work to the advantage of the college since the agents increasingly felt themselves less a part of an educational faculty than of the citizenry separated from the campus. To many the classroom represented the university, and, since the agent was not in the classroom, it was felt that he could not then be a part of the university. The colleges were guilty, too, of subdividing the staff and of ignoring, both consciously and unconsciously, the off-campus educational arm of the extension service. There seemed to be no doubt, however, about the attitude of rural people. The majority were enthusiastic and anxious for increased assistance.

Despite the development of local leadership and the growing support of the farm population, the county agent found the task too great for him to handle even with voluntary help. The subject-matter of agriculture had become so specialized that he was no longer able to be the technical advisor ready to offer some solution to every farm problem. Instead he had become an administrator of a large and expanding county program. To assist him in the technical phases of his work, the colleges sent out "specialists" in particular fields, representing most of the teaching areas of the college. As new subjects were developed, specialists were added. Whereas in 1914 there had been approximately 221 full and part-time specialists, by 1924 the number had grown to 850. In the twenties the specialists' fields included, among the most important, dairying, animal husbandry, poultry, agronomy, horticulture, agricultural engineering, farm management, marketing, rural organization, and home economics, as well as botany, plant pathology, entomology, and forestry in some states. The specialists, sometimes assisted by experts from the Federal Department, participated in demonstrations, meetings, institutes, and conferences. When they returned to the campus, they spent time in correspondence with agents and individual farmers and in the preparation of bulletins and news releases.

The experiment stations, which had come to rely on the extension service for contact with fundamental farm problems, leaned heavily on the returning specialists to keep them in touch with the local farmer. The complaint was frequently voiced that station and extension personnel were not maintaining the necessary intimate contact and exchange. Extension workers sometimes complained about the highly technical language and treatment in station publications, not readily understood by the average farmer. On the other hand, station workers found that the agents and specialists were not aware of or refusing to use the latest research findings. The obvious need for closer interrelationship helped convince many college heads that the better system of organization was one in which the three functions of the college of agriculture—teaching, research, and extension—were directed by one over-all executive with subordinates in charge of the individual areas.

Probably because of the direct and immediate contact with the local farmer, increased funds were much easier to secure for extension work than for research and teaching. This was true of all sources, including county, state, and Federal. There was a steady, sometimes spectacular, increase in the amount of extension funds throughout this period. The figure rose from $1,600,000 in 1914 to $19,151,174 in 1924. In order to assist in financing the work at the county level and to help the local community sense a responsibility for the efforts of the agent, the colleges and the Department encouraged contributions to the program by county boards or county farm organizations. This was said to place responsibility where responsibility properly belonged.

Federal financial participation increased with several Congressional enactments. The first was the Clarke-McNary Act of 1924, which appropriated funds specifically for extension work in forestry. Of greater significance to the total program was the Capper-Ketcham Act of 1928, which had the striking support of 19 national farm associations, over 80 state farm organizations, and over 120 local groups. The act appropriated a total of $1,480,000 with $20,000 allocated for each state and Hawaii, plus $500,000 each year prorated on the basis of rural population and matched by state or local funds. The Bank-head-Jones Act of 1935 authorized an additional $8 million for extension in the first year, and annual increases of $1 million until the maximum of $12 million had been reached. Funds were divided among the states and Hawaii in much the same fashion as in the Capper-Ketcham legislation except that the apportionment following the initial sum was based on farm population rather than rural. The states were not required to match the Bankhead-Jones money.

At various times during this period, particularly during World War I and the depression of the thirties, supplementary funds were provided in a variety of forms to increase extension personnel for the emergencies. In general, the amounts varied from year to year and were included as a part of the Agricultural Appropriation Act. The total extension income from all sources had risen from 3.6 million in 1915, after the Smith-Lever funds became available, to some 58.5 million in 1948. Obviously extension had prospered better than any other division of the Land-Grant Colleges.

By 1914, prior to the passage of the Smith-Lever Act, the records showed that 240 counties in twenty-seven Northern and Western States had county agricultural agents, and that forty-two of the forty-eight states employed approximately 1350 men and women in county extension work.[10] Three years later, in 1917, the total number of those engaged in the work had grown to 4100, of whom 1117 were women. The number of counties with agricultural agents totaled 1434, of which 537 had home demonstration agents. In these early days of county work, the stress was almost entirely on production. There were seed corn testing demonstrations, poultry culling demonstrations, vaccinations of hogs, and other programs and projects to encourage production. Chester C. Davis observed that "the success of Extension in those days was measured in terms of so many chickens culled, so many hogs vaccinated, so many callers at the office, so many projects completed. The wires and pulleys and strings were more in evidence than the idea or the principle behind them." [11]

The county agent was not at all sure of the value or wisdom of his program. In his uncertainty and the uncertainty of his supporters, he found sufficient insecurity to want to move on to another type of position. County work was not regarded as a life occupation. The county agent who resigned in 1919, for instance, had served an average period of but one year and seven months. Gradually, however, those who stayed realized that there would be no one way in which to carry on the work and that there was a certain challenge in pioneering and experimenting. The agent elicited and found support for local meetings to replace the formally organized Farmers' Institutes. He began to relate his teaching to local conditions and found that his presence on the scene afforded that long-sought and necessary follow-up which had been missing from the Institutes.

His first real call to service came with America's entry into World War I. Almost overnight he became the busy government exponent of vitally necessary production as well as conservation. He set to work organizing county farm bureaus to help stimulate food production and soil conservation. With the home demonstration agent, he organized programs to show ways of conserving food and clothing, to demonstrate home production through gardens, to assist draft committees, to sell war loans. His day became so full and the demands made upon him so great that the Federal government enacted emergency appropriations to add to his number and to place people like him in counties previously without agent assistance. In less than six months the number of his colleagues increased by 50 per cent. By 1919, over 75 per cent of the counties had county agricultural agents, and 35 per cent had home demonstration agents. The results were immediately apparent. By the end of the war period, cooperative extension had proven its value. Though its staff numbers were depleted with the withdrawal of emergency funds, it had not lost in stature.

Cooperative extension now entered its second phase of development within this period. The war was over, and the number of extension personnel in the counties was cut. Not until the Capper-Ketcham funds were made available in 1928 would the numbers grow again substantially. With the developing farm depression of the early twenties, cooperative extension changed in character from an agency promoting production to one concerned primarily with economic problems of the farmers. Agents and specialists were engaged in solving problems of standardization, of storage and transportation, of marketing and consumption. Farm and home income and accounts were frequent topics of discussion. Land utilization became a subject of concern. Farmers were encouraged to spread their crops in order to avoid the dangers of intensive farming which meant complete dependence on markets. New problems brought new methods, and several important changes were about to take place.

It was soon evident that individual effort on the part of the farmer was inadequate to cope with the rapid decline in farm purchasing power. From the days of the earliest institutes, cooperative extension had been attempting to raise the sights of farmers. As soon as it had become evident that the farmer could exist no longer in an isolated and self-sufficient setting, extension had tried to expand "the horizon of the farmer from his cattle and his plow to the community, the county, the state, the nation, and the countries of the world" and give him "outlook, vision, and pride in occupation." He had been encouraged to work with his fellow-farmers not only on problems of the soil but on problems of community life. Group emphasis had been promoted through a great variety of activities, such as automobile tours, field meetings, promotion of legislation, and discussion of the rural school. It was natural, therefore, for agents to think of group action as one of the best possibilities for solving depression problems.

Across the country swept a great wave of enthusiasm for cooperative effort. In agricultural areas this took the form of cooperative marketing. Farmers turned to the agents to help them organize cooperative buying and selling groups. Farmers believed that one great cause of their economic suffering was the large share of the profit taken by the middleman. To avoid his participation in the marketing process, farmers and agents organized and managed cooperatives in fields representing most of the major crops. Kuhn points in Michigan, for instance, to the Michigan Milk Producers, the Michigan Potato Growers, and the Michigan Livestock Exchange which became sufficiently strong to survive the depression days and to continue successfully to the present day. In many cases the agent served as the manager of the "coop," arranging for the purchase of farm supplies in sufficient quantity to reduce the price for the individual farmer and arranging for the sale of his products through cooperative outlets. At the same time the agent was encouraging the farmer to increase his efficiency, to pay greater attention to food and feed crops which could be consumed at home, to regulate his production to fit the market demand, and to develop practical methods for improving his declining standard of living. The emphasis changed rapidly from production increase to efficiency increase.

By far the largest single group movement of the twenties was the spread of the number and power of the "Farm Bureaus." We have seen that extension came to rely on local leadership and to encourage group action. We have seen that Farm Bureaus in the counties had been organized in scattered places before the war and then developed in increasing numbers during the war. In some places the organizations grew out of community clubs or activities known as Crop Improvement Associations, Better Farming Leagues, Farm Improvement Clubs, and County Farm Associations. A central advisory board was set up to work with the agent. At first the groups were of an educational nature under the guidance of the agent. As they developed, their character changed. The relationship to the agent often became one of direct supervision of his efforts. With the development of cooperative marketing, local organizations engaged in business and commercial activities to which the agent lent advice.

As time passed, extension sentiment regarding organized activity changed. At first extension personnel had thought that formally organized groups were not necessary. Soon, however, with the encouragement of the Federal Department, agents recognized the value of their moral and financial support and set to work helping to establish more and larger Farm Bureaus. In 1916 the county agent leaders at their annual meeting had "recommended the standardization of the various types of county organizations along the lines that experience has proven most effective and that in reports and literature the above type should be called the 'Farm Bureau.'" The movement started particularly in the North and West and spread through the South. In some states Farm Bureaus were considered to be of such importance to the work of the agent that their formation became a condition for the assignment of an agent to a county. A few states went so far as to pass legislation requiring this procedure. By 1919 there were 796 counties in 31 states with Farm Bureaus. The paid membership totaled 409,481.

The first Farm Bureau had been started in New York State, and to this state fell the responsibility for further substantial development. By 1917 New York had thirty-nine active county Farm Bureau organizations and had established a state federation. Other states followed.

It then became apparent that agricultural problems were not confined to local or even state lines. As a result of an initial organization meeting at Cornell University early in 1919, all states with Farm Bureau organizations were invited to a second national meeting in Chicago in November of the same year. Thirty-five states were represented at the Chicago meeting. The result of their deliberations was the formation of the American Farm Bureau Federation. Extension had played a large and important role in the birth of this national body which eventually became by far the largest single farm organization in the world.

There had been mixed feelings about the wisdom of the relationship between Farm Bureaus and the extension service from the very start. As local Farm Bureaus became more powerful and much more interested in both business and legislation, the agents recognized that their efforts were becoming less and less educational. Some states began to change their attitude toward the relationship, claiming that the farm organization was no longer "simon-pure." They felt, in the words of B. H. Crocheron in 1925, that "the child had left the leading strings of its father and had strayed away with other and different advisors." In spite of this scattered feeling, however, the period witnessed a strengthening rather than a weakening of the relationship. The 1930 Office of Education study listed 29 states as specifying that the Farm Bureau be one of the cooperating agencies in the counties. Furthermore, where it existed, it was usually the chief agency. The study reported that in 13 states cooperation with the Farm Bureau was required by law, and in 19 states "the public does not differentiate between the terms 'farm bureau work' and 'extension work.'" The study concluded that "Without question the farm bureau has played a larger part in the development of the agricultural extension program in the United States than all other organizations combined." The secret and ritualistic nature of the National Grange had prevented a close tie-in with this older national farm group. In the two decades of the tens and twenties, then, extension and the Farm Bureau movement grew up together. The significance to American agriculture of their parallel growth can never truly be measured.

By the end of the twenties, cooperative extension had become a large and active force. In 1927-28 county agents were established in 2300 counties, home demonstration agents in 1300, and county club or assistant county agents in 242. Voluntary leaders, both men and women, totaled 237,817. As a result of extension efforts, the agents listed over 4,660,000 improved farm and home practices in the one year 1928. The budget was said to be $20,397,560, of which 35.5 per cent came from county sources.

The countywide duties of the agent were amazingly varied. He was expected to conduct demonstrations, hold meetings, organize and supervise 4–H club work, assist the farmers with marketing problems, and, in general, raise the educational, social, economic, and spiritual standards of the people. He was expected to keep the farm people abreast of the best methods recommended by the college for all phases of agricultural activity. His work was not without fault. The years immediately following would answer some of the needs; others would remain unfilled to the present time. In any case, the collapse of the stock market brought a new and different role, and a far busier one, to the agent who was now well established in rural circles.

In 1929 the Federal government attempted to deal with farm prices for the first time on a large scale. In that year Congress passed the Agricultural Marketing Act, setting up the Federal Farm Board. But the Act was inadequate to stem the tide. Far from being stabilized, farm prices dropped to record lows and surpluses rose to record highs. The great depression of the thirties had started, and new government programs would have to be found.

To some extent, cooperative extension was not ready for the deep depression which followed the collapse of the stock market. Together with the colleges, it had failed to formulate, either in its thinking or on paper, any comprehensive program for agriculture based on sound economic principles. Perhaps this was too much to ask of a slowly maturing educational agency without experience in public policy making. In any case, the long history of emphasis on production would not serve it well. Even the later value given to marketing was little more than the pooling of production; it had no semblance of control or conservation. Little thought had been given thus far to distribution. Extension techniques and understanding appeared inadequate, too, for what lay ahead. Extension activities had been mainly of a service nature. So one in their midst had complained at an Association session as late as 1931, "Many of the county agricultural agents and agricultural specialists are incapable of thinking otherwise until they are yanked out of the ruts of self-esteem and complacency and given a background through graduate study which will help them to think in terms of human welfare." Graduate study would not be necessary, however; the depression would soon do it.

Despite these faults, extension had shown itself able to respond to change. The relatively small crisis of the twenties had been good training ground for the severe collapse of the thirties. The colleges, together with the Federal Department, had built a sound organization of trained personnel, as well as accumulated valuable information and source material. The experimental years of their childhood and adolescence gave them the security necessary to act with confidence in the tragic days ahead.

In the early days of the depression, the Federal government turned almost automatically to the cooperative extension service for advice and assistance. At first it was felt that problems could be solved mainly through education, and extension was obviously the educational arm of the government. Emergency relief could be carried on without excessive cost through the existing agency. It was not until a few years later that desperate government organizations moved into extension territory. In the beginning, however, the task was one of education. The colleges were urged to recognize the extent and character of the emergency, its possible duration, and the necessity for sound, scientific research and extension work in agricultural economics which might influence public policies in such fields as taxation, school support, highway development, and rural electrification. New teaching programs and new methods would have to be devised to make the extension program sound economically and adapted to national as well as local conditions. A coordination of extension effort to meet the economic situation was no longer merely desirable but vitally necessary. The previously effective demonstration technique was not adaptable to the new situation which found the farmer concerned less with insects and plant diseases than with his position in a creditor nation. His interest in economics formerly had been confined to his own ledger; now it would have to include some understanding of national and international monetary standards. To meet this situation, extension came to rely heavily for the first time on the discussion method.

Those who had lamented the agents' lack of understanding of human welfare soon saw the agent dealing for the first time with farmers of the lower income and lower ambition levels. Extension personnel realized that their efforts had not been reaching many of the people who most needed their help. Out of the contact came a strong social concern. The vague and previously expressed concept of the farm as a family unit suddenly became terribly real. To help the farmer, his wife, and children find at least some good in a bad situation, the arts, recreation, and cultural studies were brought into the extension program.

Once again the extension worker was reaching more people. His efforts were not always accepted with enthusiasm. In 1931 he was described by the "opposing noisy element" as a "white-collared theorist." There was some agitation to abolish extension but little came of it. It did serve, however, the useful purpose of forcing a re-examination and, in the end, an improvement. Cooperative extension, like all public agencies, was sensitive to criticism and usually profited from it.

With the Democratic victory in 1932 and the arrival in Washington of the New Deal early in 1933, striking changes were made in the government's approach to the depression problems. Almost immediately emergency legislation was passed and so-called "action agencies" set up to deal directly with specific issues. The emphasis was no longer on education as the chief method of solution. As President Charles E. Friley later described them, "The common feature of all [action] programs . . . is that they depend for results on means other than or in addition to education—on inducements which are immediately and tangibly remunerative or punitive." Cooperative extension was faced with an important decision: should it limit itself to the now traditional educational emphasis or should it become the focus of all the new activities which appeared to touch the lives of farmers in a more vital way? The initial decision, soon proved unworkable, was an attempt to combine the two. The acceptance of responsibility for a new type of program without additional funds would result in giving it priority over the old.

The first Federal program to be undertaken was embodied in the Agricultural Adjustment Act of 1933. Immediately a "propagandic campaign" was deemed necessary to acquaint the farmers with the need for such a program, and the underlying economic philosophy upon which it was based. The Agricultural Adjustment Administration turned to the Extension Service as the field agency best prepared to perform this service, and it imposed on it "certain responsibilities which could not, even with the most liberal classification, be termed educational," in the words of one land-grant educator.

Beginning in 1933 the Agricultural Adjustment program was administered and directed in the states by the Land-Grant Colleges. Directors of extension were designated state administrators, with the agents serving under them in a similar county capacity. Chester C. Davis, the Administrator of the Agricultural Adjustment Administration, spoke plainly and forcefully of extension's choice in the matter:

There are thousands of people cooperating with the county agent's office who never before were interested in his work. If you are to maintain and provide services for these people you will perhaps find it necessary to reorganize your methods, and forget some of your old activities. If such an adaption of the county agents' service is not regarded as desirable, there is the alternative that some one else may be established in the counties to handle administrative matters, and the county agent be left free to do purely educational work.[12]

The choice was thus clear and simple, and yet filled with overtones not previously heard in extension circles.

Administrator Davis was correct in his prediction of the consequent increased contacts thus made available to extension. Extension found benefit, too, in its new relationship to all of the farmer's problems, including an understanding of underlying world conditions. The break from the traditional had been made, and one Extension Director concluded, "While many may have been deeply concerned as to just when we would return to a regular program, no doubt they are beginning to realize that we never turn back—that this movement is but paving the way to a new educational program." In one form or another in the programs which succeeded the original AAA, the county agents and state staff continued to have a direct relationship.

Within a year and a half after the New Deal had been established in Washington, the Secretary of Agriculture, Henry A. Wallace, called upon the Land-Grant Colleges to undertake an entirely different kind of function than they had known before. They were asked for the first time by the Federal government to play a role in public policy formation. In an address to the land-grant convention in 1934, Secretary Wallace asked for help and, at the same time, minimized the dangers that colleges might face in replying. He commented, ". . . the Land-Grant College people and extension workers are themselves to a considerable extent members of a body which does extend over the years, and which to a very considerable extent can originate and formulate, through its influence on the great rank and file of our people, policies which will go beyond this particular Administration." [13] In the years of the deep depression to follow, the land-grant role in determining policy mainly took the form of increased and intricate relationships with the many multiplying agencies of the New Deal. In 1936, for example, in addition to a reduced traditional program, the extension service was working cooperatively in most of the states with the Agricultural Adjustment Administration (later Agricultural Conservation and Domestic Allotment), the Soil Conservation Service, the Rural Rehabilitation and Resettlement Administration, the Rural Electrification Administration, the Rural Housing Administration, and the Farm Credit Administration. In connection with the Farm Credit Administration, as an example, extension workers were organizing production credit associations, acquainting farmers with their services, handling emergency crop and feed loans, and carrying out the farm debt adjustment program.

As the new agencies grew and as extension became overburdened, Federal authorities began moving directly into the states. The Land-Grant Colleges became deeply concerned over the duplication of effort and the obvious by-pass of the colleges which, by agreement, were intended to represent Federal interests within the states. The Association appointed a Special Committee on Duplication of Land-Grant College Work by New Federal Agencies. Its name was as long as the concern was deep. As examples of duplication, the Committee cited in 1934 the activities of the Federal Emergency Relief Administration agencies in rural home demonstration work and the Federal Soil Erosion Service in research, demonstration, and extension work in soil erosion control. In the following year, 1935, the convention was marked by extended discussion of interrelationships and conflicts, and by promises of Federal officials to avoid duplication with extension.

As time passed, the duplication increased and so did the resultant problems. The colleges complained of the appointment by action agencies of educational subject-matter specialists directly working in the field, of salary increases for action agency personnel which threw out of line the compensation of extension personnel, of a lack of extension funds to meet the requirements, and of strings attached to those funds which were made available. The colleges and their Association at first requested and then demanded clarification of their relation to those programs "in which rehabilitation, conservation, or adjustment in agriculture is forwarded through the use of power legislatively conferred upon some action agency to utilize for its success, grants-in-aid (such as parity or conservation payments), the power of taxation or the police power." [14] The situation was not helped by an obvious and growing concern among college and extension personnel that the agencies had gone too far. They became worried, for instance, over too liberal lending policies which increased the farmer's indebtedness. As the irritation over duplication grew, their silent opposition also grew.

Attempts were made to define the land-grant position in the dispute. Obviously the situation was delicate and fraught with all kinds of consequences for the colleges which had been established by national and state mandate. A committee of the faculty of Iowa State College brought forth a widely quoted statement which read in part:

Any attempt to describe the role of the land-grant college in governmental agricultural programs should be predicated on the fundamental proposition that, through independent research and educational establishments, these institutions are enabled to provide and disseminate disinterested information, counsel and measurement pertinent to such progress and that these services are so valuable and vital in a democratically organized society that they should never be jeopardized or encroached upon in any way. Apart from this, the colleges are free to give wholehearted cooperation to the federal and state governments through their research foundations and their machinery for the dissemination of information.

One thing must, however, be recognized from the very beginning. No cardinal program of agricultural betterment is ever enacted without its becoming identified by the general public with the political party in power at the time of its adoption. Consequently it becomes a matter of great delicacy to show with precision how the land-grant college can make a significant contribution to the success of a program and yet avoid loss of the perfect detachment and objectivity, which under all circumstances, it should maintain.

Committees had been established by the Association and by the Department to study the relationships. After two years of work, a conference was called to present for consideration a plan of action. On July 7, 1938, representatives of twenty-seven institutions and of the Department met at Mount Weather in the hopes of reaching agreement. The discussion was frank and informal. The leadership was provided by Dean Carl E. Ladd of Cornell for the colleges and Milton S. Eisenhower for the Department. The result was the first substantial meeting of minds since the beginning days of the depression. It was agreed that the extension services of the colleges would take the leadership in building agricultural programs through analysis and planning starting at the local community level. To coordinate all public assistance to farmers, a system of local and state land-use planning was devised, with the state director of extension serving as chairman of the State Land-Use Planning Committee. The county agent would be the executive officer of the county committee. These program aspects of the agreement were short-lived, however. Within a few years Congress eliminated the supporting funds, mainly due to the opposition of the American Farm Bureau Federation which viewed land-use planning as a possible beginning of a new farm organization. In spite of this, the Mount Weather Agreement stands historically as a milestone in the attempt to settle differences and as a further indication of the ability of the colleges and the Federal Department to iron out difficulties and to work together to an unusually high degree of mutual cooperation and support.

Home Economics Extension

The second major division of cooperative extension, home economics, had paralleled the growth of agricultural work. The same influences were there, the same crises, and much the same response. In only one important regard was there a difference. In home economics, extension work actually preceded research. No definite agencies for home economics research had been established by the time there were many home demonstration agents active in the field. As a consequence, the home economics extension workers were forced to find the answers while compiling the questions. Their needs led to the further development of home economics research.

Funds for home demonstration work multiplied tenfold in the period from 1914 to 1922. Nine per cent of extension funds had been allotted in 1914, compared with 18 per cent for 1922. At the time of the passage of the Smith-Lever Act, there were 349 county home demonstration agents. By 1936 the number had grown to 1916 agents and assistants affiliated with fifty-one colleges within the Association and all seventeen Negro institutions. In addition, the extension faculty on the campus included in that year 444 state home demonstration leaders, assistants, and specialists. The organized home demonstration groups throughout the states numbered 41,504 with a membership of 950,927.

World War I was the first cause of home demonstration expansion. As in agriculture, home demonstration agents were added on an emergency basis. In the development of organized groups to assist the agents, some form of Home Bureau paralleled the Farm Bureau. The agents planned programs to demonstrate better methods of food storage and conservation, as well as a beginning emphasis on nutritive values. Rural health and personal hygiene were important topics. When the flu epidemic descended in 1918, agents and farm wives soon found they could practice to great benefit what they had learned. The First World War also witnessed a growth, albeit short-lived, in urban demonstration work. Increased supplies of wheat were found necessary for American servicemen and their allies, and civilian consumption had to be reduced. The home demonstration agents undertook a foods and nutrition program in large cities. City house-wives were thus assisted for the first time by women trained in foods and nutrition work.

With the end of the war came a reexamination of the purpose and function of home demonstration work. In order to plan for the future, particularly in the North and the West, the colleges and the Department cooperated in a survey of ten thousand farm homes. The survey disclosed urgent problems where help was needed:

. . . the shortening of the working day, the lessening of labor, the improving of home equipment (particularly by rearranging the kitchen and installing running water, power, and a modern heating system), and promoting of higher standards of comfort and beauty in the home, the safeguarding of the health of the family (especially by better selection and preparation of food, more intelligent care of children, and sanitation of the home and its surroundings), the developing of money-yielding home industries, and the more satisfactory allotment and expenditure of the family budget. There were also problems connected with the farm family and the school, the church, and organized recreation and social life, as affected by modern transportation and communication, which tend to relieve isolation and to tie farm homes and rural communities to the villages and the cities.[15]

It was obvious, then, that home demonstration agents had plenty of work ahead. Soon after the survey had been completed, however, the farm depression of the twenties settled on the nation. Signals were switched and the home demonstration agent concentrated on showing farm women how to dress and beautify homes without lavish expenditure, spend their small income, utilize labor-saving methods and equipment, and develop home crafts for additional income. As in agriculture, the emphasis soon changed from production to conservation.

The home demonstration agent followed the lead of the agricultural agent in developing sources of local leadership. The fostering of leadership among rural women was to become one of the major contributions of home economics extension. The agents were quick to place as much responsibility on local women as the women proved they could carry without detriment to the program. The technique served to strengthen organizations of farmers' wives and home demonstration clubs. Within a few years, college leaders found it wise not to place an agent in a county even if funds were available unless the county were ready to assume some sort of cooperative responsibility in an organized way for her employment. By the end of the twenties it was reported that enough progress had been made so that it had become increasingly difficult to tell farm women by their dress when they came to town. In 1927 alone, the women in 297,000 rural homes were taught costume designing, hat making, and adaptation of dress goods.

With the beginning of the great depression of the thirties, home demonstration work appeared to be on a relatively sounder footing than agricultural work. Proportionately more farm women had been reached under a more systematic and effective program. The only criticism seemed to be that home economics extension was too standardized to adjust easily to changing conditions and local needs. The criticism was not repeated later. Home economics extension responded quickly to depression needs. In the twelve month interval between 1933 and 1934, the state reports listed a 37 per cent increase in the number of farm families reached and an equal increase in the number of improved practices adopted by the families. The depression emphasis on the family as the farm unit served home economics extension well and gave it a reason to extend its efforts. Farmers, their wives, and children were regarded as partners in the building of the extension program. The agents passed along information on low-cost foods, on clothing repair and renovation, on methods for inexpensive recreation and entertainment. Their work was popularly received and helped considerably to strengthen their role in the rural community. As the depression stretched on, the agents broadened their approach to emphasize habits, attitudes, and philosophies of life which might bring strength to depressed people. The work of the agents was well described by Mrs. Lucille Rust of Kansas State College:

The home economics extensionist, primarily a teacher, has a most difficult but extremely satisfying teaching job. Her school may be an entire county, a district or a State. Her classroom is wherever a meeting place can be arranged. Unless a specialist and often then, she must be prepared to give instruction in any and all phases of homemaking. She must not only be a leader but develop leadership in others. She must be a personal advisor, encouraging and helping many through trying periods of emotional and mental stress. She must have a deep understanding of rural life and its problems and likewise rural people.[16]

The lot of the home demonstration agent and her supporting specialist was not an easy one. She was asked to show the same results as her male counterpart under equally difficult conditions. But her perseverance brought her high regard. One agent was said to have been called to the office of the county sheriff who told her, "Miss Grace, I can't sleep at night for thinking of you driving all over this county in all sorts of out-of-the-way places with no protection. Take this gun and I will swear you in as a deputy and you can use it if it is necessary. I'll sleep better if I know you have it." [17]

Boys and Girls Club Work

Extension work with boys and girls had expanded steadily in the years immediately following the passage of the Smith-Lever Act. Though the leadership was inadequate to cope with the numbers, the boys and girls continued to flock to the clubs. The First World War caused the numbers to spiral suddenly. Over half a million youth were enrolled in 1918. Following the war, the totals dropped back to 222,137 in 1920. But, in spite of the depression, 4-H Club work quickly expanded to its wartime figure by 1924. Numbers continued to grow in the late twenties and early thirties until in 1936 the total stood at 1,145,508.[18]

The withdrawal of emergency funds which had supported the employment of many new agents during the war forced club leaders to reexamine the program. Ruby Green Smith concluded that "this real blow to many of the enthusiastic supporters of club work was the beginning of a sounder and broader program. Gradually public support increased; methods of organization were perfected; recreation, health education, and community service were added; and the whole program was studied with regard to sound, long-time aims and objectives and the means of attaining them." [19] The emphasis in the early years on garden, corn, canning, pig and poultry clubs with the objective of profit-making turned to the promotion of life enrichment programs. Recreation, camping, soil and wildlife conservation were stressed, along with appreciation of music, the arts, and particularly drama. In 1927 at a meeting of the club leaders, a pledge was adopted for national use: "I pledge my head to clearer thinking, my heart to greater loyalty, my hands to larger service, and my health to better living, for my club, my community, and my country."

Commercial concerns were still continuing to capitalize on club work by offering prizes and awards in return for the advertising and good will which might result. The problem for the colleges and for club leaders and agents was vexing and not easily solved. Unfortunately, during the depression of the thirties, club work in any form suffered from the pressures put upon agents to perform government service. Somehow, however, 4-H work continued to grow and to gain great stature among the rural people. In many states it was regarded as the heart of cooperative extension work. The continuing interest and support of local leadership was largely responsible.

Engineering Extension

In the meantime, during this period, engineering extension was making a slow beginning. The meagerness of the program was caused by the lack of Federal support and insufficient demand from industry. In 1910 only the University of Wisconsin, which was well imbued with the extension idea in all fields, was paying much attention to engineering extension. Other institutions slowly developed the work and by 1920 more than half of the land-grant institutions were carrying on at least some form of engineering extension. Among the most progressive, Penn State, for instance, inaugurated correspondence instruction which led to the preparation of the extension division's own textbooks and to an additional form of instruction known as the "Home Study Plan." Correspondence courses covered a wide variety of subjects, including those of the technical, high school, and college entrance grade, as well as college courses paralleling those offered in similar subjects on the campus. The location of many of the Land-Grant Colleges in small towns and agricultural areas, however, prevented them from developing closer and more effective services to industries and trades. The growth of vocational schools in the larger cities made engineering extension less of a necessity. Thus the contact with industry was limited largely to college preparation of engineers and industrial leaders.

In the twenties engineering extension seemed to make some headway. Among the major forms were practical short courses, correspondence instruction, night courses, specialized conference sessions, package libraries, and lecturers, and the offering of engineering advice. The program remained small, however, as shown by the figure of $311,451 spent in all states on engineering extension in the year 1929 compared to $12,758,067 expended in thirty-six states on cooperative extension in the same year. The need was evidently there but it would take special encouragement and demand before it would be filled and then still inadequately.

General Extension

General or University Extension developed more slowly than cooperative extension in most institutions and for many of the same reasons as engineering extension. No Federal funds were forthcoming for liberal arts or industrial extension and state allotments were insufficient to build a strong program. Unlike agriculture, general extension could not be related to profit gain and was without any organized lay group to back it. One of the more unique aspects of land-grant history is this almost complete void of support from the business world, including such organizations as chambers of commerce. Their only place in the total picture was to give early support to the agricultural extension movement. As a result, Land-Grant Colleges took no special leadership in economic and business education or extension. The historic tendency was to stress agriculture and home economics and to give an almost equal place to engineering only in its instructional phase. General extension, which might have developed a strong industrial and cultural program in almost all states, was considered by the colleges to be more a part of the program of state and urban universities. Where it appeared in Land-Grant Colleges, it was asked to pay its own way, resulting frequently in an imbalance in the offerings. Until more recent times and in only a few universities did it ever have a teaching staff of its own. It was dependent, instead, on the resident faculty and, as a result, came off second-best. Consequently, general extension never developed a set of concrete aims tied to specific purposes in the usual pattern of land-grant growth. Land-Grant Colleges have been a part of the general or university extension movement but never a particularly unique part.

Louis E. Reber, one of the first and strongest supporters of general extension, surveyed the progress to 1920 and reported what he termed "marvelous growth":

Thirty-three [Land-Grant Colleges] report well-organized departments of correspondence and extension class instruction; 10 record well-developed lecture and lyceum bureaus, while many supply lectures from faculty upon demand; 8 describe strong departments of forum teaching and library extension, and 12 others are doing work of the latter type; 20 have introduced a visual instruction service; 12 are doing a considerable amount of well-organized work in community development; 6 have established bureaus of municipal information; and 5 are conducting post-graduate medical work. Several report cooperation of general with agricultural extension, and many carry on some form or forms of university extension without distinct organization for it.[20]

With the war over, the national adult education movement emerged in strength and form. By 1926 the American Association for Adult Education had been organized with funds largely from the Carnegie Corporation. Throughout the twenties the emphasis in many universities, including the Land-Grant Colleges, was on home study. Kansas State College reported, for instance, that between 1921 and 1928 approximately 900 million words were written by students and sent to instructors for grading and comment, enough to make a library of from 7000 to 8000 volumes. The Office of Education survey found correspondence study an accepted method of teaching procedure enrolling 34,615 people in correspondence classes in 26 of the Land-Grant Colleges. The emphasis nationwide was said to be on "a new discipline of refreshing inspiration and pleasurable study," rather than on strict academic lines. The colleges responded by offering popular courses which could attract sufficient enrollment to pay for themselves. There was little inclination to subsidize much more than the administrative work. The growth was steady but slow. It was not until 1934 that the Penn State Board of Trustees formally created a separate division of Arts and Science Extension, and yet Pennsylvania had been one of the most active from the beginning.

THE ASSOCIATION

The growth and development of the colleges were clearly reflected in this period in the activities of their national association. Even the changes in name of the Association mirrored what had been happening in the colleges. From its organization in 1887 until 1919 it was known as the Association of American Agricultural Colleges and Experiment Stations. From 1919 until 1925 it bore the name of Association of Land-Grant Colleges. In 1926 to this was added "and Universities." It would not be changed again until 1955 when it became officially the American Association of Land-Grant Colleges and State Universities. The dropping of "agriculture" from the title in 1919 was chiefly the result of the return to the fold of engineering. Mechanic arts had not played an important role from the very beginning. It was often ignored in the sessions which emphasized agriculture. Even the papers presented on the subject were not printed in the Proceedings except by title. Engineering dropped out of the Association completely after the turn of the century and organized its own Land-Grant College Engineering Association which functioned until 1916. In that year an Engineering Division of the Association assembled for the first time. Obviously with engineering back in the ranks the Association could no longer continue to be called "Agricultural." With the change in name in 1919 came also a reorganization which finally vested the legislative functions with the presidents of the colleges and retained the sections and divisions for discussion and report purposes. It would take some years before all would be happy in the new grouping. Some blamed, for instance, not only the opposition of the state universities but the disinterest of the Executive Committee of the Association for the failure to obtain Federal aid for the engineering experiment stations.

As the years passed, however, the Association gained the support and cooperation of all of its many segments. The proper coordination of extension, research, and resident teaching was a frequent topic of discussion in land-grant meetings. In 1936 the Deans of Graduate Work in the Land-Grant Colleges met with the Association for the first time. It was not until after the Second World War, however, that liberal arts became a recognized member.

During the depression days of the thirties, the Association and its several committees acted as a clearinghouse for the problems brought on by the economic crisis and the many attempts to solve them. Deliberations at the annual meetings frequently centered around current farm problems of a national nature. The Convention of 1930, for example, was devoted almost entirely to discussion of the farm price situation. In 1927 the Association began a practice which would bring it recognition and great benefit in the years ahead. It appointed a special committee to report on the agricultural situation. A second report was issued in 1932. President W. C. Coffey noted that these reports "have been quoted time and time again as sources of reliable information by practically all agencies, groups and individuals sincerely interested in the welfare of agriculture. They have been one of the most stabilizing influences in these very unstable times." The Association was also influential in bringing about the passage of the Bankhead-Jones Act of 1935. The Committee on College Organization and Policy helped pilot this important Federal measure through Congress.

Throughout these difficult years, the Association was singularly fortunate in its ability to enlist the help of highly competent land-grant educators at all levels. The college presidents who became Association presidents, as well as those who served often for long periods on Association committees, looked upon Association duty as a primary obligation as well as a pleasure and honor. For fifteen of the years, from 1929 to 1944, they were assisted by the Association's able Secretary-Treasurer, Dean Thomas P. Cooper. There was close cooperation, too, between the Association and major farm organizations, including the American Farm Bureau Federation, the National Grange, and the Farmers' Union.

Not all was completely harmonious between the Association members and the separate state universities. President W. E. Stone of Purdue had observed in 1916 that "whenever in recent years legislation is proposed in the interest of the Land-Grant Colleges, it immediately meets with a certain opposition in Congress, and usually the opposition can be traced to those State Universities not connected with the Land-Grant Colleges." [21] There was talk in 1926 of combining the Association and the National Association of State Universities, but actual steps in this direction would not be taken for some time to come. So, too, there was a call for more sympathetic cooperation between the colleges and the Negro colleges which were not members. The question of Negro membership in the Association was first raised officially in 1934. Again, years would pass before the question was answered in the affirmative.

The Association continued to promote closer cooperation between its member institutions and the United States Department of Agriculture. It was instrumental in 1923 in obtaining a reorganization of the Department for better service to the colleges. In that year the States Relations Service was abolished and separate Offices of Experiment Stations, of Cooperative Extension Work, and of Home Economics were established. Within the institutions, the Association continued to promote graduate study, one of its early interests. The results were apparent. Whereas in 1898 only 35 doctor's degrees had been conferred by the Land-Grant Colleges, in 1935–36 the number was 859, or 31 per cent of the national total.

THE PERIOD IN RETROSPECT

There was no doubt that this period had been one of difficulty for the colleges as well as the nation. In 1924 the President of the United States, Calvin Coolidge, had told the colleges:

I look upon you as the group in whose hands rests a greater responsibility for the destiny of American agriculture than can fairly be attributed to any other single body. The great chain of the colleges and universities under your care and guidance are institutions of practical economics. They are much more than merely agricultural colleges. They are also concerned in the diffusion of a wide general culture, as all properly directed education must be. Their interests are broad, scientific, and practical. . . . They have done a truly wonderful work, which has aimed at rescuing agriculture from an almost chronic status as the Cinderella in the industrial family, and placing it on a higher plane of scientific accuracy and permanent prosperity.[22]

Before many years were out, some of his words were to have a hollow ring, but others stood up under the test of time. And, in this period, time had tested well the Land-Grant Colleges. It had thrust upon them three great crises. Their response was proof of their ultimate strength and wisdom. They were ready now to serve a nation soon to be plunged again into tragedy. This time there would be little hesitation, little fumbling. They had learned to stand fast through trial and error. Their great friend, President Edward A. O'Neal of the American Farm Bureau Federation, had told them, "I see the effect of your work on the people, and I see its effect on action and thought of the people. A great many of the philosophies of some of our elder statesmen have fallen down. But your institutions have not failed. . . ."[23]

7

Maturity, 1938-1956

AMERICA had just begun to recover from the great
depression when, on September 1, 1939, Hitler moved the German
Army into Poland, thus signaling the start of the Second World War.
Whereas the war of 1918 had been confined to Europe, this soon was
to become a global conflict. Eventually only a few countries remained
neutral. In America, nothing like it had been felt before; it involved
every segment of American life. The Land-Grant Colleges, now so
much a part of the American nation, could not remain immune.
Their role in wartime and in the uneasy days to follow would be the
largest they had ever played in service to the people. Within a few
months after Congress had declared war in 1941, the Association's
Executive Committee was ready with a resolution presented in behalf
of the colleges: "They offer to the Nation, through the appropriate
military and civilian channels, all of their facilities for such essential
scientific, technical and professional training and research and other
educational activities as may be necessary for the success of the country's war effort." The national and international services of the colleges would not be confined to the war years alone. Recovery from
the impact of the war would bring new responsibilities. The emerging
"Cold War" and consequent confined conflicts, such as that in Korea
in the early fifties, resulted in permanent uncertainty for the world,
the nation, and its colleges.

THE PERIOD IN PROSPECT

By the end of the thirties and prior to the war, America had become as highly industrialized as any nation in the world's history.

The population ratio of 85 per cent rural and 15 per cent urban had reversed itself within a period of a hundred years. Cities were larger and life more complex than man had ever dreamed possible. Both industry and farm were producing enough to fill domestic needs and to export huge quantities of food, machinery, and manufactured products to foreign nations. The Second World War hastened all of the changes which had been occurring more slowly during the first four decades of the century. The output per man-hour on the farm in 1951 was 86 per cent above that of 1930 and 45 per cent above 1940. In 1900 one farmer was producing enough for himself and seven others; by 1951, he was supplying food and fiber for himself and fourteen others. All of this was being accomplished with fewer and fewer farm workers. Industry had aided agriculture by inventing and producing thousands of inexpensive labor saving machines and devices. Whereas there had been 246,100 tractors in use in 1920, there were 3,860,000 plowing American land in 1950. With the depression over and prosperous war economy in full force, standards of living changed. In their daily lives as well as in their bank accounts, the American people were now receiving the full benefits of the industrial revolution.

This entire modern period of the Land-Grant Colleges was marked by increasingly greater agricultural productivity. The years of American peace shortly before formal entry into the war saw excellent crops produced in huge quantity. There was still some bitterness over the Federal program. A president of the land-grant Association in 1939 had complained, "Where 'once the embattled farmers stood, and fired the shot heard round the world,' may become merely the gathering place of an eager group awaiting the arrival of the pay checks of a beneficent government." Farmers soon, however, were busily involved in war production. Together with the colleges of agriculture, they were called upon to reach production goals of unprecedented magnitude. There was no longer any doubt whatsoever about their dependence on the world beyond them. By 1952, the United States with 6 per cent of the world's population, was producing annually more than 40 per cent of the world's goods.

In their continuing response to these national needs, expansion and maturity came to the Land-Grant Colleges. With the exception of the war years, from 1933 through the foreseeable future increasing enrollment would be one of the major problems of all Land-Grant Colleges. In some states enrollment in the five years from 1933 to 1938 rose almost 100 per cent. The distribution of students according to fields of study had changed substantially, too. In the Land-Grant Colleges in 1938, courses in arts and sciences enrolled 35.7 per cent of the student numbers; engineering, 18.3 per cent; agriculture, 12.0 per cent; teacher preparation, 8.4 per cent; commerce and business, 7.7 per cent; home economics, 6.0 per cent; law, 1.6 per cent; medicine, 1.9 per cent; and others, 4.5 per cent.[1] Agriculture continued to drop in popularity so that by 1947 it constituted only 8 per cent of total land-grant enrollment.

The war years brought inevitable changes in the student population. The Federal government turned to the Land-Grant Colleges more than to any other type of educational institution for the on-campus establishment of war training programs. In 1943, for instance, the colleges were training in organized military programs some 100,500 members of the armed forces. As we shall see, this was only one of many war services of the colleges. It caused dislocation; many were not satisfied with the handling of the programs, but there was no doubt that the Land-Grant Colleges were being used and used effectively.

With the end of the war and the establishment of the "right" to further education for the returning veteran, the number of students nationally attending institutions of higher education jumped by almost a million. The Land-Grant Colleges assumed a large share of this burden. Enrollments swelled to greater heights than ever before. War-surplus apartment houses were relocated on the campuses, and trailer camps built for married veterans. Temporary houses were constructed to accommodate the increased number of faculty members. Quonset huts were obtained to house single students, and additional buildings of all types were constructed. Despite the building activity, however, the colleges found dormitories and classrooms flooded with students. As public institutions, the Land-Grant Colleges felt perhaps more keenly than most the obligation to make room for every qualified veteran as well as civilian student. Educational standards suffered to some extent; not all learning conditions were ideal; but there was little doubt that the obligation had been met.

As the postwar bulge ended, the colleges settled down to a more normal pattern. In 1951–52, the land-grant institutions were enrolling 421,000 students. They represented 17.2 per cent of all students in all types of institutions of higher education in the country. Of all earned degrees, the Land-Grant Colleges were conferring 21.4 per cent and about 38 per cent of all doctorates. In engineering this included 37 per cent of all bachelor's and first professional degrees, approximately half of all master's degrees, and two-thirds of the doctorates. In agriculture it included more than 82 per cent of all undergraduate degrees, 97 per cent of master's, and 100 per cent of the doctorates. In home economics, the colleges were educating 40 per cent of the bachelor degree holders, 54 per cent of the master's, and 82 per cent of the doctor's. In veterinary medicine, the Land-Grant Colleges educated 96 per cent of the degree winners. In addition, they were supplying 20 per cent of the medical doctors, 33 per cent of the pharmacists, and 15 per cent of the nurses. There was no doubt about the quantity of their operation; quality was another problem, not just germane to the land-grant institutions, however.

In addition to the degree program, the colleges continued to provide extensive offerings on the short course level. The Committee on Short Curricula in Land-Grant Colleges and Universities reported in 1947 that twenty-one of the institutions, including the Negro colleges, were offering programs of a short course nature in one or more fields besides agriculture. Sixteen were engaged in more than one field of study. The total short course enrollment was 28,740.

The modern Land-Grant College and University was thus a far broader interpretation of the original intention of education for the "industrial classes." It had come a long way from the struggle for place and function in the latter half of the nineteenth century. The first focus on agriculture and mechanic arts had been expanded to include all of the functions of the modern university, including some which were unique to the land-grant system. This was true not alone of the Land-Grant Colleges associated with and an integral part of the state universities, but of those which operated as a unit distinct from the existing state university. Many of these "separated" colleges had grown into the stature of another state university. The most striking example was Michigan State offering 126 different areas of study, of which 65 were also on a graduate level. By 1955, this early Land-Grant College had become a university in name as well as function. It enrolled 15,500 students taught by a faculty of more than 2,000 including teaching, research, extension and adult education personnel. Its internal divisions were nine—Agriculture, Basic College, Business and Public Service, Education, Engineering, Graduate Studies, Home Economics, Science and Arts, and Veterinary Medicine. Its campus covered 570 acres, plus 3,230 acres of adjacent experimental farms. Its physical plant with 130 permanent buildings and nearly 1,000 temporary structures, was valued at more than seventy million dollars. The acorn buried in 1855 had branched into the majestic oak of 1955.

As the Land-Grant College had become more a part of the lives of the people, its instructional function had expanded. In a number of states, the campus as such was but one central unit with a number of branch divisions in other communities within the state lines. Adult education was considered by many land-grant educators to be the responsibility of every department, not just agriculture, home economics, and engineering. New fields were opening. At Cornell, by legislative enactment in 1944 and 1945, a School of Industrial and Labor Relations had been established. The School would operate both at the undergraduate and graduate level and encompass the three traditional functions of teaching, research, and extension.

The colleges were expanding in other ways, too. By the end of the thirties, they had accepted their important responsibility in the formulation of public policy in agriculture. Participation was justified on the basis of their existence as national and state agencies of education. It was as clear an indication as any of the final and complete emergence of higher education from the Ivory Tower. The colleges were quick to recognize the limitations of this new role. In 1940 President F. D. Farrell had declared that they "are not and never should be policemen, promoters or propagandists. The Colleges are scientific and educational agencies. If and when such an agency becomes a policeman, a promoter or a propagandist, it ceases, in some degree, to be either scientific or educational." The colleges conceived of themselves rather as forces for intelligent understanding among all people.

Aside from a few previous steps, the first real indication that the colleges had assumed a function in shaping national attitudes and policy came with a report in 1944 of a special Association committee on postwar agricultural planning. The report called for "basic long-run national policies to lessen instability of income resulting from variations in production and demand." It recommended the establishment of policies to place agriculture on a "satisfactory, self-sustaining basis," and for "policies to promote higher levels of consumption and nutrition." It emphasized the important "relationships between our foreign trade policy and domestic agricultural policies." The committee's conclusions and recommendations deviated from the current government policies. The ideas expressed were not new, but it was the first time that many of the conclusions had been given public support by a group of agricultural research workers and administrators. In the following year, 1945, the committee asked the colleges to face squarely their postwar function:

The conclusion seems inescapable . . . that in the period after World War II farmers are going to have an enormous interest in public policies related to agriculture, not only as regards farm prices, but also as regards the many government programs that deal with the welfare of farm people, such as production, control, credit, conservation, foreign trade, etc. The Land-Grant institutions and the U. S. Department of Agriculture thus face the necessity of deciding whether they will give leadership in college and extension teaching, and in research, in this broad field of public policies related to agriculture.[2]

The colleges obviously felt that it would be virtually impossible to escape an interest and participation in any government program for the future.

The 1945 report further suggested possible courses of postwar action for the colleges. Its summary follows:

Resident Instruction—The curricula of all Land-Grant Colleges should include courses that adequately cover the field of general public policies related to agriculture.

Experiment Stations—. . . greater attention and more resources ought to be devoted to the analysis of broad public questions and policies that bear on rural welfare. Research might also be directed towards the development of more effective extension methods and techniques in respect to these matters.

Extension Service—It is especially necessary that those who are responsible for extension policy make certain that in the years ahead their programs give emphasis to these public policy questions. In most states this decision will require broad adjustments in the whole extension program, and will necessitate the allocation of more personnel and funds to this field.[3]

The committee reports, especially in terms of national policy, were widely used and praised. Most farm magazines carried feature articles and editorials commenting on the reports. Daily newspapers and trade journals gave space to the conclusions, particularly of the 1944 report. Congressional committees summoned before them representatives of the Association to elaborate and comment on the committee conclusions. Obviously the colleges had made a strong initial step in undertaking the new function. Their leadership was recognized if not always followed. An editorial in *The New York Times* in 1953 paid high tribute:

If this country has failed notoriously to develop a sound program since the end of the Second World War, it has not been for lack of constructive and realistic proposals from the Land-Grant Colleges. Long before the time arrived when the stop-gap legislation of war-time was to have been scrapped, the Association of Land-Grant Colleges and Universities set up a Committee on Post-War Agricultural Policy. That report, published in 1944, called for a gradual liquidation of the program of artificial incentives for high production, frowned on the idea of general curtailment of production and set as its ultimate goal the free market.

While it has profound educational influence, however, that report was handicapped by one infirmity. It was based on broad economic and social considerations, and ignored the panaceas so dear to the hearts of farm Congressmen. But history suggests that sooner or later even the most obtuse Congressman comes to realize that in a nation of free people documents of this kind never really die. That is because, unhappily for the politicians in a free nation, one can only run away from the truth; he cannot hope to destroy it.

The colleges which had been found lacking after the First World War were ready for the more immense problems which would follow the Second. They were no longer merely keeping abreast of national developments; they were now exerting their leadership. The Federal government continued to rely on the help which the colleges had found possible to offer without becoming politically involved. This new educational role would not be easy. It demanded careful and sound planning. Nevertheless, the colleges had indicated forcefully their willingness to play the part. To this day effective methods are still being studied and evolved.

Financial Support and Relationships

Before examining in more detail what took place within the colleges during this period, it would be well to review for the last time their sources of support. By 1951 the contribution of the Federal government to the maintenance and support of the colleges amounted to approximately $50 million annually. This was divided approximately three ways: $5 million for campus instruction, $12.5 million for experiment stations, and $32 million for cooperative extension. In terms of funds for resident instruction, each state (and the two territories of Alaska and Hawaii) received automatically $70,000 in each year, the total sum comprising approximately $3.5 million of the $5 million. The remaining $1.5 million were distributed on the basis of population. Direct Federal support for resident instruction for all of the colleges amounted to approximately 2.3 per cent of the total expenditures for such instruction. In addition, the colleges received annually $1,774,666 as endowment income from the original Morrill land grants, or 0.8 per cent of expenditure for resident teaching.[4]

The principle of Federal support is an important one to the institutions, although the ratio of Federal to state funds continues to change. For many years the Federal government had practically matched the state support. In recent times the increase has been met largely by higher student fees and state appropriations. The colleges have come to rely on student fees as an increasingly important source of income. In a number of states direct tuition charges are levied. In others, student fees account for substantial sources of income, although there is increasingly little distinction between fees, as such, and tuition.

With increases in state support have come tendencies toward greater state control. The power of the Governor and of the executive branch of the state government has been extended by law in a number of states. State control has been active in such areas as purchasing, academic and nonacademic personnel appointments, publications, and accounting. In a survey conducted in 1953, President A. L.

Strand of Oregon reported that, of the forty-seven institutions replying, twenty-two indicated that they "have lost some degree of control of their internal affairs to some outside governmental agency, and
seventeen feel that there is a definite trend toward exactment of more
controls. Only two report controls receding." [5] As the state higher
education picture has become more complex, a number of states have
created over-all boards or commissions to centralize control, with the
avowed purpose of preventing needless duplication of program and
facilities. Texas, Oregon, Georgia, New York, and North Carolina are
examples of states in which the land-grant institution is now a part,
in one fashion or another, of a statewide system of publicly supported
higher education. With the same purpose in mind of preventing
duplication and waste, a number of states and of institutions have
entered into so-called "regional compacts" for providing special and
technical education which individual institutions or states by themselves could not undertake to offer.

THE CURRICULUM

Gradually and largely through the efforts of these colleges, the
democratization of higher education has taken place within an expanding nation. The colleges have long since abandoned the notion
that their purpose was to produce either a small intellectual elite or,
to the other extreme, practical farmers and tradesmen. The aristocracy
of higher education has vanished except in a few private colleges
which maintain the concept as a means of self-justification and
morale. The products of the Land-Grant Colleges are too much a part
of life to consider themselves academic aristocrats.

With democratization in the nation as well as the colleges had
come many other important movements. New occupations had been
developed, living had become more complex, knowledge of all types
had expanded, and there was in higher education, as in all life, a
resultant disunity. The long-sought abstract body of truth, once
found, had proven far too large for any one person to comprehend.
The result was specialization, and with specialization came intensifi-
cation. The age of the expert had arrived. To this was added universal
anxiety over what was happening in a world which attempted periodically to tear itself apart. There were many who felt that education
should be making a far more substantial contribution to enlighten-

ment and understanding. But where could education turn? Obviously science alone was no longer the key to human progress. Science had brought specialization, and specialization had bred many evils, not the least of which was a great proliferation of course offerings in the colleges. A curriculum study at the University of Minnesota in 1941–42 reported, for instance, that more than 3500 separate courses were being offered in that one institution, an increase of 25 per cent over the offerings of five years earlier, and double the number provided twenty years earlier.[6] Even vocational education, with its relatively simple occupational emphasis, found itself with a multiplicity of subject matter, much of which lacked correlation.

The depression of the thirties had focused attention on human needs and the forces of society which affect human aspirations. The economic and military state of the world took the place of the depression in increasing the longing for something new in education. Educators began asking whether knowledge was actually of greater importance than attitudes and values. Their confusion was compounded by one of their ranks, Robert Maynard Hutchins, who, in the mid-thirties, unleashed a stream of criticism against the aims and methods of education. He criticized colleges for wanting too much to be instruments of service to society, for neglecting the pursuit of knowledge for its own sake. He wrote, "The notion of educating a man to live in any particular time or place, to adjust him to any particular environment, is therefore foreign to a true conception of education." [7] He called for a return to the classics and the liberal arts as the center of education.

But most educators found little comfort in the efficacy of the liberal arts. They doubted that possession of knowledge by itself was automatically the key to understanding and progress. They noted the error in thinking that mere study of certain subjects spontaneously makes a student liberally educated. They recognized, in the words of a land-grant Association committee in 1940, that, "The width of range in subject-matter courses is no guaranty of a liberal education unless the student consolidates his information and training into an intelligent whole. . . ." There was fear that the liberal arts were not sufficiently relevant to the problems of the times to accomplish all that Chancellor Hutchins claimed they would. Even liberal arts had been affected by the vocational emphasis, and the colleges could not prevent the students from thinking primarily in terms of occupation. There was no doubt that liberal education had a significant contribution to make, even the most significant in the eyes of many. It continued the important fundamental education which had not been completed in high school. It emphasized attitudes and values as no other subject-matter seemed able to do. But, still, this was not the effective solution. Something new would have to be found.

General Education

To meet society's complex needs and, at the same time, to deal effectively with the increased volume of available knowledge, educators turned more and more to a concept and a method commonly designated as "General Education." It differed from the traditional liberal arts in degree but not kind. The President's Commission on Higher Education in 1947 attempted to define the difference: "General education undertakes to redefine liberal education in terms of life's problems as men face them, to give it human orientation and social direction, to invest it with content that is directly relevant to the demands of contemporary society. General education is liberal education with its matter and method shifted from its original aristocratic intent to the service of democracy." [8] The intent was to counteract overspecialization. General education as a subject of discussion emerged in the late thirties and reached its height in the late forties after the emphasis given it by the President's Commission. Intelligent discussion and action immediately encountered three serious obstacles, according to President Edmund Ezra Day. The first was widespread disagreement over the nature of the learning process. The second was the inevitable competition of specific educational interests. To these difficulties was added excessive generality of statement in the formulation of objectives. And anyone who attempted to make sense out of much of what was said would readily agree. As Dr. Day concluded, "Excessive generality of terms is a persistent ailment of educational planning." [9]

General education was to be interpreted in many different ways by many different people. Some thought it to mean a common body of knowledge which every student should be expected to study. Others put the emphasis on the student in terms of "effective living" or "life orientation." Whatever the interpretation, however, all seemed to agree that it meant a unifying process, tying together "making a life" and "making a living." General and vocational education would then be integrated, each giving meaning to the other.

The issue, as it emerged, was not the end in view but the means of attaining it. Various methods were tried: extension of time devoted to the educational process, provision for more electives, requirement of a basic set of courses before specialization could begin. Colleges encountered the opposition of faculty who resisted any change or who still demanded their department's "place in the sun." All in all, however, there was no doubt that a trend had developed toward more liberal than practical education.

The Land-Grant Colleges played an important part in the discussion of and experiments with general education. They recognized that "specialization is the easy road in the intellectual journey of life," but that it "contributes to the development of a stratified and compartmentalized society which, more than any other single factor, is making it difficult for democracy to succeed." They noted that their graduates were all too frequently uninformed, dogmatic, and biased. So, in the further words of C. B. Hutchison at the 1944 convention:

It is not enough that a man be able to build a Golden Gate Bridge, he must be a responsible citizen as well. It is not enough that one be a competent producer of food and fiber—a first-class husbandman of the good earth; it is not enough that one understand the intricate mechanism of soil and plant relations upon which crop production depends; it is not enough that one know how to apply the modern techniques of genetics to the improvement of plants and animals. None of these abilities, important as they are to the welfare of mankind, are sufficient unto themselves. They must be accompanied by other qualities essential to responsible citizenship, and unless the Land-Grant Colleges provide opportunity for their students to develop these essential qualities they will fall short of the goal envisaged in their original charter—the liberal as well as the practical education of the industrial classes. . . .[10]

Through the years the colleges, because of their public nature, had felt a particular responsibility for the development of informed and understanding citizens. They felt that training in social leadership was equally important to the gaining of technical know-how. They were fearful, in the words of President John A. Hannah, that their students would leave "with the mistaken notion that everything in life can be reduced to a mathematical formula and their relations with their fellow men determined by slide-rule calculations." The emphasis was on the students' capacity to think, to judge critically and without bias, and to make intelligent decisions.

Experiments continued as the discussion led to more definite concepts. A number of land-grant institutions appointed special faculty committees to investigate curricular possibilities. Some devised survey or comprehensive courses; others attempted to find a core of studies in the midst of curricular plenty. "Synthesis" was the by-word of the new approach. It was attempted at the freshman and at the senior level. Some tried to revise and broaden the content of the established courses. Comprehensive courses were introduced to take general education out of the hands of curriculum-makers in the various internal divisions of the college.

To study the recommendations of the President's Commission, the Association created a special committee which prepared in 1948 a Manual of suggestions and questions for use by the individual institutions. In the eyes of the committee, the Land-Grant Colleges could choose one of three directions in their future educational efforts. The first would be to continue essentially along present lines with occasional new courses being offered to meet the need. The second was called "educational dualism"—treating general education in a separate category by providing adjustments in purposes, courses, curricula, and methods. The third, and the one favored by the committee, was a "unitary approach or synthesis as a solution of the problem as a whole." This was termed "comprehensive education" based on the total experience and total philosophy of the institution. The committee recommended a "central or unifying concept, seeking an effective synthesis or educational totality." [11] Thus it was felt that the Land-Grant Colleges could bring to bear on a student's educational experience the vast array of educational resources found in the function and curricula of the colleges. To be personally and socially competent would depend upon the individual's proficiency in communication, achieving and maintaining an adequate philosophy of life or value system, developing sound attitudes, and exhibiting maturity in managing emotions. How much the Land-Grant Colleges took to heart the committee's recommendations cannot be judged at this short distance. Suffice to say that interest in general education as a subject for discussion died out by the mid-fifties. It was probably talked to death. Perhaps it continues to be on the minds of the more perceptive and concerned. Certainly American higher education, including the Land-Grant Colleges, has not yet solved all its curricular problems or reached a near-satisfactory conclusion. Experiments undoubtedly will continue to flourish.

The Liberal Arts

For emphasis rather than from neglect, special attention has not been given in this study to the role of the liberal arts in the Land-Grant Colleges. The liberal arts historically have been an essential part of the land-grant movement, but never a unique part. Whereas the colleges pioneered in the development of new subjects such as agriculture, engineering, veterinary medicine, and home economics, they accepted the traditional heritage of the liberal arts. Their approach was never essentially new or different. In many instances liberal studies were an accepted part of the college scheme from the very start. In others, the emphasis was so heavily on agriculture that it was not until modern times that liberal education came into its own. As a result, not a few institutions were identified popularly as "cow colleges," perhaps justifiably so until recent decades. Both enrollment and offerings in land-grant liberal arts have grown substantially since the twenties, going beyond enrollment and offerings in other areas of study. This growth is too recent to evaluate properly. Future historians will be better prepared to chronicle the substantial change.

The place of the liberal arts in the land-grant scheme has been a subject of frequent controversy over the years, particularly in those land-grant institutions which are not a part of an existing state university. Until recent times the controversy has stemmed from the existing state university's fear of its work being duplicated by an institution which, in its opinion, should be limited specifically to agriculture and the mechanic arts. Several factors have tended to mitigate this problem. In some separate Land-Grant Colleges the historic emphasis on the liberal arts has brought acceptance without much question. Washington State College, for instance, has a long history of emphasis on English literature and languages. In other cases, the liberal arts grew out of a need for service courses in the more professional subjects and then became a unit of their own. In still others, the development of the liberal arts was a result of filling unmet needs. At Michigan State, as an example, Kuhn reports that "the applied science and liberal arts division were created primarily not to provide a general education for students in the technical curricula, for that had always been present, but to educate people for a variety of previously neglected occupations." [12] Whatever the reason for development, the growing concern over the need for general education tended to dissipate the attitude that there was no place for the liberal arts in the separate Land-Grant Colleges. In the present day, then, the liberal arts have a central place in the land-grant scheme.

Despite the fact that the Land-Grant Colleges have not developed a unique system of liberal education, they have affected profoundly the existing system. Their emphasis on functional education has tended to make the liberal arts generally less formal and other-worldly and, consequently, more related to the immediate needs of the students and of modern life. There is no doubt, too, that the land-grant work in the sciences has revolutionized the scientific phase of liberal studies. The laboratory method, for instance, is now accepted by all liberal arts colleges, whether or not related to land-grant institutions.

In turn, the liberal arts have contributed to the development of those subjects which are considered to be more unique to the Land-Grant Colleges. The Association's Committee on College Organization and Policy commented in 1940 that "we obviously are far short of [the realization of liberal and practical education] in certain of our curricula; we have achieved, however, because of this mandate [in the Morrill Act], an essentially 'liberal' attitude and aspiration in almost all the colleges. And this will save us from serious deterioration." The liberal arts have thus prevented the Land-Grant Colleges from becoming mere trade schools with utility as the primary purpose. By stressing the traditional academic approach, liberal education has kept the colleges from becoming too practical. The modern liberal arts have made a contribution, too, in their concern over human values. This concern, as we have seen, has seeped down into the more professional curricula. In general, then, it could be said that the liberal arts in the Land-Grant Colleges have been more valuable historically for what they have prevented than for what they have produced in terms of a new and different concept of education. They continue to serve in increasing fashion as the academic heart of the Land-Grant College idea.

Agriculture

By the time the forties had arrived, agriculture was a specialized and professionalized curriculum. Although the colleges continued to produce graduates who actually returned to the farm, the emphasis was on related professions, such as teaching, research, commercial agriculture, and extension. The colleges had left behind them permanently the notion that their four-year course had, as its main purpose, the return of farmers' sons to the farm. The public, however, continued to think of the primary work of the colleges as the training of "farmers," even though this historically had never been their major effort or result. It was obvious that agricultural study could no longer be termed vocational and practical but had become professional and scientific.

The complete realization of this trend brought home to agricultural educators the need for a reexamination of the curriculum. In general, agreement was reached on two points. Agricultural study must become less of a handicraft and more fundamental, with stress on the basic scientific subjects; application would follow with occupation. Secondly, agriculture must stress less of the how, and more of the why. The humanities and social relations should have recognized and well-protected roles in the curricular offering.

The colleges of agriculture in the modern period had become institutions almost in themselves. Enrollment, for instance, in the first term of 1953–54 ranged from 5 in Alaska to 1690 in Iowa. Ranking behind Iowa came Cornell with 1558; Pennsylvania with 1435; Ohio, 1394; Oklahoma, 1351; and Texas with 1268. The median enrollment was Maryland with 519, while the mean was 592. This was in contrast to the total of 101 youngsters who had enrolled at Michigan State 96 years before.

As the four-year course became more professional, the colleges felt more keenly the responsibility for continuing to offer curricula of less-than-degree length. By 1949 short non-degree agricultural courses were on the increase in the Land-Grant Colleges with twenty-eight of thirty-four reporting institutions indicating more demand. Nine institutions were listed as running courses ranging from one term to two academic years. Twenty-four reported short courses of one week or more, but of less than a term's length. Thirty had organized courses varying from a few days to a week, some conducting as many as seventy-seven such courses in a year's span. They varied in kind from training courses for young farmers to refresher courses for those with experience in such areas as livestock judging, dairy herd improvement and testing, and greenskeeping. In one institution alone, Oklahoma A. & M., the short course department cared for approximately sixty thousand persons who came to the campus for any subject which was judged important or valuable to the population of the state.

Thus the short courses had become an effective device for serving the people in the many areas envisaged in the original Morrill legislation. They served, too, to fill the highly important land-grant function of training practical farmers. As an indication of their success, a Michigan State survey in 1948 found that over 85 per cent of former short course students were directly engaged in agriculture and operating farms of larger than average size.

Engineering

Engineering, too, would respond to the educational changes of the times. The first reaction to specialization was a surge in the number of undergraduate curricula, each designed to train the student in some one particular phase of engineering subject-matter. Some colleges reported as many as thirty or forty distinct curricula. It was a vain attempt to meet the demands of occupational diversification in modern industry and commerce. As time passed, the colleges recognized the futility of attempting to prepare students for every occupation that modern industry appeared to require. The emphasis changed to finding a core of fundamental subjects which every engineer needed, then providing specialized training in broad engineering fields, and leaving to the employer the task of specific skills related to the job. The depression had its effect, too, by paving the way for increased sensitivity to the need for such studies as economics and the humanities. Gradually more and more engineering educators recognized that the engineer must know more than technique or even scientific fundamentals; he must have intelligent understanding of the importance of his work and its significance in the lives of men as well as relationship to the world of which he is a part. Among the first Land-Grant Colleges to take constructive steps in this direction was the Massachusetts Institute of Technology. In 1936 it prescribed two semesters of General Study in the sophomore year. The student was allowed his choice of one of four areas: History of Western Civilization, History of Science and Thought, Esthetics and Arts, or Social Science. He would enlarge upon his chosen field in his junior and senior years. This was said to integrate nontechnical studies, to keep alive student interest in general fields, and to concentrate the attention of faculty and students upon the importance of general studies in preparation for a specific career.

In the years to follow, the Society for the Promotion of Engineering Education continued its studies begun in the twenties leading to the Wickenden Report. It issued a number of new reports on liberalizing the engineering curricula which received wide attention in the Land-Grant Colleges. The first of the new reports, appearing in 1940, was entitled "Aims and Scope of Engineering Education." It advocated strengthening of the sciences and the allotment of 20 per cent of the undergraduate curriculum to the humanities. Further studies included the so-called Hammond Report in 1944 on "Engineering Education After the War" and the "Humanistic-Social Research Project" of 1955.

The most significant change in engineering education in the pre- and postwar periods was the resultant move toward liberalizing the curricula. Engineering educators were concerned with a better mastery of fundamentals. They noted once again, as they had periodically throughout the life of the colleges, the difficulty of students in the study of engineering because of the lack of preparation in basic mathematics. They wanted, too, "to infuse the fundamental concepts of the humanities and social sciences necessary for modern citizenship in a democracy at a time when engineers must realize their responsibilities as social agents." And they had come to realize that specialization must be left to graduate work or to industry. Engineering graduate work was regarded as important to the development of research talent. In increasing fashion, there came an interdependence of graduate study and the Engineering Experiment Stations.

The interval of the war forced the colleges to train their sights on specific war purposes rather than professional preparation. In 1940 Brigadier General C. R. Huebner of the Army Services of Supply had told them, "When we win this war, we will have time to come back afterwards and secure more education. But now we must concentrate on the training which we needed the day before yesterday." The colleges in the war years provided intensive and specialized training for service men assigned to the campus. Their problems were not eased by a lack of trained faculty, many of whom had been called into the armed services or to industry. Teaching staff reductions varied in institutions from 10 to 65 per cent. The war training operations, however, served the useful purpose of showing the colleges the possibility of new and liberalized curricular offerings. The Navy V-12 program was particularly successful in making this contribution to long-range engineering education. The war period was followed by increased study and experimentation. By no means had all the answers been found for engineering education, nor all the attempts made which it deserved.

Home Economics

Home economics, in the meantime, was still growing up. It had been struggling with a 95.7 per cent increase in enrollment in the six years from 1934 to 1940 at a time when the total enrollment of women students in colleges had increased but 55.5 per cent. Despite the increase in students attempts were made to develop a body of scientific matter which could be treated objectively and thus, once and for all, remove from the curriculum all semblances of sentiment and indoctrination. To do this, home economists set to work to develop competent staffs and to urge that each teacher also undertake research and each research worker be also a teacher. Their efforts were, in the main, successful, and the period is noteworthy for the emergence of home economics as a fully accredited and accepted part of the academic family.

Home economics had always depended heavily on the liberal arts and thus its principal objective came to be the imparting of a home-centered liberal education. The development of fields of study such as family life and child development helped home economists to recognize that their work was more than a skill and that it involved people and interpersonal relationships. This recognition carried over into fields such as nutrition, in which not only the nutritive value of food was determined but the effect of environment upon attitudes toward preference and upon digestion.

During the war home economists contributed by attempting to meet the demand for trained women in a wide variety of fields hitherto restricted to men. Course content and methods were modi- fied to prepare women for effective service in essential war activities. The war also created problems in child care which became a lasting pattern in the society which emerged from the war. The dislocation of homes, the problems created by working parents, and the disorgan- ization of home-centered life were questions for which home econo- mists would continue to seek the answers. The war, too, served the useful purpose of focusing industrial attention on the value of nutri- tion to the health and efficiency of workers.

Today home economics, which had developed largely in the Land- Grant Colleges, is in a secure academic position, respected for its contribution to science and to human welfare. It is preparing women in increasing numbers for home-making as well as professional careers in school and college teaching, research, dietetics, extension work, commercial firms, and nursery schools.

Graduate Study

Graduate work, by the end of the thirties, had become an accepted part of the pattern of the Land-Grant Colleges. Master's degrees were conferred in one or more fields in almost all institutions at the rate of approximately five thousand a year. More than half of the colleges conferred doctorates to the number of approximately nine hundred a year. As the colleges became universities, the graduate schools found their previously ill-defined place in the pattern of advanced study and research. They then contributed to the increasing stature of the universities. The report of the President's Commission on Higher Education called upon graduate schools in the postwar period to undertake three major tasks: the training of research personnel, of experts for a host of services in nonacademic fields, and of teachers for all levels of higher education. These the graduate schools of the Land-Grant Colleges were satisfied they were accomplishing, although they recognized much room for improvement.

As they grew, they expanded opportunities for off-campus study in keeping with the philosophy of the colleges to bring education to the people rather than requiring the people to come to the campus. In 1949, out of forty-five institutions reporting, twenty-nine indicated that graduate study was offered through extension courses. A few institutions had gone so far as to establish off-campus graduate centers in major cities. Many of them, working with their General Extension divisions, were conducting workshops for graduate students to bring additional assistance to those who were attempting to combine full-time work with part-time study.

In the post-war period the Land-Grant Colleges added a wide variety of new majors in graduate work. Each year saw an increase over the previous year. As an indication of the expansion, thirty-three land-grant institutions reported a total of seventy-seven different new majors for master's or doctor's degrees in the two years from 1948 to 1950. The land-grant record is particularly outstanding in the field of natural sciences. The National Research Council in 1955 reported that eight Land-Grant Colleges were among the first twelve institutions in numbers of doctorates awarded in the natural sciences during the period 1946–50. The twelve institutions had awarded more than half of all the natural science doctorates during this period. On the basis of undergraduate origins of successful doctoral candidates during the same period, the list of the first twenty institutions included thirteen Land-Grant Colleges or Universities. The colleges had been successful in combining their extensive research undertakings with expanded graduate study.

Veterinary Medicine

The end of the war brought a sharp increase in the number of colleges of veterinary medicine. In three years from 1945 to 1948, seven new schools were founded, only one of which was not a part of a Land-Grant College or University. This brought the total to seventeen, of which two were non-land-grant. The new land-grant schools were located at Georgia, Missouri, Oklahoma, Minnesota, Illinois, and California. Besides the formally established colleges, some twenty-four land-grant institutions had departments of veterinary medicine in their colleges of agriculture or experiment stations, although these, of course, were not degree-granting units. They continue to contribute, however, to the number of students qualified to undertake graduate veterinary work.

With the Land-Grant Colleges playing the dominant role in veterinary medical education, it was natural for the colleges to expand into veterinary research and extension. By 1950 cooperative extension work in veterinary science was a part of the extension program in eighteen states, with a total of twenty-seven veterinary specialists employed to work with doctors as well as farmers. The veterinary extension program emphasized improved animal health. The colleges sponsored annual conferences for veterinarians, conducted specialized short courses, and sent their faculties throughout the state to speak at county and regional meetings. In addition, a pathological laboratory was established and consultant services made available. Much of the work was carried on through practicing veterinarians, individually and in associations. The veterinary extension staff worked directly, too, with livestock sanitary officials, livestock owners, other extension staff members, public health officers, and with farm youth groups. Demonstration projects before organized farm youth groups included such subjects as farm sanitation, essentials of effective quarantines, proper disposal of dead animals, and disinfection of premises. In addition, the adult and junior work stressed good hygiene, sanitation, and other elements of maintaining the health of farm animals as well as understanding the contributions of veterinary science to the livestock industry.

In research, too, the Land-Grant Colleges were contributing to veterinary medicine. In 1952 the total amount spent for animal disease research in the United States, by all agencies, amounted to $10,978,301. Federal agencies spent $1,930,146; agricultural experiment stations and colleges of veterinary medicine, $3,248,383; and private industry, $5,809,772. It was thus evident that the colleges and the stations were carrying the bulk of research not undertaken with proprietary motives. Veterinary research would not only benefit the farmer and the animal owner but the consumer and the citizen as well. Its aims were many. The over-all objective was to help the production of more and better food for human consumption. One direct result would be better meat at less cost through the reduction of animal losses from parasitism and malnutrition. Research was deemed necessary, too, because many animal diseases could be transmitted to men. Veterinarians had discovered at least eighty-three such diseases. Attention was focused, therefore, on control and eradication particularly of the major types, such as tuberculosis, anthrax, glanders, and rabies. Finally, veterinary research had benefited and would continue to benefit all branches of medicine, partly through the stimulation of investigators to carry on for human welfare what the veterinarians had begun in terms of animal welfare.

In the present day, the demand for trained veterinarians continues. The supply is still inadequate, particularly in those states or regions without a college of veterinary medicine. The veterinary graduate can move easily into the field of small-animal practice or he can find a position where he is needed even more in the state and national regulatory and disease control programs, in public health activities, or in poultry disease work. Wherever he goes, he will find that most of his colleagues are graduates of the Land-Grant College veterinary program.

Military Instruction

By the end of the thirties, world conditions had forced national sentiment away from the desire to abolish military training in the colleges and to the demand for more effective defense preparations. All but two of the Land-Grant Colleges continued to require military work at least in the first two years. Forty-nine institutions reported in 1938 that they were enrolling 57,000 students in the basic course, 8,900 in the advanced course, for a total of 65,900 in training. The War Department had assigned some 350 officers on detail with these units, a far cry from the struggling days of the previous century. In some land-grant institutions Naval ROTC units had been established in addition to the Army.

The chief prewar military concern of the colleges was the lack of academic standards in ROTC courses. The Association's Committee on Military Organization and Policy reported each year its continuing struggle "to persuade the War Department to enable us to bring these courses, in equipment and teaching personnel, more nearly up to the standards maintained in all other departments of instruction." The Committee almost despaired of forms of persuasion and, by 1939, had come to the conclusion that threats were its only recourse. In its report of that year, the Committee concluded that "it may even be necessary, since all other forms of persuasion have failed to secure adequate support to let it be known that unless there seems to be some prospect, through a plan definitely disclosed by the department, of improvement, we shall be obliged (italics) to consider the possibility of no longer giving credit toward a degree for R.O.T.C. courses." For their part, the colleges estimated that they were contributing more than $375,000 each year in their maintenance of ROTC units over and above what it would cost without such units. The amounts per college varied from less than $1000 up to a figure in excess of $44,000. They concluded rather testily that "parsimonious and inadequate provision for training Reserve Officers of our Army, amid generous expenditures for other no more essential activities and interests, ought to continue no longer." One of their greatest interests was for the provision of adequate drill quarters, storage, and staff quarters for ROTC units, to be financed by Federal appropriation. The facilities were said to be grossly inadequate. In addition, the equipment which was available was termed practically obsolete for modern military operation.

Despite these handicaps, the colleges were ready to play a tremendously important and enlarged role in the beginning years of the Second World War. In the period from 1920, when the ROTC had been formally established by the National Defense Act, to the outbreak of the war, a total of 159,800 reserve commissions had been granted through land-grant ROTC units. Just prior to the war, the Army was receiving officers at the rate of 10,000 per year from the ROTC. With America's entry in 1941, the War Department was forced to lean heavily on ROTC graduates. During the initial stages of mobilization, some fifty per cent, or about 75,000 of the officers in the Army were obtained from the advanced ROTC graduates of Land-Grant Colleges and state universities. Some years later the Secretary of the Army, Frank Pace, quoted then Chief of Staff General George Marshall as saying, "Just what we would have done in the first phases of our mobilization and training without [the ROTC graduate] I do not know. I do know that our plans would have had to be greatly curtailed and the cessation of hostilities on the European front would have been delayed accordingly."

As the war stretched on, the ROTC graduate continued to be an important and essential part of the military effort. More than 104,000 previously commissioned ROTC graduates served on active duty in the Army, including the Air Corps. In 1943 Brigadier General Edward W. Smith, Army executive officer for Reserve and ROTC affairs, was quoted as saying, "The Land-Grant Colleges and Universities constitute the very heart of the ROTC system. The Reserve officers produced by ROTC are, in effect, the life-blood of the present Army of the United States. . . . Their performance has been most gratifying and has received the expressed commendation of the highest authorities in the War Department."

In the postwar period the Department of Defense expanded rapidly and widely its college reserve program. Up to this time the Land-Grant Colleges had been the backbone of the reserve system. Now new Naval and Air Force ROTC units were established in a number of other public as well as private institutions. President J. L. Morrill of Minnesota stated in 1948 that the expansion had "erased the Land-Grant identity, so conscientiously maintained, so proudly cherished." Despite the appearance of other units in other colleges, the land-grant institutions, with their compulsory basic feature, continued to produce more than half of all reserve officers for the Army and Air Force. Together with many non-land-grant state universities requiring basic ROTC, as well as other state institutions, they graduated and commissioned as high as 80 per cent of all reserve officers in any given year. Though their historic identity with military training had been lost, they continued to be the foundation of the expanded college reserve program. General Omar Bradley, then Chairman of the Joint Chiefs of Staff, told them in 1952:

. . . I feel that your Land-Grant Colleges and Universities are a keystone of the civilian-military relationship in our democracy. Under the Morrill Act of 1862, and the National Defense Act of 1916, we have developed a partnership that furnishes the greatest part of the practical instruction in military education for the young men and women who provide the pool of military leadership in any emergency.[13]

To many land-grant educators the praise of high military leaders was not enough. ROTC problems continued to vex the colleges. "Unfortunate actions and policy determination" caused "widespread fear among the Land-Grant institutions for the future strength and service to the nation of the ROTC pattern of former years," in the words of the 1954 report of the Association's Committee on National Defense. The Committee listed the uncertainty as to quotas in the Army and Air programs, the failure to secure support for bills to stabilize the programs, the failure to provide Federal assistance for housing ROTC units on the campuses, and the uncertainty of the continuance of units newly established in many colleges and universities. It concluded that "student, faculty, and administrative dissatisfaction over the resulting difficulties and uncertainties caused several of our Land-Grant Institutions to debate the wisdom of continuing required military training." The words had a familiar ring. Obviously the Department of Defense, though outwardly appreciative of ROTC work, was not yet ready to support it completely and without reservation. It is a remarkable fact in land-grant history that the colleges have been so patient, so determined to live by the provisions of the 1862 legislation, and so anxious to continue military training as a part of their national service function, in the midst of this continuing discouragement and lack of adequate support.

RESEARCH

Significant changes took place in the research pattern and program of the Land-Grant Colleges during this period. Basic research had been curtailed during the war in order to concentrate the college facilities on war projects of immediate concern. The amount of national expenditures during the war years and in the period to follow increased substantially. Whereas 900 million dollars had been spent throughout the nation on research and development in 1942, the figure for 1952 rose to 2 billion, 900 million. The war had taught the colleges several research lessons. In the concentration on immediate war projects, the colleges found how little of the necessary basic research had been undertaken in the years preceding the war. Since industry was concerned primarily with practical results, national support of basic and fundamental research would have to come from public funds. In addition to this lesson, the colleges learned from the war even more vividly the value and importance of conducting cooperative research with industry. The benefits to both were obvious.

In the postwar period the Federal government expanded greatly its support of college research in existing fields and in fields not hitherto explored. Between 1947 and 1949 Federal research funds going to colleges and universities throughout the country practically doubled. In 1949 the National Military Establishment was spending over $53,000,000 on research and development, the Atomic Energy Commission over $81,400,000, and the Department of Agriculture over $18,600,000, on research in the colleges.[14] The land-grant institutions received an unusually large share of these amounts. They recognized the advantages of Federal and industrial research in turning their interests from purely state-centered programs to ones of far greater national and international significance. In 1951 President John A. Hannah told them, ". . . here there is an opportunity for accomplishments on behalf of mankind potentially far greater than stands to the credit of all of the Land-Grant Colleges and Universities combined after almost 90 years of service to the American people."

The dropping of the atomic bomb on Hiroshima during the war had signaled a change in many of the old research patterns. After the war, radioactive isotopes, by-products of the atomic energy program, became available to the colleges. Their great value lay in their tracer action, allowing a scientist for the first time to trace some of the most intimate details of chemical reactions and of living processes. By 1953 about 90 per cent of the Land-Grant Colleges were using isotopes in research work. In addition, the Land-Grant Colleges were cooperating extensively with the Atomic Energy Commission in its important efforts. Some 185 contracts between the AEC and 44 land-grant institutions were in force in that year when the Chairman of the Commission, Admiral Lewis L. Strauss, told the convention that the Land-Grant Colleges were setting "the highest standards of research to be found anywhere." Again, one cannot help but compare this modern achievement with that early day when Professor Isaac Roberts had dug up the dead horses and placed his class "on the windward side."

The modern Land-Grant College by no means restricts its research efforts to its organized "stations." Many faculty members, including a large number in the liberal arts, undertake research both as a part of and in addition to their teaching assignments. The results of a study at the University of Minnesota reveal a situation typical of the average Land-Grant College. In that one institution it was found that three-fifths of all full-time academic staff members were working on one or more research projects which required an average of twelve hours a week. The projects ranged "from the identification of white dwarf stars, the development of a psychological 'brand' barometer, the improvement of the shortening value of lard, and the appraisal of various substances for sealing riveted joints, to the courtship experiences of college students." [15]

Agricultural Experiment Stations

The agricultural experiment stations, already well established by the thirties, continued to expand in program and function. By 1940 more than four thousand scientists, some full-time and some part-time, were engaged in agricultural research in the stations. Under the authority of the Bankhead-Jones Act, the Federal Department had established in the period between 1935 and 1939 nine regional laboratories, six of which were in association with individual Land-Grant Colleges. The program of the college stations had broadened from the problems of the individual farmer to include all those associated with the entire national agricultural industry. In addition, the stations were engaged in activities affecting both commercial industries which process and handle agricultural products and the consumer himself, who is the ultimate recipient of all agricultural produce. In one year the stations had issued 686,647 copies of 571 bulletins numbering 4221 pages.

Cooperative research efforts also continued to expand. By 1940 there were at least 1350 cooperative projects carried on by the Federal Department and the stations, some involving a number of states. The development of cooperative research had come as a result of a joint Association-Department committee which had been at work since 1913 and which, over the years, had found new methods of cooperation, strengthened the old, and encouraged both parties to eliminate duplication through cooperation. Interstate cooperation had not developed as fast as efforts between the Department and the states. By this time, however, the benefits of cooperative work were apparent to all. One system of agricultural research had emerged instead of a number of independent and uncoordinated agencies.

The rapid development of the stations during the twentieth century had taught them a number of lessons which would not have to be learned again when war came once more to the American people.

Through the years they had evolved methods which made possible the sudden and substantial increase in farm production during the war. They were able, too, to develop new techniques and products to meet specific war needs. Not only were the stations called upon to increase production for the war but to help the farmers raise new and difficult crops. Their war efforts included increased emphasis on the control of insects and diseases, on plant and animal breeding, and on animal nutrition to safeguard the health of necessary livestock. The stations worked on new methods of food preservation which would also insure no loss of vitamin content, on labor-saving equipment, and on the maintenance of crop yields in the face of a severe labor shortage. The stations cooperated with the Department of Agriculture in a nationwide study of better methods to conserve sixty-nine different foods. As early as 1943, the Vice President of the United States and former Secretary of Agriculture, Henry A. Wallace, had complimented the stations on the effectiveness of their war efforts. He said, "It is only because of the extraordinary technological discoveries of the U. S. Department of Agriculture and the State Experiment Stations in soil management, crop breeding, and livestock feeding that we . . . have been able so far this year to ship food abroad at an annual rate of about 10 billion pounds."

When the war was over and the nation's international responsibility had become clear, the stations began broadening their concern to deal not just with the needs of America but of the world. New emphasis was placed on organized basic research. New tools, such as the electron microscope and radioactive isotopes, became available. The Department's Report on the Experiment Stations in 1952 noted, "These have made it possible to probe more deeply into many phenomena of nature, such as the functioning of various organs in the animal body, the mechanism of plant and animal nutrition, and the various chemical and physical interchanges that take place in the different kinds of soil under the management and cropping practices followed by farmers."

In the mid-fifties the agricultural experiment stations in the Land-Grant Colleges included a total of 500 substations and field stations located in various parts of the states. Printed publications in 1952 included 797 bulletins, circulars, and reports; 4612 articles in scientific journals; and 551 miscellaneous publications. In addition, 617 popular and 749 technical reports, bulletins, and circulars were processed by the stations. The number of new and revised research projects begun by the states with Federal funds amounted to approximately 700 for the year 1953. Altogether some 4500 projects were under way with an average of 16 per cent concluded annually.

New Federal funds had become available to the stations in 1946 with the passage of the Agricultural Research and Marketing Act, an amendment to the Bankhead-Jones Act. The emphasis was on applied research, and the amount, when appropriated, would almost triple the Federal funds previously available to the state stations. By 1953 Federal funds for the experiment stations amounted to over twelve million dollars while non-Federal support, including state funds, totaled some sixty-two million. The Federal total had been raised to nineteen and a half million by 1955. In that year Federal legislation involving the experiment stations was consolidated into one act, following the earlier lead of the consolidation of cooperative extension acts.

Although attempts have been made, it is questionable whether the achievements of the stations could ever be measured in monetary terms. A report entitled "Research and Related Services in the United States Department of Agriculture," prepared for the House Committee on Agriculture in 1950, estimated that research had resulted in an increase in farm income of more than ten billion dollars annually, or about one hundred times the present annual cost of all agricultural research in the country. Achievement is perhaps better stated in terms of results. They have, for instance, done pioneering work in conservation research and education. The spectacular rise of the soybean industry in the United States is directly attributable to station efforts. The number of acres planted to soybeans had risen from less than 3 million in 1929 to 15 million in 1953 which accounted for well over a third of world production. The new varieties developed were better adapted to the soil and climate in various parts of the country and provided higher oil content, as well as being better suited to machine processing.

Two of the most important achievements of the experiment stations have been the development of hybrid corn and the discovery of streptomycin. Hybrid corn has been called the "food production miracle of the twentieth century." It is said to have increased corn yields by about 30 per cent and to have provided an extra thirty-five pounds of pork for every American citizen. It added one billion dollars to the value of the Nation's corn crop, and gave the Nation the equivalent of one full extra year's crop during the crucial war years of 1941–45. In dollars and cents, its value has probably repaid the entire amount spent through the years on all agricultural research. At the New Jersey Station, Jacob G. Lipman's early fundamental investigations of soil microorganisms, begun some fifty years previously and carried forward in later years by his former student, Selman A. Waksman, led in 1943 to the discovery of streptomycin by Dr. Waksman and his associates. Scientists since have proven that this revolutionary new drug affects directly many diseases such as tuberculosis, tularemia, plague, influenzal meningitis, bacteremia, and various virulent urinary tract infections. In recognition of the significance of his work, Dr. Waksman was awarded a Nobel Prize. Its significance to commerce, in addition to the larger importance to human welfare, can be seen from the report that, within three years after the discovery, industry had constructed new buildings for its production in a dollar value one and one-half times as great as the entire cost of operating the New Jersey Station from the time of its establishment in 1880 through 1948.

Undoubtedly each state station could add important items to the list of achievements. As one example only, the University of Idaho drew together what its station had accomplished over the years: Developed and introduced disease-resistant field beans for Idaho farm production which saved Idaho's bean industry; originated the Idared and Idajon apple and Lamida cherry; developed a nationally recognized brucellosis (Bang's disease) control; developed control of potato ring-pot and other potato diseases; introduced improved grain cereal varieties—wheat, oats, barley; developed control of such animal parasites as sheep and wood ticks, cattle grubs, and lice; adapted use of phosphate fertilizers to increase quality and yield of Idaho crops; determined sources of mechanical damage to potato tuber and developed improved harvesting equipment for reducing such damage; developed post treating methods estimated to save Idaho farmers more than a million dollars in the next twenty years; and developed effective control for lygus bug in Idaho's alfalfa and red clover seed industry.

Although the stations could look with pride upon their past, their future contained many new challenges. It was obvious that America's economic farm crisis had not been solved. Much more needed to be known concerning consumption and distribution. Scientifically, too, the fight against insects and diseases was not over. Agricultural research in the Land-Grant Colleges obviously can continue to make important contributions to human welfare.

Home Economics Research

Home economics research, in the meantime, had continued to expand. Among the more outstanding contributions had been the improvement of the nutritive value of foods through varied selection based on research, more exact knowledge of nutritive requirements, information on food habits and their relation to the economic status of population groups, standard specifications for consumer goods, functional house plans, improved designs for household equipment at low cost, and a better understanding of family relationships and their problems.

The war soon made obvious the need for increased strength and breadth in the home economics research program. It increased the emphasis on research in foods and nutrition, almost to the exclusion of other types of research. Home economists were asked to advise on quantity cooking under wartime service conditions, on the nutritive value of available and potential food supplies to help guide production and rationing policies, and on better methods of food conservation in storage. In addition, they attempted to find new means to prolong the life of products curtailed because of war production and to design serviceable clothes and uniforms with better wearing quality under special conditions.

The research program in home economics continued to expand in the postwar years. A fivefold increase in the number of projects was reported in 1949, as well as a broadening of the subject-matter base. Foods and nutrition, with special emphasis on human nutrition, comprised two-thirds of the projects. The other third dealt with a variety of fields: housing, textiles and clothing, household equipment and home management, consumption economics, family life, and education. Home economics research, like all areas in home economics, was challenged by problems resulting from the changing pattern of life. The future held almost limitless possibilities for work. Research in the past had struggled to make home economics a science and a profession and to place it among the respected members of the academic family. With that now accomplished, home economics research could pay less attention to its stature and more to increasingly significant accomplishments.

Engineering Experiment Stations

With the depression over, engineering experiment stations in the Land-Grant Colleges began to grow in number and importance. A low point had been reached in 1934 when only $764,271 were made available for engineering research. By 1937–38 the figure had increased to $1,633,648. In 1945 the Association reported forty-four active stations in operation. By 1946 they had published nearly 2500 bulletins, in addition to a large number of papers in the transactions of engineering societies. In the following year, thirty-seven of the stations reported over seven and a half million dollars available for research, not including the large sums budgeted at the Massachusetts Institute of Technology. The functions of the stations included scientific investigations and industrial research, disseminating information on results, training research workers, co-operating with graduate schools in graduate study programs, and rendering whatever service they could to industrial concerns, manufacturers, and professional engineers, particularly in the solution of broad fundamental problems.

Attempts had been made periodically to obtain Federal support for the engineering stations, but it became obvious that the day had long since passed when the Land-Grant Colleges as a group could be so favored. In 1942 the land-grant institutions gave up the attempt and helped to form the Engineering College Research Association in co-operation with the separate state universities and certain endowed institutions. It was designed to bring together all interested institutions to work in common for the promotion of engineering research in all qualified schools. As a result, a transition was made from effort in behalf of legislation of a strictly engineering nature to that benefiting all of science. The results were successful later in the forties with the passage of a Congressional act establishing the National Science Foundation, although none of the colleges was satisfied with the amount of funds made available through the Foundation.

World War II marked the turning point in the attitude of the colleges and of industry toward industrial-university research. The value of the stations was demonstrated in the closing years of the war when research in such important industrial fields as aeronautics, electronics, metallurgy, ordnance, and power was started. By 1949 there had been a five- to tenfold increase in available support. To guide the colleges in the management of industrial research, President James R. Killian, Jr., of the Massachusetts Institute of Technology suggested three principles:

1. The primary purposes of an educational institution are to educate men and women and to increase knowledge and are not to compete with industry in industrial or development research.

2. Sponsored industrial research should be closely related to the normal program and recognized objectives of the institution.

3. Imposition of restrictions on publication of research results, either for secrecy or patent reasons, can become incompatible with the basic concept of an educational institution as a source and distributor of knowledge.[16]

Many of the colleges felt that industrial research should thus be limited to those projects which contributed to the effectiveness of instruction and the routine testing of the past should be reduced to a minimum. Others looked upon the small industries of their states as the backbone of the state's economy and the principal units to be served by the colleges. Otherwise, small industry might be without research facilities.

The engineering experiment stations are a relatively late addition to the land-grant scheme, at least in size and number. Nevertheless, substantial contributions have been made in a brief span of years to such diverse fields as ceramics, aeronautics, communications, electronics, television development, flood control, fuels, hydraulics, highway construction, farm equipment, irrigation, construction materials, metallurgy, power generation and transmission, diesel engines, refrigeration, sanitation, transportation, waste disposal and utilization, weather forecasting, and work simplication. Perhaps more than any other function of the Land-Grant Colleges, engineering research work will be affected by the greatly enlarged possibilities in the availability of atomic energy machinery and by-products. The first two universities to have nuclear reactors of their own for engineering research and teaching were land-grant institutions, North Carolina State and Penn

State. A whole new era of accomplishments and contributions has begun, but it is too soon to assess its lasting value.

EXTENSION

Cooperative Extension

The modern Land-Grant College conducts extension work in three major divisional areas: cooperative extension including agriculture and home economics, engineering extension, and general or university extension. In the course of twenty years the number of professional personnel in cooperative extension had nearly doubled. By 1941, there were 9000 trained and experienced extension workers in the colleges and in the Federal Department. A county agricultural agent was located in practically every important agricultural county in the country. The agents were working directly with at least 700,000 local leaders.

The work of the agent by the end of the thirties had become largely planning, organization, and administration. It had shifted considerably from the earlier times of individual and group demonstration work. Nevertheless, the number of farm people reached by the agents continued to climb. In 1938 the agents influenced directly the work of 6,362,000 people, including 3,445,000 farmers; 1,240,000 farm wives; 425,000 wives in small towns; 1,192,000 4-H Club members; and 60,000 farm young people. Cooperative extension in the late thirties and early forties became greatly concerned over its inability to reach more farm young people. A special Association committee was established to define problems and suggest better methods. It was an area of effort previously neglected, and the neglect was showing. The national committee worked closely with similar state committees.

This period in cooperative extension has been called a time of "economic analysis." Outlook conferences for extension personnel had been started by the Federal Bureau of Agricultural Economics as early as 1925. In the depression days and the recovery days to follow, the conferences assumed greater importance. As a result of the Mount Weather Agreement in 1938, county agents were directed to set up land-use planning committees designed to develop coordinated land use programs. Because of the shortage of personnel, extension became somewhat less than enthusiastic about the program, which eventually was abolished through lack of Congressional support. In two regions of the country, beginning in the thirties and continuing to the present day, extension lent a helping hand to two important national developments. The first was the great Tennessee Valley Authority whose administrators recognized the value of extension work and arranged to deal closely with extension personnel on the common problems of the Valley. The second was the cooperative work on phosphate resources in the western states.

The period witnessed a distinct change in the organized affiliations of cooperative extension. As late as 1939, at least seventeen or eighteen states specified the county Farm Bureau as the agency at the county level to cooperate in extension work. Due in part to the continued activity of the Farm Bureau in commercial and political fields and to the opposition of the National Grange, the disaffiliation movement which had started earlier began to reach its height. In 1948 the Joint Committee on Extension Programs Policies and Goals commented:

This committee expresses its conviction that it is not sound policy for extension to give preferred service to any farm organization or to be in a position of being charged with such actions. The committee is further convinced that it would be in the public interest for any formal operating relationships between the Extension Service and any general farm organization such as the Farm Bureau to be discontinued at the earliest possible moment.[17]

Although many recognized the wisdom of such a break, it was not an easy one to make for the two agencies which had grown up together. The arguments for and against were heated and bitter in some states. In the mid-fifties the last few remaining states took the step toward disestablishment.

As the war came, extension found that its years of trial and error would prove invaluable in the sudden call for help. In 1941, the Federal government turned again to extension as its rural educational arm. Secretary of Agriculture Claude Wickard issued a Memorandum on February 11, 1942, assigning to the extension service the responsibility for all education in agriculture and home economics of a wartime nature. And M. L. Wilson told the land-grant representatives, ". . . the people on the land must understand our national need. They must know why we need more milk and more hogs, and why we don't need more wheat or cotton or tobacco. A great job of education needs to be done, and we must not overlook any phase of it. . . ." Extension wartime activities included assisting with national drives of all kinds, including scrap metal and salvage, war bonds and stamps. The county agent helped with price control and rationing. He carried on programs designed to increase war production goals as well as civilian conservation of essential food and fiber. He worked with the state extension offices on the acute farm labor shortage. Once again a national emergency had brought a challenge to cooperative extension, and, in its response, it gained. As a result of a directive from the Secretary of Agriculture, county agents established a "personal-contact system" involving some 650,000 voluntary neighborhood leaders to supplement the large number of local extension leaders. The method was used so that it might be possible to spread information to every farm family, regardless of how distant the farm was from the community center. The neighborhood-leader plan brought extension into contact with a number of families not previously reached.

The extension war effort was so successful that the executive body of the land-grant Association took an unusual step in 1943 "to record its public expression of high commendation" of the extension effort "in behalf of the vital national program for increased food and feed production and in the management of the current critical farm labor problems." The Association representatives noted that "extension programs on the community and state levels have been carefully planned, and intelligently and patriotically executed." The resolution called particular attention to the "remarkable success of the extension agencies, in cooperation with federal agencies, in developing a sound and efficient farm labor program throughout the nation." It noted that this success had proven "a major factor in assuring for the year 1943, one of the largest food and feed supplies in the history of the United States."

In this period of continual expansion, cooperative extension gained additional Federal support from three Congressional acts. In 1939 Congress passed the "Additional Extension Work Act" which was later amended in 1944. In 1945 the Bankhead-Flannagan Act was passed "to further develop the Cooperative Extension system . . . and particularly for the further development of county extension work." It was the most specific legislation to date regarding the type of extension to be undertaken. The third piece of legislation, the Research and Marketing Act of 1946 (commonly called RMA), expanded the work of extension particularly in the marketing field. It led to increased urban contact in the furnishing of marketing information and suggestions to consumers. Attempts were made to obtain better buying practices and better utilization of food products. Demonstrational programs, financed by funds from the act, were arranged to show better marketing methods and practices.

The new legislation did not help in the least to reduce the confusion stemming from the Federal acts regarding cooperative extension. Some funds were outright grants; others required offset. Some were permanent and continuing appropriations; others were authorized annually. Some went directly to the states; others were included in the Federal Department of Agriculture budget. Some were based on rural population; others on farm population. Still others were apportioned equally to each state. The situation was confusing at best and led to unnecessary amounts of state, college, and Federal bookkeeping. The first mention of a possible codification of the separate extension laws had occurred as early as 1932 when the Association appointed a committee to study possible solutions. After extended deliberations, Congress finally took action in 1953 to consolidate the legislation. The new law, as an amendment to the original Smith-Lever Act, was entitled Public Law 83 of the Eighty-third Congress. It is known popularly as the Hope-Aiken Act. It repealed all of the separate laws, with the exception of the Clarke-McNary Act of 1924 relating to extension forestry work and the Agricultural Marketing Act of 1946 which included provision for extension in addition to a number of other non-extension stipulations. In the new act an open-end appropriation clause permits each session of Congress to allocate the amount for extension work.

The Commission on Intergovernmental Relations found that the proportionate contribution to extension work from the several sources for fiscal 1954 included Federal—36.0 per cent; State and college—37.8 per cent; County—23.6 per cent; and other local sources—2.6 per cent. The national total of cooperative extension funds from all sources amounted to $89,531,000.[18] The President of the American Farm Bureau Federation had estimated in 1947 that "of every dollar spent for extension work, 69 cents is spent at the county level, 29 cents at the state level, and only 2 cents at the federal level." It was obvious, therefore, that the majority of funds from all sources was returned directly to the county-level work with the people. The individual states varied in the number of workers and the amount of funds received from the Federal government and from the state. In 1948 the smallest cooperative extension staff maintained by a Land-Grant College was reported to be Alaska, with eight professional extension workers and a budget of $48,950. Texas was listed as the largest, with 709 professional workers and a total budget of $3,042,010.

The modern period brought some lessening of the tension between cooperative extension and other governmental agencies attempting demonstration and educational work in the states. Many of the depression agencies had been abolished. The colleges, however, were still disturbed over the duplication with those that existed. In the late forties they put the blame on the Federal Department and, as a result, the relations between the colleges and the Federal Department were far from harmonious. As an illustration, in 1947 the Association Senate adopted a statement presented by the Association's Committee on Extension Organization and Policy:

There is evidence that there is now being waged a relentless campaign to convince the public and the Congress that the Land-Grant Colleges have failed to live up to their responsibility to the people and that they are now incapable and unwilling to carry forward an aggressive program for the agriculture of the nation. . . .

We maintain that it is fundamentally unsound in a democracy for a Federal agency to by-pass a State agency having similar responsibilities in working with and serving local groups and individuals. . . . Much of the confused situation and lack of coordination in the operation of agricultural agencies stems from the Office of the Secretary of Agriculture which has failed to follow the established policy of Federal-State Cooperation.

The chief difficulty lay with the Soil Conservation Service. The work of this service in the states led many land-grant educators to conclude that the Federal government was intent on establishing two extension services, both providing educational and technical guidance to the farmers. The duplication was termed wasteful and confusing. Eventually a written understanding of relationship was reached with the Soil Conservation Service, but dissatisfaction and some tension continues.

A joint committee of the Association and the Department succeeded in 1954–55 in reaching agreement on a revised Memorandum of Understanding between the colleges and the Department. The new Memorandum brought up to date the document which had been in effect over the years. It made more explicit extension's educational role and provided also a more definite method of settling differences. Provisions which had appeared in subsequent legislation were included in the new Memorandum, together with recognition of new practices. The Memorandum of 1914 had sought to establish the cooperative extension service; the new document emphasized its maintenance and continuance.

By the end of the forties extension had become a recognized profession of its own. Its highly specialized work made certain skills and training necessary. At least eight Land-Grant Colleges had recognized the wisdom of advanced graduate study for professional extension workers and had established graduate training. The typical agent was now a farm-reared graduate of an agricultural college. He had in his background some experience as a teacher or professional worker in a commercial agricultural enterprise. He was expected to have competence in applying the principles of education and of psychology to extension work, although few of the agents had, to this point, undertaken formal training in psychology and education. He was further expected to have the ability to organize rural people and to lead them as well as train their leaders. He was asked to bring rural people together for the purpose of analyzing local problems and developing a county program toward their solution. He was expected to deal as effectively with youth as with the aged. He should know how to evaluate the effectiveness of his work and be willing to change, despite inclinations to the contrary. In general, he had won the affection and support of the great majority of rural people.

By 1953 all but some 44 agricultural counties in the United States had agricultural agents, totaling in number 3062. In addition, there were 2589 home demonstration agents. The ratio was 3 county extension workers to each 1800 farm families. The topics covered in some way by extension ranged from economics to engineering to agronomy to community life, marketing, vegetable crops, and zoology. As the work expanded, extension had been forced to abandon much of its demonstration efforts on the face-to-face basis. It came to rely more on mass media, on volunteer teachers, and on new techniques. In the postwar period, partly as a result of its wartime program, it recognized that it must expand its efforts to include urban dwellers on the grounds that farm and city homes were constantly coming to be more similar. Consumer information and the emphasis in the post-war period on marketing led the agents into the cities. It was pointed out that the Smith-Lever Act, extension's original charter, had not specified rural or farm people but "the people of the United States . . . not attending or resident in said colleges." By 1950 cooperative extension in most states had reached into urban communities to meet the growing demand, although it would be a long time, if ever, before urban work matched the rural program.

As extension grew vertically, it expanded horizontally to include new areas of subject-matter. By now, four broad fields of emphasis could be observed. The first was the traditional emphasis on production. In the postwar period this took the form of stress on balanced farming or individual farm and home planning, as it was called in some states. It was intended to involve the whole farm and home rather than individual problems in isolation. It was designed to develop farm income-producing enterprises, conserve soil and water resources, develop the farm home, and improve rural standards of living, all as part of one comprehensive program. The second modern emphasis was on marketing in rural and urban areas, and the third on public policy formulation and discussion. It was regarded as an urgent assignment of extension to acquaint the average farmer with the national and international agricultural problems. It was felt that democracy could progress only in the degree to which citizens were informed. Among the topics listed on which rural people needed information in order to render intelligent judgment were price and production policies, food distribution and nutrition, regulation of monopolistic practices, labor and management policies, international relations, and monetary and fiscal policies. The farmer was expected to understand how surpluses could be handled, whether production controls were inevitable, the implications of various methods of price supporting, the benefits of Social Security, and the question of foreign trade and its relation to domestic economy. There was some hesitancy over entering too actively into the field of public policy discussion. There were those who felt that it was too controversial and inclined to have strong political implications. There were others who felt that it was too great an undertaking to accomplish well, as it would have to be if it were undertaken at all, in the light of the many other commitments made on the agent's time. Programs in public policy became accepted eventually on the justification that this was truly educational, in line with the essential purpose of cooperative extension. Extension should attempt only to promote discussion and to make the farmer think rather than accept solutions previously agreed upon.

Finally, cooperative extension branched into the area of human relationships, helping people to understand complex social as well as economic problems. Attempts were made to stress moral and spiritual values, the relation of the farm to the church and school, the development of a satisfying family life, and the improvement of local health services.

Home Economics Extension

In the meantime, the second of the three major divisions of cooperative extension—home demonstration work—had enlarged and expanded in much the same fashion. By 1939, some 1,118,500 women were enrolled in home economics extension work, in addition to 580,-000 girls completing home-making projects within 4–H Clubs. The fundamental aim of home demonstration work was said to be the development of rural family life in attaining a higher plane of profit, comfort, culture, influence and power through a continuing program of education. Such a program would contribute toward self-realization, economic efficiency, assumption of civic responsibility and desirable human relationships.

The war had taught home demonstration personnel the importance of community consciousness and of extending efforts from the farm kitchen into the many projects of community life. The home demonstration agent assisted with the school lunch program, with factory menus, with welfare and war agencies. She arranged well-baby clinics and special provisions for working mothers. She found, as had the agricultural agents, that her program was just as applicable to urban women as to rural women. The health and welfare of children were as important in the city as on the farm. Attractive homes and clothing appealed as much to the city woman as to the farmer's wife. The urban dweller had many of the same problems in household management, preparation and storage of food, and human nutrition. In increasing measure, the home demonstration program spread during the war and postwar years into the cities. By 1952, nine states had appointed one or more urban Home Demonstration Agents.

The field of home demonstration work expanded in concert with home economics research and teaching. The traditional pattern of cooperative extension had been to emphasize improved farming; home demonstration work made a substantial contribution to the equally important phase of improved farm living. In its emphasis on conservation and utilization of nutritious food, on economical and attractive clothing, on well decorated and inexpensively but attractively furnished homes, on community life and recreation, on child care and citizenship development, it had paralleled the work of agricultural extension and yet given all cooperative extension a continuing and important stress on more enduring home values.

4-H Club Work

The third division of cooperative extension work—the work with boys and girls in 4-H—did not undergo the remarkable expansion during this period of the other two divisions. Its growth, rather, was slow and steady. Part of the difficulty lay in the divided responsibility of agents for both farm programs and youth work. The exigencies of both the depression and the war forced the agents to turn their attention more to farm problems than to the development of 4-H Clubs. Nevertheless, the growth was satisfying. In 1939 over 1,000,000 boys and girls were organized in 74,594 clubs in 3000 counties, under the guidance of agents and of 143,017 voluntary leaders. The number of projects under way were said to be, in round figures, 1,500,000. Club work extended into rural non-farm families as well. In 1942, 21 per cent of the club enrollment was from this bracket. The chief difficulty of 4-H work, continuing to the present day, was its inability to hold the interest of the older youth. As a result, the majority of members belonged in the age grouping of 10 to 14 years.

Within ten years of 1939 the number of boys and girls reached through 4-H Club work had risen to 1,829,250, with an average of 587 enrolled in each agricultural county. In 29 states there were no specific county agents assigned to club work. The responsibility was left to the agricultural and home demonstration personnel. In the remaining states by 1947 there were 558 county workers designated as Club agents. Many others working directly with boys and girls were given the title of assistant extension agents.

The emphasis in 4-H work continued to be educational. Learning was expected to take place through the experiences of club membership. Attitudes, knowledge, and problem solving were stressed. The major objectives of 4-H work were listed by the University of Wisconsin in 1949: "To provide an opportunity for rural boys and girls to discover their abilities and interests; to help young people assume positions of leadership in the life of the community . . ; to instill a sense of stewardship for the soil and other natural resources; to learn to work and play together . . . in the give-and-take of life . . ; to deepen and enrich the love of home and family life."

Cooperative extension, understandably enough in troubled times, had put its emphasis on the more immediately urgent problems of the farm and home. Work with young people was more a matter of long-term building. Other agencies had shared in the task. As a result, 4-H work was less unique but, in the long-range program of the Land-Grant Colleges, no less important than any other phase of work. Its progressive effort directly associated with the boys and girls of the nation paid rich dividends.

General Extension

General or university extension, meanwhile, had become increasingly centered around the motives and methods of liberal education in line with the developing interest in general education. By 1951, the Land-Grant Colleges as a whole were enrolling more than 274,000 men and women in extension courses and 81,000 in correspondence courses. Several institutions had developed Centers of Continuation Study. Michigan State, for instance, with its handsome Kellogg Center, provided a gathering place for state groups as well as a center for all of its general extension program. In Minnesota in 1948–49, over 20,000 people were enrolled in evening classes conducted, for the most part, by faculty who also taught regular day classes. Eighty per cent of the enrollees were reported working toward the baccalaureate degree, and at a level of achievement comparable to full-time students. Dunaway describes the many phases of Penn State's general extension program in the modern period:

The extramural classes of the Arts and Science Division, located in more than 80 communities in the State, offer instruction on the adult level in liberal arts and scientific subjects. The larger number are of the non-credit type for those seeking cultural self-improvement, but some of them carry college credit. This Division offers approximately 100 correspondence courses, with a wide range of subject matter. Among the services it renders is the program of work offered in dramatics through the holding of dramatic institutes and through lectures and consultative service. Practical assistance in music is also made available to schools, clubs, churches, and other community groups interested in music education. . . .[19]

In many areas and through many methods, the Land-Grant College of the present day has extended its influence far beyond that originally assumed to be agriculture and mechanic arts. It serves as a meeting place and center of education for doctors, women's organizations, lawyers, bankers, teachers, municipal officers, policemen, and men and women of almost every profession. Wherever a need resembling education is shown, the colleges move to meet the need. Their anxiety to be of service and to serve the constituency in every possible way sometimes takes them far beyond the normal channels of educational endeavor and into areas educationally questionable. This is an inherent temptation in the effort of the colleges to root themselves deeply in the common life. All in all, however, the colleges have served the people in better fashion than any other educational enterprise, and the vast majority of their work has been educationally sound.

Engineering Extension

Until the decade of the forties, only a comparatively few land-grant institutions were carrying on any engineering extension program, at least on a scale at all comparable to cooperative and even general extension. The picture changed rapidly due largely to new programs developed during the war. As a result, some institutions organized separate engineering extension divisions while others consigned the work to the general extension office.

The change and expansion came about as a result of the establishment in many Land-Grant Colleges of a program known nationally as the Engineering, Science and Management War Training. The program was established in 1940 to make use of the facilities of colleges and universities in the training of technical specialists badly needed for the war effort. It was administered by the Federal Office of Education dealing directly with the institutions, and, during the course of the program from 1940 through 1945, involved the expenditure of nearly $60 million. In all, some 1.5 million people received short intensive training under the guidance of college faculties.[20] Graduate engineers were retrained to perform new and specialized tasks. Other men and women, many without the benefit of previous college training, were given sufficient instruction to enable them to become technicians, draftsmen, inspectors, testers, and engineering assistants, as well as competent workers in the fields of physics, chemistry, and production supervision. By this effort, much of which was conducted in land-grant institutions, the Land-Grant Colleges found a way to expand off-campus adult education in the technical fields, and, in the words of President J. L. Morrill, realized "at last in the 'mechanic arts' the service ideal long since attained in agricultural extension."

In the postwar years, engineering extension expanded rapidly. It consisted of off-campus instruction comparable to the beginning work on a degree program, of special technical courses of varying lengths offered both in the day and evening, of courses and conferences to fill particular needs of specialized industries and occupations, of management training conferences and courses, and of informal work in time study, job evaluation, and other fields related to industrial management. Engineering extension work was not confined to a particular occupation or profession, in the manner in which cooperative extension traditionally had operated. It sought to serve factory, business, office, and commerce of all grades and types. The program was extended in the postwar years to include consultation and advisory service as well as more formal instruction. At Penn State, for instance, the Engineering Extension Division offered more than one hundred subjects through correspondence instruction, as well as promoted study groups for both management and workers in industries. In the small state of New Hampshire, an annual industrial management conference enrolled nearly a thousand supervisors, foremen, and executives who came to the University of New Hampshire campus in the summer for a week of lectures, discussion, and mutual exchange of information. Industry has recognized and voiced its appreciation of this enlarged effort of the Land-Grant Colleges. In 1950 the Vice-President of

Standard Pressed Steel Company, H. Thomas Hallowell, told an Association session:

Programs such as the ones offered by the Land-Grant colleges and universities can help industry improve its competitive position by improving its ability to produce. This ability to produce is industry's one control of inflation. Such training programs can improve the living standards and increase the security of the workers, because a trained man is much more secure than one who is not. In this way our country, as a whole, will be benefited, and our position in world competition will also be strengthened.

Finally, then, in the modern period, mechanic arts extension had come closer to agricultural extension in form and function if not in numbers.

NEW AREAS OF SERVICE

In the years following World War II, the Land-Grant Colleges found two new areas of educational opportunity opening to them. The areas would involve all of the phases of the land-grant scheme—instruction, research, and extension—and would make even more useful the land-grant idea. One would serve to strengthen efforts at home; the other would take the colleges across broad expanses of ocean into foreign nations.

Educational Television

The colleges had been concerned with educational and informational service through the medium of radio ever since that medium had become popular in the United States. For many years the Association received periodic reports from its Radio Committee, which had worked with Federal authorities as well as with individual colleges in the attempt to make better use of educational radio. Commercial radio had forged ahead, however, and education was forced to take second-best in channels as well as programs. Relatively little of any educational significance had been accomplished through the medium of radio.

In postwar days the bright possibility of educational television loomed on the college horizon. The colleges were determined that this new medium would not slip through their fingers as radio had many years before. They set to work, individually and collectively, to capitalize on its manifold opportunities for education. In the early fifties almost all land-grant institutions were examining possible adaptation of television within and without the institution. The Committee on Radio and Television of the Association commented in its 1954 report, "In a century 'when the pictures of the world inside our heads' are derived more frequently from mass media than from personal experience Land-Grant administrators may well ponder the question of what portion and how much of the television screen they should occupy in terms of their appointed task in the furious competition of many agencies for men's minds and hearts." The land-grant administrators responded by agreeing that the land-grant task included using television to the limit of its possibilities, governed only by the ever-present problem of available funds. They recognized, in the words of President David D. Henry, that "its values were not to be measured by total numbers, but by relative ones; not by extent but by depth; not by passive listening, but by action. They saw its potential as an aid to the teacher and extension workers, and as a tool for the small community as well as the large." It was an extension of the educational system, allowing the institutions bent on service to the people to reach far greater numbers than ever before. Television was not regarded at the ultimate answer to all of education's many problems but as a stimulus to better employment of traditional techniques.

Iowa State College was the first educational institution in the country to establish a television station. Its work preceded the Federal freeze on allocation of channels which later delayed other institutions from following its early lead. Through the efforts of the Land-Grant Colleges, in association with other interested educational agencies and institutions, the government authorities became convinced of the wisdom of establishing educational stations. As a result, when the freeze was thawed, channels were allocated to a number of land-grant institutions. Slowly, one by one, the new educational stations affiliated with the colleges came into existence. In 1954 ten land-grant institutions were among the fifty-five educational institutions and agencies operating or planning to operate their own television facilities. A number of others continued to explore its possibilities and, particularly, ways of financing the new enterprise.

Many colleges were making use of commercial stations to offer educational programs.

Iowa's experience served as an important guide. Its station, WOI-TV, employed the services of full-time as well as part-time faculty members. In 1954, Iowa's President J. H. Hilton listed some of the benefits already derived, including a single program series produced by the extension and resident home economics staff resulting in 9700 letters of commendation from 47 counties (as a result of later rebroadcast); thousands of citizens enjoying a course in literature, history, or psychology given by the best professors; and almost half of the total population in Iowa given an opportunity to see and understand the why and how of research. Michigan's D. B. Varner observed that "we have taken the position in Michigan that the Extension Service can no more ignore the potentialities of television as a means of education than could the county agricultural agents in 1915 ignore the possibilities of the automobile as a means of transportation." There was no doubt that the colleges would find television a useful tool in education as well as public relations. Its further development depended on wisdom as much as finances.

International Responsibilities

The effect of the war and of subsequent events in Europe destroyed once and for all America's futile attempt to live in its own orbit, independent of life and thought beyond the American world. America's postwar assumption of international responsibilities brought another new and interesting facet to the land-grant idea. A start had been made in the prewar years in connection with the Good Neighbor Policy, but the war interrupted any lasting action. In 1942, E. J. Kyle had addressed a convention session on "The Mission of the Land-Grant Colleges in Promoting Our Good Neighbor Policies Among the Latin American Republics." He had told the delegates that ". . . every possible effort to encourage and promote the establishment of a system of land-grant colleges throughout the Latin American Republics" should be made.

As international tension mounted in the postwar years, President Harry S. Truman proposed that America have a direct hand in world affairs through the assistance she could lend to struggling nations on other continents. The subsequent Point Four Program was born partly of humanitarian desires, but admittedly it was also a bold and wise stroke in world politics. Russian friendship had cooled, and suspicions of her intentions to seek authoritarian world domination had been confirmed. The great struggle began between two diametrically opposed ideologies, and the Land-Grant Colleges were destined to play an important part in that struggle.

Within a few weeks after the first proposal of the Marshall Plan, the Executive Committee of the Association offered to the government the immediate and full assistance of the colleges. Here was a way in which the colleges, through research, extension, and teaching, could be of assistance to the farmer and the manufacturer on the other side of the world as well as those on the other side of the state. In particular, agricultural production in many underdeveloped countries had not kept pace with the rising rate of population. The colleges were called upon to undertake a production emphasis which, in many ways, they had long since abandoned. Research was needed, and then extension, and finally instruction to train research and extension staffs. The colleges could contribute by helping foreign people to build the kind of agencies and institutions which had been developed over a hundred years in America—the unique combination of government, institutions, and the people themselves cooperating in a common program. The colleges had learned, too, that production by itself was not enough. It should be coupled with the promotion of a better and higher type of rural life. From decades of experimentation, the colleges had developed techniques and planning methods which could be adapted with relative ease to other situations in other nations.

In the beginning phases of land-grant participation in the Point Four Program, the institutions loaned faculty members to the Federal government to serve as technical advisors and specialists in overseas missions. Some two-thirds of the men and women going into the foreign technical assistance program in agriculture and home economics were recruited from the Land-Grant Colleges, while most of the remaining third had been trained in land-grant institutions. The first large-scale involvement of land-grant personnel was in the occupation government of Germany. By 1949 there was scarcely a Land-Grant College in the country that had not loaned one or more persons to assist the occupation government. It was in Germany that the first attempt was made to set up an educational system based on the land-grant idea. The institution was the ancient University of Giessen where a radical departure from European tradition came with the introduction of student-training in agriculture, home economics, and veterinary medicine. Germany had been a leader in scientific research for at least a century; it needed particularly the extension concept to supply the missing link in the translation of scientific truths discovered in the laboratory to understandable and concrete methods of food production on the farm.

Efforts were being made in Latin American nations, too. In 1949 the Secretary of Agriculture, Charles F. Brannan, reported to the land-grant convention, "A couple of months ago, a young fellow named Francisco Vasquez got his name in our papers. He did it by becoming the first county agent El Salvador ever had. Francisco was trained by Extension Specialist Bill Bailey, of Colorado, and in August of this year he was sent out on horseback to the most primitive part of the country to teach better farming methods." The government program expanded sharply in the number and geographic spread of countries involved. It sent special advisory missions to collaborate with specialists of the nations on specific agricultural programs. A number of Latin American countries as well as China, the Philippines, Syria, Lebanon, Iraq, Saudi Arabia, Egypt, and Greece were receiving assistance by 1949. Secretary Brannan estimated that every Land-Grant College had one or more representatives taking part. In agriculture alone, seventy-seven different countries were involved within two years. In addition to sending experts to foreign nations, the Land-Grant Colleges served as training and information centers for technicians and specialists coming to America for advanced training. By 1950 at least three thousand visitors a year from seventy-seven different countries were studying and observing on land-grant campuses.

The international task had grown by leaps and bounds. The importance of the colleges to its success was giving willing testimony by government leaders. In 1950, for instance, Ross E. Moore, Chief of the Technical Collaboration Branch of the Office of Foreign Agricultural Relations, United States Department of Agriculture, told the colleges, "Not only are you participating; the truth of the matter is that the United States is incapable of carrying out its technical assistance commitments without you." In the early fifties, the concept evolved that foreign nations might well develop for themselves the type of institution which had served America so well. Henry G. Bennett, President of Oklahoma A. and M. College, was appointed Administrator of the Technical Cooperation Administration. Shortly after, in speaking at a land-grant meeting, he commented, "I am convinced that one of the soundest ways we can help in the long run is to assist the other countries to develop institutions like our Land-Grant Colleges, experiment stations, extension service, and credit and marketing systems. We should not try to transplant our own institutions intact to foreign soil, but rather to help other people develop the kind of institutions that suit their own particular needs." Within a short time, Oklahoma A. and M. had signed the first technical cooperation contract for work in Ethiopia, and the University of Arkansas had sent staff to the Republic of Panama to help expand and strengthen the agricultural school at Divisa. In Mexico, Texas A. and M. College was at work on a similar program in cooperation with the government. A number of other contracts were arranged between land-grant institutions and governments and institutions overseas. The object was to make the foreign institutions into centers of technical training and knowledge, as the Land-Grant Colleges had been in the United States.

The overseas work of the colleges now included four types of effort. American technicians were trained to undertake technical cooperation work abroad. Technicians and leaders from foreign nations were brought to the United States for study in the colleges. The colleges were loaning the services of faculty to projects overseas, and they were assuming direct responsibility for contract work in fields as diverse as labor management and sanitary engineering. Of the seventy-eight contracts listed by the American Council on Education as operative in 1956, the Land-Grant Colleges were responsible for forty-seven. The funds allotted to the institutions for the work often totaled well over a million dollars. At the State College of Washington, for instance, the contract to work with the University of the Punjab in West Pakistan had a dollar value of $1,600,000 and called for effort in agriculture, engineering, education, business administration, and home economics. The University of Maryland assumed responsibility for the entire technical assistance program in British Guiana on a $900,000 contract, to be coordinated with a $25 million British program for the development of that country. Its importance could be noted by the fact that the British Government had recently suspended the local constitution, governing its 450,000 population, because of the pro-Communist leanings of the legislature and administration.

The Foreign Operations Administration reported that some fifteen countries had started extension services as a part of the cooperative programs. Other countries with some type of extension already under way were reorganizing and expanding the program. In 1953, the FAO estimated that about eight thousand farm extension agents trained under technical cooperation programs visited an estimated seven million individual farms and conducted some 260,000 demonstrations. A total of 1650 demonstration farms had been established. More than four thousand rural youth clubs, with an estimated membership of 88,000 boys and girls had been organized in twenty-one countries. Agricultural colleges were operating in seven countries, and fifty vocational schools had been established in eighteen countries. Further figures indicated that the programs had helped more than forty million farmers across the world. In Peru, extension agents had set up more than three hundred committees of farmers working with more than a million and a half rural people. Programs in Formosa were said to have reached more than 90 per cent of the rural population. Egypt established an extension service on the land-grant pattern. The National Extension Service in India in 1953 opened two hundred village "development blocks," with each block serving about one hundred villages.

In that same year in Bolivia, 1500 demonstrations and meetings were attended by more than 33,000 people. Agents made 2308 farm and home visits and distributed nearly 5000 bulletins and circulars. The number of visits in Costa Rica in 1953 totaled 26,000 with 12,000 farmers reached by the demonstration method.

It thus was obvious that the Land-Grant College idea had become worldwide. The effort was not without some sacrifice on the part of the colleges, as well as difficulty and frustration due to Congressional uncertainty and administrative red-tape. Nonetheless, it was a new and rewarding function for the college which, by now, had come to serve the people without much thought of cost. In addition to government contracts, some of the land-grant institutions had undertaken overseas work under contract with various foundations, particularly the Ford and Rockefeller Foundations. As early as 1947, the British

Ambassador to the United States, Lord Inverchapel, had expressed the thanks of the world's nations. He told the Association delegates, "In the true international spirit of the arts and sciences you have made this wealth of new knowledge truly available to all men. In doing so you have made a handsome contribution to the progress of mankind—not only in this great country of yours but also across the world as a whole."

THE ASSOCIATION

The Association, which had played such an important and significant role in the life of the institutions, continued to serve in increasing effectiveness. The present day finds it a valuable forum for discussion and exchange of opinion, a clearinghouse for all matters of importance to the member institutions, and a strong voice for their concerns. Its organization grew again in concert with the developing institutions. A section on Graduate Work was organized in 1939, and in 1945 the constitution was revised to include the arts and sciences for the first time, at least in formal fashion. The benefits to be derived from this latter addition were thought to be twofold, operating to the advantage of the liberal arts in the colleges as well as to the professional subjects. President J. L. Morrill commented in 1949:

. . . a new Division of the Arts and Sciences was established in this Association, but not with the idea that the liberal arts traditionalists need just another meeting-place. The aim was to infect our liberal arts people with an urge to make their subjects more functional, more relevant to the problems of daily life more serviceable to our students in training for specialized, not scholarly, careers . . . Professional, technological, and agricultural education—mainstays of the modern Land-Grant college task —must take larger account of humane values. They must be taught in a more meaningful social context.

The Association in 1946 chose for its permanent Executive Secretary-Treasurer to work in its permanent Washington office Russell I. Thackrey, a man with a background of experience in land-grant institutions. Since that year, the individual institutions as well as the organized group have been ably and skillfully served by this capable executive. Further expansion included the creation of a division of Veterinary Medicine in 1948, and the establishment of a Council on General Extension and a Council on Instruction. It was not until

1954, some sixty-four years after the Second Morrill Act had passed, that Association doors were opened to the Negro Land-Grant Colleges.[21] After years of discussion and maneuvering, the Association Senate in that year voted to make membership available to all of the land-grant institutions. The seventeen Negro colleges joined within two years thereafter. In 1955 the name of the Association was changed to open membership also to state universities which were not Land-Grant Colleges. This step had been taken after years of negotiation to combine the Association and the separate National Association of State Universities had failed to produce positive results. The new name became the American Association of Land-Grant Colleges and State Universities.

Among the more important committees of the Association has been the Committee on Federal Legislation which analyzes bills before Congress, presents testimony in behalf of the membership before Congressional committees, and brings to bear upon government agencies and the Congress the full weight of the colleges' great influence. The Committee on Extension Organization and Policy, and its counterpart for the experiment stations, have a long history of useful service in policy making and in acting as spokesmen. To indicate the wide range of interests, there exists such committees as Irrigated Agriculture and Water Resources, National Defense, and Radio and Television. A joint land-grant and Department of Agriculture committee on training for public service has functioned effectively and influentially since 1936. The Association has also been active and influential in obtaining passage of the National Science Foundation legislation, in setting up an Agricultural Communications Center, and a National Agricultural Extension Center for Advanced Study. Its leadership has been lent to such educationally significant projects as the attempt through the forties and into the fifties to bring order from the accreditation confusion. As a result, the National Commission on Accreditation was established to the great benefit of the land-grant member institutions. As each year passes, the Association extends both its influence and its service.

IN RETROSPECT

One hundred years had passed since the first two land-grant institutions opened their doors to the sons and daughters of the industrial classes in order that they might gain both a liberal and a practical education. The doors had been opened in the midst of a virgin Michigan forest and in a buried and desolate section of Pennsylvania. The modern Land-Grant College and University is a far different educational institution in a far different nation. In recent years, it had continued to expand in function and size. It had responded to the needs of the nation during the recovery from a depression, during the most disastrous war man had yet experienced, and during the difficult days to follow. It had emerged as a strong instrument for world peace. Before we close, we shall pause briefly to look at the Negro colleges, and then to examine the philosophy of all these institutions.

8

The Negro Land-Grant Colleges

AMONG the sixty-nine institutions receiving some of the benefits from Land-Grant College legislation are seventeen Southern colleges listed by the United States Office of Education as "attended predominantly by Negro students." In their own way, they are as unique in American education as the other fifty-two Land-Grant Colleges and Universities. Historically they have developed under entirely different conditions and with handicaps unknown to the other fifty-two. They are the product of a social and economic pattern of a particular region rather than a nation. The Negro institutions have been and continue to be operating under a time lag of some fifteen to twenty-five years behind the other institutions with which they share the name "Land-Grant." Their progress since the mid-thirties, however, shows ample promise of an erasure of that lag.

The first Negro Land-Grant College was Alcorn University, established by the State of Mississippi in 1871. It received in its beginning years three-fifths of the benefits of land sales from the Morrill legislation of 1862. In 1878, the state changed its name to the Alcorn Agricultural and Mechanical College and assigned to it one-half of the land-grant endowment. It was located in one of the three states which were to make the attempt to apportion a share of the 1862 benefits to Negro education. The other two were South Carolina and Virginia. South Carolina in 1872 granted income from the fund to Claflin University, a private institution, although the fund was not used for educational purposes. It later established a state-supported Negro college at Orangeburg. In like manner, Virginia in 1872 gave half of its receipts from the land sales to Hampton Institute, another private

257

institution, and later established a Negro Land-Grant College of its own.

Despite these three indications of interest in sharing the 1862 funds, the majority of Southern states took no action in behalf of Negro land-grant education until, in a sense, they were induced to do so under the terms of the Second Morrill Act of 1890. The act provided:

That no money shall be paid out under this act to any State or Territory for the support and maintenance of a college where a distinction of race or color is made in the admission of students, but the establishment and maintenance of such college separately for white and colored students shall be held to be a compliance with the provisions of this act if the funds received in such State or Territory be equitably divided as hereinafter set forth.

Here, is, then, both an injunction against discrimination and a specification that "separate but equal" satisfies the mandate. The Southern states had no alternative but to share "equitably"; the act did not say that the sharing must be "equal." With the exception of Alcorn, the 1890 Morrill Act was the principal instrument for the establishment or designation of all of the Negro land-grant institutions. In effect, it accomplished for the Negroes of the South what the first act in 1862 had accomplished for the men and women of other races.

Following 1890, the Southern states had four alternatives for action to meet the requirements of the law. They could establish new Negro Land-Grant Colleges under state control; they could designate an existing private college for Negroes as the land-grant institution; they could name an already existing state-supported Negro institution as recipient; or they could take over a private Negro institution as the state college. Those states in which a private Negro school was designated as the Negro land-grant institution and later established as such included Mississippi (1871), South Carolina (1896), and Virginia (1883–1920). The states which designated the existing state-supported Negro institution as the Land-Grant College were Alabama (1875), Arkansas (1872), Florida (1887), Kentucky (1877), Louisiana (1880), and Missouri (1866). Those which assigned funds to private Negro schools under conditions of acceptance and which later took over these schools as state institutions, were Maryland (1887), and Tennessee (1913). The states which established new Land-Grant

Colleges under state control were Delaware (1891), Georgia (1890), North Carolina (1894), Oklahoma (1897), Texas (1879), and West Virginia (1892). The picture was at best confusing.

SPECIAL CONDITIONS AND PROBLEMS

Both in the early and in the succeeding years, there were social and economic conditions in the Southern states which affected profoundly the course of Negro education at all levels, including land-grant higher education. The Negro was seldom self-employed; he was cither a tenant on a farm or a domestic servant. His wage-earning capacity was controlled in many cases by factors other than ability. Even in industry his place was restricted and confined. The social aspects of living particularly worked against an interest in advancement through education. Among the major factors which prevented the growth in Negro education of the type earlier championed by the other Land-Grant Colleges was the lack of dignity associated with daily labor. As Chapman observed, "It was . . . not easy to persuade the children and grandchildren of slaves in 1890 to accept a type of education which emphasized the practical arts." There were many in the South who felt also that public funds used in behalf of Negro education would be spent wastefully on men and women who, because of their personality and lack of ability, could not benefit in proportion to the cost.

In most Southern states the private Negro school and college preceded by some years the public institution. As a result, the private colleges had a dominant influence on the subsequent Negro Land-Grant Colleges. The church colleges, for instance, had long emphasized "cultural" instruction with very little, if any, place given to vocational training. The early Negro Land-Grant College conformed to this accepted pattern. As the denominations became less able to meet the demand, however, the church colleges faded in importance to a sufficient extent to allow the public institutions to gain the place and prestige prerequisite to expansion in scope and function.

Not the least of the problems of the Negro Land-Grant College was the lack of any adequate system of Negro public education in the South. Public high schools were a later growth in only the larger cities. As late as 1915, there were but sixty-four public high schools for Negroes in the Southern states, and only forty-five of them offered a four-year curriculum. The secondary enrollment in that year was 20,234 with 11,527 Negro students in private schools and only 8707 in public schools. The Negro Land-Grant Colleges for many years, therefore, performed the function of elementary and secondary level work. In 1914 the colleges enrolled a total of 5997 students, of whom only 12 were of collegiate grade. The number included 3367 in elementary level work and 2618 in secondary school grades. Not until 1930 did the college enrollment exceed that of high school. These institutions suffered from other effects of the retarded Southern Negro educational picture. An obvious example was their inability to obtain adequately trained teachers. For faculty they depended largely on graduates of Northern colleges, most of which were land-grant and which did not bar Negro students, but even this source was insufficient. The colleges faced great difficulty not only in finding instructors but in the ability to pay them adequately. In 1924 Wilkinson reported a great disproportion in physical equipment and in salaries paid between the white and the Negro colleges. In general he concluded that Negro faculty were receiving only about one-half as much as others of similar training, ability, and service.

According to the few historians of the Negro Land-Grant Colleges, the conditions in the colleges prior to the First World War were deplorable. The period following their designation or establishment was one of stagnation and inactivity. State support was meager, often less than the Federal contribution. No effort was made to encourage improvement or enlargement. Gandy reported that, ". . . many of the buildings became dilapidated and ramshackled. There was practically no equipment for teaching such as laboratories and maps. Many of the colleges did not have even an adequate supply of blackboards in their classrooms. The living conditions of the students and teachers was unsanitary and breeders of dissatisfaction. The teachers were woefully underpaid." [1] The total value of the combined plants of the colleges in 1914 was estimated to be $2,507,434. Income from the Federal grants was $281,030, with state appropriations amounting to $368,487. By 1925, plant value had risen to $7,979,848, and state support to $1,455,260, still a sharp contrast to the development and increased support of the other fifty-two land-grant institutions during this period. Enrollment in the Negro colleges increased only slightly in relative terms in contrast to the other colleges. In 1910–11, the

Negro institutions enrolled 8138; in 1915–16, 10,613; and in 1920–21, 11,527. By 1953 the total resident enrollment of students of college grade was 21,975.

The decade of the thirties found the Negro colleges in increasingly better shape. Whereas as late as 1930 only three of the seventeen institutions could meet the standards established by accrediting agencies for libraries, by 1940 only two were below standard. During this time, public interest and concern had been stimulated by a number of reports emphasizing the lack of attention to adequate Negro higher education and the sorry facilities of the colleges. Two surveys by the United States Office of Education, one extending over the early twenties, and the other published in 1930, helped the states to realize their previously inadequate assumption of responsibility.

EMPHASIS ON TEACHER-TRAINING

The principal function of the Negro Land-Grant Colleges, in contrast to the other land-grant institutions, has been largely that of teacher-training. It was dictated in some measure by the growth of public and private educational facilities for Negro youth and the demand for teachers, as well as by social restrictions on other professional fields which Negroes might enter. With the private Negro colleges oriented toward the pure liberal arts, it fell to the land-grant institutions to take the lead in the education of more and better teachers, although in these colleges, too, primary emphasis continued to be placed on the liberal arts. In graduate study, for instance, in 1953 the education majors numbered more than four times the combined enrollment of the other three fields in which graduate students were reported. As a result of this emphasis on teacher-training, the operation of summer session work became an important part of the Negro Land-Grant College program. The emphasis on teacher-training was a primary factor, too, in leading the Negro Land-Grant Colleges into the traditional land-grant fields of agriculture, mechanic arts, and home economics. A large percentage of the Negroes in the South worked on the land. The colleges directed their attention toward teacher-training at the secondary level, however, rather than toward college educated farmers and research scientists. The percentage of agricultural graduates entering teaching runs to over 90 per cent in some of the Negro Land-Grant Colleges. The same situation exists in engineering and home economics, largely because of the lack of other teaching opportunity in these fields. There has been a traditional emphasis on "learning by doing," in part made necessary by the lack of adequate educational background of the students and by the demands of the profession which graduates enter.

The Negro colleges have never given strong emphasis to the traditional land-grant subjects. For many years the number in agriculture was relatively small, and instruction in mechanic arts was limited to manual training and trades. Negro graduates found it difficult to find employment at any other level, and the colleges themselves were handicapped by the lack of equipment so necessary to professional engineering training. Until recent years the work has been given almost entirely on a high school level and has consisted of mechanical drawing, automobile mechanics, carpentry, masonry, building construction, power-plant engineering, printing, and industrial management. The development of home economics has been slightly more consistent with the non-Negro land-grant institutions. With the increased interest in nutrition and child development, home economics graduates found more demand for their services. By mid-century college offerings in agriculture, home economics, and engineering were rapidly increasing and improving, partially due to a genuine desire to improve status and to make realistic the separate but equal provision.

Until World War II, there was little military training provided in Negro Land-Grant Colleges. Since then, the United States Office of Education has emphasized the obligation of the institutions to offer military instruction, whether or not an ROTC unit is provided through Federal assistance. The Department of Defense has established units, with varying degrees of success, in most of the institutions, despite the reluctance of the various branches of service.

FINANCIAL STRINGENCY

The colleges have been held back as much by financial stringency as by social conditions. Davis reported that in 1937 "the white land-grant colleges in 17 Southern states maintaining separate schools expended $13,360,598 of Federal funds in or through white institutions while only $504,767 was spent in Negro institutions." [2] Works and Morgan observed that, whereas the Negroes constituted 23 per cent of the total population of the 17 states in 1930, as late as 1935–36 the Negro colleges received only 6 per cent of the funds apportioned to the states for the support of Land-Grant Colleges.[3] The fact that they received what they did was due largely to the requirements of the Second Morrill Act and subsequent Federal legislation. The Federal funds for resident instruction continue to be important and significant parts of the income budget of many of the Negro Land-Grant Colleges, although state appropriations have increased markedly in more recent years. There is no doubt that educational standards in the Negro colleges have suffered because of lack of financial support, and that opportunities for Negro study in a wide variety of fields have been curtailed on both economic and social grounds.

LACK OF RESEARCH AND EXTENSION

The chief complaint of the Negro colleges has been their inability to obtain what they consider to be their equitable share of funds for extension and research. They claim that, as a result, they are deprived of a stimulus which has come to other institutions by virtue of extended work in extension and research. In the main, Federal as well as state research and extension funds in the seventeen Southern states have gone to the "white" institutions, although some attempts at different distribution have been made within most recent years. The work of the "white" institutions has undoubtedly benefited the Negro citizen of the state; the Negro colleges, however, prefer to share in extending the benefit. The President's Advisory Committee on Education in 1939 laid the blame in part on the practices of the Federal Department of Agriculture. The committee study commented:

The most liberal interpretation that can be made of the situation indicates that the Negro has been discriminated against in the administration of the Smith-Lever Act in the South and that this discrimination has occurred in spite of the fact that there was sufficient basis in the legislation for the United States Department of Agriculture to have prevented it. It is not clear that a completely separate administration of funds for Negroes and white persons is desirable, owing to the difficulty of dealing with the counties, but it is evident that the administrative procedures and practices that have been followed have not given equitable results. It appears probable that if equity is desired it will have to be provided for in legislation.[4]

The same situation has existed in the allocation of research funds, although the Negro colleges have only recently become interested in undertaking research work. The solution eventually may be a division according to capability. The arguments for centralization of effort in extension and research are cogent. So, too, it must be recognized that white agents and research scientists serve the Negro population in a fashion which does not deny the Negro farmer and housewife extension and research services. Aside from desires for racial equality, the major argument of the Negro colleges for a share in the agricultural and home economics undertaking is a logical one. We have seen how extension and research have both contributed substantially to the present non-Negro colleges. Presumably the Negro land-grant institutions could derive as much benefit and thus strengthen their program. The colleges have also made known their dissatisfaction with another element of alleged discrimination—the lack of Negro members on governing boards of the Negro Land-Grant Colleges. As late as 1940, only three of the seventeen institutions had Negro board members with voting power. Since that time there has been a slight increase in the number of Negroes so appointed.

Their Role and Their Contribution

The Negro Land-Grant Colleges have been and continue to be called upon for the rendering of service, both in quality and quantity, far beyond that usually expected of institutions of their size and stature. The seventeen states in which the colleges are located are populated by the great majority of the nation's Negroes, most of whom live in rural areas, leaving to the Negro land-grant institutions a staggering job of raising the level of living and working conditions. This they are asked to do in association with the "white" institutions but also with the recognition that living and working standards depend largely on the white population which employs the Negro.

Despite the immensity of the task and these many handicaps, the Negro Land-Grant Colleges have succeeded, through the conviction and determination of a core of hard-working educators, in making a contribution to the life of their race which otherwise would never have been made. In themselves and through their graduates, the colleges have struggled hard and successfully to raise the educational level of the Southern Negro. In this manner, they have extended the influence and prestige of the Negro and thus bolstered the efforts of

the more talented of their numbers who had been hindered by preju-
dice and lack of opportunity. They have proven, too, the wisdom of
government assumption of responsibility for the higher education of
the Negro, and the contribution which the educated Negro can make
to the state and to society. State support of Negro higher education
is now an accepted practice in the South. It has come a long way
from the original assumption that Negro higher education was alone
a responsibility of philanthropic and missionary endeavor. The colleges have also, through their efforts and their program, afforded a
needed measure of dignity to the common pursuits and professions
of life in which the Negro, like all people, must be involved. In recent
years they have followed the pattern of all higher education in the
trend away from the purely vocational and in the emphasis on quality
of life. This combination has helped to raise the sights of the Negro
who had considered himself doomed to unrewarding toil.

As the more difficult years have passed, the Negro Land-Grant Colleges have come into a period of increasing recognition of their importance and place. They have proved, in the words of President
Rufus B. Atwood, that they are capable "of performing a respectable
collegiate service" to their clientele and that they are "something
more than inadequate, make-shift jokes, parading in the name of
colleges." No more significant indication of their present position can
be found than in the full acceptance of the Negro institutions as
members of the highly respected and jealously guarded American
Association of Land-Grant Colleges and State Universities. This step
was taken in 1954 with the assent of the majority of the member institutions, including most of the Southern "white" colleges. The
Negro college presidents had long been associating together in their
own separate organization which resulted from a conference at Tuskegee Institute in 1923. The group, with the constant encouragement
of officials of the United States Office of Education, had been of great
value to the institutions.

THE FUTURE

The future of the Negro institutions, however, remains in doubt.
It is an open question what will happen eventually to the separate
Negro colleges as a result of the United States Supreme Court de-
cision invalidating the long-held separate but equal approach. There

are those who feel that the Supreme Court decision negates the provisions of the Second Morrill Act which led to the compulsory establishment of the separate institutions if a state did not wish to admit Negroes to its "white" Land-Grant College but still wanted the benefits of the act. With such invalidation, it leaves only a prohibition within the terms of the act against any funds going to institutions which discriminate. Whatever the outcome and whatever the future, the Negro Land-Grant Colleges should feel some measure of pride over the obvious success of their struggling efforts in behalf of their race. Against numerous obstacles and with many encumbrances, they have contributed in their own fashion to the philosophy of service which marks all of the land-grant institutions.

9

Some Philosophy and Some Conclusions

A n attempt has here been made to show how a unique system of American higher education evolved over the years from the times rather than from a sudden revelation of a new type of educational endeavor. One cannot expect to find in the thinking of one man or the legislation of one act historical evidence of an eventual result. Evolution marks the Land-Grant Colleges—a gradual, slow, but steady evolution reflecting the needs of the nation. Sometimes the colleges were ahead of need, sometimes behind, but almost always they responded in some fashion to national demands and changes. There are those who have attempted to penetrate the mind of Congress in 1862 or the thinking of men like Turner, Morrill, and Knapp, and who would have us believe that the land-grant scheme was a vision ahead of its day. Such attempts do not do justice to the thoughts and the struggles of the many who could not be mentioned in this study, but all of whom contributed in ways large and small to the evolution of a system of education so distinctly American.

The Land-Grant Colleges were not the result of a popular movement, called forth by a landslide of public sentiment. They evolved, instead, from a gradual awakening of education to fill the needs of an expanding and increasingly complex country. For all this the nation can be grateful. It is fortunate that such instruments as the

267

Morrill Act offered no more than an idea. It remained for the institutions to develop in character and program in concert with the developing nation. The colleges were the product of many forces in a democracy—social, political, economic. They began in a time of national peril, and they continued to develop with the changing nation, especially in periods of crisis. They started at the secondary school level and developed into complex organizations devoted, in part, to graduate study and pure research in many fields. They were intended at first to train the sons of farmers and mechanics; they became instruments of broad public service to every class and kind. Although they maintained a national pattern, their individual internal function became sufficiently flexible to suit the needs of particular states and regions. They began as colleges with limited purposes; they emerged as universities in purpose and fact. This was the evolution of the land-grant idea.

THE LAND-GRANT PATTERN

Although each institution is individual, certain characteristics mark them all. From these characteristics emerges a clear and unique pattern, sometimes termed a trilogy of American ingenuity. The colleges represent a break from tradition—in purpose, in type of control and support, in curriculum, in admission standards. Carl Becker described in his own institution the nature of that break from tradition:

The quality and flavor of this freedom is easier to appreciate than to define. Academic is not the word that properly denotes it. It includes academic freedom, of course, but it is something more, and at the same time something less self-regarding, something more worldly, something, I will venture to say, a bit more impudent. It is, in short, too little schoolmasterish to be defined by a formula or identified by a professional code.[1]

The three legs on which the tripod stands are instruction, research, and extension. Here is an attempt to apply intelligent understanding to every aspect of living. In instruction, most of the colleges look upon undergraduate education as their primary purpose, from which graduate study, research and extension emerge as natural adjuncts and sequences. In instruction, too, the colleges have emphasized and attempted to practice the equality of all subjects. Each is reputable and all must stand under the ultimate test of usefulness to society.

Because of the early emphasis on agriculture, the colleges are known popularly for their agricultural endeavors and fruits. It is a matter of time and of public information to remedy a present misconception.

Under the stress of changing times, the colleges came to identify research and extension as functions coordinate to instruction. The end in view was "the performance of broad public services and participation in activities designed to serve both immediate and long-range needs of society." [2] Chiefly because of an early lack of subject matter for instruction, the colleges accepted a responsibility for the creation of knowledge. The responsibility for dissemination followed naturally. We have seen some of the struggle to keep this responsibility free from supervision and regulation, both from without in terms of government authority and from within in terms of performance.

The colleges have not always been successful in the complete integration of the trilogy of function. The tendency has been to develop isolated phases. This remains one of the major problems of administration. It will be solved in proportion to the emphasis given in individual colleges to the over-all goals. The Land-Grant Colleges have an opportunity to develop unity among trustees, faculty, students, and alumni, if all the constituent parts are made aware of this brand of education which has as much to offer as any other system. Conviction and enthusiasm over the unique land-grant scheme must be shared if the colleges are to realize their potentiality.

Social Consciousness

If there is one characteristic which most vividly marks the change of the Old World scheme into the New World pattern, it is the prevailing social consciousness of these institutions. Almost from the beginning, they were more concerned with service than with traditional academic criteria. In 1912, during the celebration of the 50th anniversary of the Morrill Act, President William Oxley Thompson had said, "The tendency . . . to operate an institution for the sake of maintaining standards is all wrong as I see it. An institution is to be operated for the good it can do; for the people it can serve; for the science it can promote; and for the civilization it can advance." The Land-Grant Colleges have attempted this ideal of service in every phase of their extensive program—in the advancement of agriculture, science, art, and industry; in the training of students as citizens; in the search for useful new truth; and in the relationship of the college to the life of the people. Their zeal has been almost missionary.

In a real sense, the colleges have become a mighty educational team rooted in the conviction that people, no matter of what level or kind, are of the utmost importance. They are proud and jealous of this prevailing social consciousness. To them, it is the long-missing, priceless ingredient of higher education in service to the nation. The basic unit of the social idea is the individual person. The colleges have told themselves that no academic achievement, technical skill, or educational technique is more important than the human being involved. In stressing the individual, their attention has not been centered on a mass, seething and groping toward some far distant light. In their literature and in their speeches, land-grant educators have sought to emphasize the typical individual looking for help along his way. Perhaps it has been a student, or a farmer, or an industrialist, or a housewife, but whoever he is and wherever he is, the colleges have attempted to be for him a symbol of the American educational dream. In their philosophy, the colleges have endeavored to represent the conviction that the individual citizen has dignity and importance not only in the sight of God but of man as well. Thus they seem to say that their moral right to exist depends upon the degree to which this conviction controls every program, every course, every project, and upon their ability to turn out citizen graduates who, by their living, demonstrate their belief.

Only in a democratic nation could this kind of philosophy prevail, for it is directed toward the people and not the state, despite the interest of government in founding and support of the colleges. In effect, they are much less state institutions than their outward form would lead us to believe. One of their presidents, Edmund Ezra Day, gave definition to the land-grant function as an instrument of the state in service to the people:

The rights of the state derive from the interests of the people. In other words, the state is an instrument with which the common good is promoted. It remains merely a means; back of it lies the end—the well-being of the people. This conception of the relationship between the people and the state . . . is, in a sense, the very cornerstone of our political structure. The state is never supreme in American thought. The interest and the well-being of the people are what give the state its ultimate reason for existence.[3]

The Land-Grant Colleges thus are committed to the concept that the state and the nation prosper in proporion to the development of the individual.

This social consciousness is of such strength in the thinking of the colleges that they look upon their ability to serve as the supreme criterion, and on the degree to which the ability is put to useful service, they rise or fall. They pride themselves on close relationship to the needs of the people. Their devotion to an education suited to the land and time reaches sometimes the point of relinquishment of other ideals. In an address in 1931 on "The Spirit of the Land-Grant Institutions," President W. J. Kerr told the colleges, "That land-grant institution, in fact, that most fully surrenders itself to the state and nation in a spirit of service, that institution shall truly be greatest among us." Service, in the eyes of the colleges, is a direct and practical response to public demands. Often it is not what the people *should* want but what they *do* want. The test is their ability to change with the changing needs of the people.

The fruits of this philosophy are shown in the growth of such instruments of service as research and extension. Thus they feel that, whereas the Old World regarded its educational institutions as the conservative backbone of society, the New World demands of its public colleges the ability and the desire to adapt themselves continually to changing times and, where possible, to anticipate society's needs. The colleges have not always been aware of the dangers inherent in this approach. Their attempt to keep current has sometimes delayed their progress and their long-range ability to serve.

On occasions, the expenditure of time, money and effort has caught up with the need just as the need changed. They have run the risk, too, of serving one public faction at the expense of others. So, too, their attempts to be all things to all men have sometimes led them to be accused of operating as "academic service stations." There are those who feel that their program is unrealistic and incompatible, that they cannot be institutions of higher learning and, at the same time, operate effectively in the marketplace. They have justified their position on the basis of their unique function in the integration of knowledge with life, wherever life may be. This desire for the intimate relation of learning with living has carried the college into the factory, the farm, and the home.

In instruction, the social consciousness has strongly emphasized utility. Subjects have been introduced and taught on the basis of their practical value. To this has been added the constant concern of the colleges over training for citizenship. President Frederick L. Hovde in 1954 echoed the high-minded intentions of the colleges which, unfortunately, remain too often the theory rather than the practice: "Every student, given the experience of higher education, must be taught, impressed, and so stimulated that he will give, throughout life, a real part of his intellect, energy, and time to the process of making democracy work, not only for his own benefit but also as proof to men everywhere that democracy can be achieved and through it the noblest aspirations of man can come to fulfillment."

In research, social consciousness results in the attempt to undertake only those efforts which have, as their ultimate purpose, the good of humanity. The scientists in the laboratories are urged to be concerned with the well-being of the largest portion of the human family. As early as 1892, President W. L. Broun observed, ". . . whether working with retort, microscope, or pruning or dissecting knife, you are working to ameliorate the condition of human life, and by showing how better to subdue the earth, to bring increased prosperity and happiness to the homes of the people, you are working not for self, but for the good of humanity."

Extension joins research in its humanitarian concern. The people are said, for instance, to be agriculture's basic resource, and, whereas production and income are important, "the necessity for helping people learn how to develop themselves and how to enjoy living are fields which cannot be overlooked." [4] In recent years, extension has come to put primary emphasis on the interests and needs of people, relegating methods and tools to secondary place.

The colleges pride themselves on this closeness to the people. They believe that the confidence and trust in which they are held are the result of their sensitivity to changing challenges of changing times. And thus they feel that there is no room for a dominating Ivory Tower on a land-grant campus. Where some colleges have regarded and continue to regard such a Tower as a point of pride, the

Land-Grant Colleges consider their greatest asset to be the confidence of the people. They are wary, too, lest they lose this confidence by erecting Ivory Towers in their midst. Instead they intend to be ready always to meet change. To maintain this confidence, in the words of President John A. Hannah, "it must always be cultivated and fertilized—cultivated through continuing useful services and fertilized with new ideas, new programs, new developments, to meet the ever changing public need."

Public confidence and trust is not easily won. Once won, it is held not without effort. From the beginning the colleges have never shied away from their public nature. They have, instead, attempted to be both national and state institutions. In their thinking, responsibility and opportunity are synonymous. Since they were born as a result of society's concerns, they consider themselves agencies of public progress, responsible for the ever-increasing enlightenment of those concerns. To realize such an accomplishment, they recognize, depends upon their objectivity and integrity.

Contributions to the Land and Time

Perhaps most important of all the contributions of the Land-Grant Colleges has been the conservation of human resources. This is seen in their substantial achievement of a democratization of higher education. They have believed from the beginning that intellectual capacity and achievement are not confined to those privileged by wealth or position. The fruits of this belief are apparent in the numbers of substantial leaders as well as enlightened citizens whom they have trained and returned to the cities as well as the villages and farms. They pride themselves on the graduates who have "quietly and effectively served their communities in unspectacular ways" and who have raised "the tone of American life without fanfare or the usual forms of public recognition."

So, too, they have added to the nation's supply of scientific and professional manpower. In recognition of their contribution, the report of the National Manpower Council in 1953 observed that "the most important, single governmental step in connection with the training of scientific and professional personnel was the Morrill Act of 1862, which laid the basis for the country's extensive state college and university system." [5] Not the least of their achievements has been one hard-earned. In terms of human resources, as we have seen, they have kept faith with a vague provision for military tactics in their original charter. Only in recent times has this service been recognized properly. In 1954, President Dwight D. Eisenhower told them:

. . . I am one of those who can bear sincere witness to the efficacy of that training and to the very great services you people and your predecessors have rendered to the United States of America on the field of battle, and I think I would be remiss in my capacity as Commander-in-Chief if I should fail to pay my tribute to all of that great body of individuals who have graduated from the military sections of your colleges and from those who dedicated their talents to helping in that education.

Their contribution has included, too, their lifelong service as strongholds of scientific investigation and thought. To them, as much as to any single group of institutions, goes the credit for the acceptance and appreciation of the potentiality of science to enrich human life. The results of the benefits of science and technology in all fields have expanded beyond measure the nation's material resources and raised substantially the standard of living. The contribution to agriculture, for instance, has not been limited to the farmer. The public has derived the ultimate benefit in better produce and lower prices. In general terms, President W. J. Kerr listed the extent of land-grant service to all men:

. . . great circles of helpful service . . . radiate from these centers— service that has changed deserts into gardens, redeemed abandoned lands, evolved new and more profitable crops, multiplied production, created new industries, conquered disease, destroyed pests and plagues, harnessed natural power and thereby increased human efficiency, guided agriculture and business, made science the handmaiden of the housewife as well as of the captains of industry, revealed the processes of nature, and put into the hands of man the tools that enable him to work with natural law in shaping his own destiny and that of his country.

Many of the contributions of the colleges now are so taken for granted that their origin has been forgotten. The benefits are not always direct, of course. As an example, one can point to the retired professor of physiology and applied botany, Benjamin M. Duggar, who left the University of Wisconsin after years of service to join the staff of Lederle Laboratories. Within a short time, he had discovered on a soil sample the first strain of a new species from which aureomycin was later obtained. It is safe to assume that there is not a single American citizen who has not been affected in some beneficial way, either directly or indirectly, by the scientific leadership of the Land-Grant Colleges.

The development of rural leadership, of the stimulus to mental growth of the rural people, is another obvious contribution. In reporting on the extension consolidation bill in 1953, the House Committee on Agriculture commented that "the Cooperative Extension Service, devoted to agricultural education, has contributed as much or more than any other Government agency to the improvement of rural life and to building the character of American youth . . ." The result of the college effort has been a gradual change in the attitude of farm people toward education and the uses of science. Derision and skepticism have given way to appreciation and acceptance.

The Land-Grant Colleges have contributed substantially to the pattern of American education. In their adherence to the philosophy of educational service, they have helped to change, to the benefit of student and nation, the purposes and programs of educational endeavor at all levels. Certainly they have influenced profoundly the public and private school system by their attempts to combine the liberal and practical in one curriculum and one student. They have established a respected place in American education for study in engineering, science, agriculture, home economics, and veterinary medicine. In their insistence on the equality of studies, they have wrought deep changes in all collegiate enterprises. In their willingness to undertake educational experiments, they have forced American higher education to keep more abreast of the times. In their acceptance and use of science as an important element in the general body of knowledge, they have helped to change the character of liberal arts in both private and public institutions. They have stimulated the tremendous growth of the American state university in quality as well as size. As President J. L. Morrill has observed, the impact of the Land-Grant Colleges on the democratization of higher education "made both possible and plausible the recommendation of the President's Commission [in 1948] that college enrollment in this country later be doubled." The future support of education at all levels "will proceed from the proof of enormous returns upon the national investment in the Land-Grant enterprise." In a real sense, then, the contributions of the Land-Grant Colleges to education have only begun to be felt. Their pattern is of the future, in America and in all free nations.

Federal Participation

An unusual feature of the land-grant scheme is the joint founding and subsidy by both Federal and state governments. The Federal interest has been justified on the basis of the national character of both agriculture and industry. Research and extension involved regional and national rather than purely state concerns. Federal interest was necessary to insure the continuance of fundamental research; state support might lead only to work on immediate and practical problems, the solution of which would be impossible without continued basic research. Federal participation was essential, too, to the cooperative character of both research and extension programs. The Land-Grant Colleges might never have come into existence, at least in their present form, had it not been for the Federal stimulus. A few states had begun the establishment of schools or colleges of agriculture by the time of the passage of the Morrill Act, but it is probable that not all would have followed suit. The Federal grants served the useful purpose of providing a common bond among the institutions. The Hoover Commission concluded:

The land-grant colleges have been an outstanding example of federal promotion of state leadership and initiative. The very large local support as compared with the relatively small present federal assistance is witness to this fact. . . . We have demonstrated through these programs that the federal government can promote specific causes in the fields of education whereby initiative and responsibility can be properly retained by the states.[6]

The Federal grants represented a distinct change from the previous pattern of Federal subsidy. Prior to the Morrill Act, Federal legislation was far from specific either in purpose or in control. Grants were made only with broad intentions. The 1862 Act, however, defined the objectives and created a new element of some supervision. The Commission on Intergovernmental Relations noted that "the first provision for Federal audit was in an 1895 amendment to the Hatch Act" and that the Smith-Lever legislation "contained further innovations . . . introduced apportionment formulas, dollar-for-dollar matching, and the requirement for advance approval of State plans by the National Government." [7] Despite the restrictions, however, the colleges have generally regarded Federal interest and control as a steadying influence, offering benefits and stimulation. Together with state participation, the scheme provided the institutions with a precautionary device discouraging complacency and self-satisfaction. Almost all land-grant legislation contains provision for amendment, suspension, or repeal, in effect serving notice to the colleges that continued subsidy depends on performance.

The Federal participation is an unusual example of decentralized control with matters of national interest locally sponsored and left primarily in the hands of those more familiar with local needs and conditions. Though the fear of Federal control of education has often been voiced, the land-grant history is an example of effective and fruitful relationships. With minor exceptions, there appears to have been no serious effort ever made by the Federal government to dictate curriculum or operations. Instead, the Federal grants often have enabled the colleges to resist state and local pressures. The land-grant Association has been another powerful factor in this maintenance of independence and authority. The Association has provided the leadership in discussion and negotiation and has been a constant watchdog over the interests of the member institutions. American tradition had favored from the start local control of educational matters and the separation of political interests from educational endeavor. Together with other factors, this has kept interference and control within bounds.

Grants for resident teaching have been the least subject to control and supervision. Through the years the Department of the Interior (and now the Department of Health, Education, and Welfare) has interpreted the legislation to mean Federal jurisdiction only over the proper expenditure of funds and not over quality. After detailed exploration, the Commission on Intergovernmental Relations concluded that the grants serve the useful purpose of "a benchmark against which the future posture of the Federal Government can be measured in relationship to higher education throughout the country

—namely, Federal financial assistance without any trace of Federal control of State educational policies, programs, and processes." [8]

Extension funds present a different picture in the provision for substantive and fiscal review and approval. Work plans and budgets must be submitted in advance and, according to the Commission's study, involve "considerations of balance and relative emphasis among projects, as well as considerations of a purely fiscal nature." This is accomplished, however, in an atmosphere of mutual cooperation and respect, as well as with continual communication and consultation. The United States Department of Agriculture has recognized the local nature of cooperative extension work and has limited its leadership to advice and persuasion, particularly with respect to relative balance and emphasis among programs, suggesting changes primarily where general national or state interests are involved.

In much the same fashion in research, the state is free to determine the problem to be studied, but must subject it on an annual plan basis to advance review and approval by the Federal office. Only infrequently over the years has Federal inspection resulted in interference with independence. As a result, the cooperation between the colleges and the Department of Agriculture has been regarded generally as a highly successful example of Federal-State relationships. Again after considerable study, the Commission on Intergovernmental Relations found the arrangement so satisfactory that it recommended no change. In terms of benefits, the results of Federal expenditure have been far beyond that normally expected from the relatively small amount of funds expended.

State Relationships

Historically, Federal initiative and interest have stimulated extended state support. In most of the Federal legislation there is either an implied or a stated obligation imposed upon the states either to match or to go beyond the Federal subsidy. As the institutions have grown, the states have assumed an increasingly larger share of the cost of operation. The colleges generally have regarded state support as a trust, imposing upon them responsibilities as well as opportunities. In addition to state support, the colleges have come to rely in increasing measure on student tuition and fees for a share, large or small, of their income, despite original intentions to provide education without charge.

The increased measure of state support has made the colleges more susceptible to the dangers of political interference. They have often protested that, since education concerns itself with all truth, the insitutions must be free to deal with any matter affecting human welfare in the manner in which they choose. President F. D. Farrell in 1940 stated well their case:

We should never forget that as scientific and educational agencies the Colleges are obligated to discover and disseminate truth; and that means the whole truth, in so far as it is known, and not merely such fractions of the truth as support a particular contention or belief, or as serve a particular special interest. It means unpleasant truth as well as pleasant truth. Only by telling the truth can we do our full duty as scientific and educational agencies. Only so can we be fair to the public, which looks to the Colleges for unbiased, reliable information. If we are to retain the respect and confidence of the public—not to mention our own self-respect—we must maintain unfalteringly our intellectual integrity.[9]

Primarily, difficulties have arisen out of the desire of governors and legislatures for more effective management of funds. President A. L. Strand commented in 1953 that "this is the point where an impairment of the authority of institutional governing boards is interposed, and where their judgment as properly constituted elements in the State government is countermanded in favor of the judgment on educational matter of officers quite removed from the educational scene and often not familiar with institutional objectives." He observed that "the mechanisms of control that have been created in State governments are a snare and a delusion," and that more money has been spent to save money than if the institutions had been left free. He concluded that "it is undeniable that education and research prosper in an atmosphere of freedom—even when appropriations are meager—and falter and lose their force and spirit when hampered by confining regulations."[10] With increasing support necessary due to increasing enrollments, the problems of the colleges in this regard unfortunately are bound also to increase.

THE IDEA IN ACTION

Instruction

The traditional aim of land-grant education has been a two-fold concern for the development of society and for the development of the individual to serve society. The attempt has been made to interweave learning and living. The Land-Grant Colleges have applied to higher education what President J. L. Morrill has called "the challenge of useful relevance." The Land-Grant Colleges have developed from institutions which were little more than trade schools. In this development, what was originally vocational education with emphasis on occupations has become professional education with the goal of broad training to fit a number of life careers. The colleges are not preparing plumbers and mechanics but engineers; not cooks and seamstresses but home economists; not so much practical farmers on the land as agricultural scientists. To do this, they have attempted to stress the fundamental disciplines above the practical techniques, the sustained pursuit of scholarship above the vocational art, and social consciousness above the narrow concern for employment and self-preservation. To them, social progress depends upon the highest degree of professional training. It is through his life work that an individual makes his contribution to society, and organized society has a major obligation to provide the kind of education from which it ultimately gains the most. President Edmund Ezra Day observed that "no free society has a real future in which an interest and a devotion to work does not constitute one of the prime, moving urges." The modern theory of progress for more and better "things" demands a central spot for professional education. To these colleges, then, all education is, in essence, professional, on the assumption that democratic life depends upon the contribution of each individual to the welfare of all and that the individual makes his contribution through his profession.

In this framework of thought liberal education, too, is regarded as useful. It helps to impart an understanding of principles underlying the practical. It gives over-all meaning to particular purposes and activities. President Lewis Webster Jones summed up the land-grant concept of liberal education by saying, "Liberal training, if properly conceived, is an attitude, a moral and humane approach to all knowledge, affecting people's lives and work; it is not something separate, academic and remote; and it is in the highest degree useful."

In so conceiving the function of education, the Land-Grant Colleges have recognized their particular responsibility for graduating citizens as well as professional men. As public institutions, they are aware of their obligation to add to the nation's leadership more than a fair share of responsible citizenry. Training for democratic citizenship, however, cannot be relegated to one course or confined to one experience, nor is it found just in the more liberal studies. The colleges believe that science and its application to life have as much to say about democracy as, for instance, the study of language and literature. To accomplish their assumed task, the colleges have attempted to achieve citizenship training through a broad institutional approach and through the opportunity of extracurricular experience. It is a worthy but elusive goal. There has not been sufficient success in dealing with the potential impact upon the student of the total educational experience. It is partly a result of specialization and partly a result of the vagueness of the appointed task.

The colleges appear to need course pruning and combining and a better synthesis, not by the addition of new courses but by reexamination of the old. There is need, too, for faculty who, in the words of President Virgil M. Hancher, "see their subject matter in relation to the whole field of modern learning and modern civilization." Hancher concludes:

In an institution possessing such teachers and likewise possessing an imaginative and intelligent student body, liberal education is bound to occur, whether the subject is contracts or classics, physics or politics, anatomy or art, soils or sociology, history or hydraulics. To use words which may have become slightly shopworn and overworked in recent years, we need teachers who teach with a sense of the "infinite and urgent." We need teachers who teach their subject matter not only as a means for developing techniques and skills, vitally important as these are, but also as the means for opening vistas which will challenge and inspire the student's imagination.[11]

This training for democratic citizenship through education denies the study of knowledge just for the sake of knowledge, denies the acquirement only of specific skills, and places education in an understanding relation to both society and the individual. Education becomes more concerned, therefore, with the development of values and attitudes.

Research

If knowledge is not to be pursued for the sake of knowledge in the land-grant classroom, so in the research laboratory, science is not investigated just for the sake of science. Here lies one of the fundamental difficulties of land-grant research efforts—the proper balance between the pure and the applied. As we have seen, most research began with practical problems. The inability to find solutions resulted in the emphasis on fundamental research knowledge. The practical results were only as valid as the fundamental work on which they were based. The famous Babcock butterfat test resulted from previous work in organic chemistry. The success of efforts to control disease, both plant and animal, came from the science of bacteriology. The discovery of hybrid corn was based on theoretical genetics. Streptomycin and aureomycin came after years of research in the processes of growth and reproduction.

The problem of the colleges in their research endeavors is to provide the balance between the fundamental and the practical and among all fields of learning. There remains an imbalance in the obvious stress on physical science research; the social sciences and the humanities, in the light of modern problems, need as much if not more attention. Man's ability to control human affairs has not advanced in the same measure as his ability to control the physical environment.

Extension

Ultimately land-grant extension work faces the same test as instruction and research—the right mixture of the practical with the theoretical. The demand for immediate results often runs the danger of obscuring equally important long-range objectives. In essence, all land-grant extension is essentially the same—concerned with the educational and cultural advancement of the people in their efforts to make a living and a life. In bringing the force of knowledge to bear on daily life, the colleges have contributed substantially to the common eagerness of the American people to learn more and to do better. The colleges are not content with offering only the immediate and practical. Their concern has led them to offer in extension much more than techniques; the emphasis is rather on values and attitudes. The stress on the individual as the basic unit has shown itself most graphically in cooperative extension's contribution to the development of a highly individualistic rural society in America. The individual family farm has been the bulwark against the movement toward the large corporate agricultural enterprise.

The development of adult education work has been one of the major contributions. Historically it has been confined largely to three main divisions: cooperative, including agriculture, home economics, veterinary medicine, and boys and girls club work; engineering; and general or university extension. It has paid rich dividends in activating the social ideals of the colleges and enabling them to reach the individual. To be true to its assumed task, the Land-Grant College of the future might well expand its extension endeavors to include every college and subject-matter department within its framework. As we have noted, the liberal arts in some land-grant institutions have failed to find their true role in keeping with land-grant philosophy. The faculties in the humanities and the social sciences have attempted with frustration to emulate the older private colleges. They fall back on the notion that their power lies in making themselves felt among only the few who should be accommodated within a "true community of scholars." The conviction sometimes lacking in the land-grant liberal arts might well be found in an increasing awareness of the role the liberal arts can play beyond the classroom in the lives of all the people.

Labor leaders have complained, too, about the lack of labor extension and research. In 1955, for instance, the Director of Education of the United Automobile Workers, Congress of Industrial Organizations, told an Association session, "There are no universities and colleges centered in a network of county agents and home demonstration agents, pitifully few short courses, no demonstration projects, no annual fairs to present visually to workers and their wives evidences of their work during the year or of the application of new ideas to their labors. . . ." Labor has been sharply aware of the preference shown to agriculture and industry, although certainly no other group of institutions has given as much attention to labor's needs.

The Land-Grant College of the future may well prosper in proportion to its ability to serve all classes and kinds, in keeping with its stated aims. It will necessitate the discovery of new methods and techniques, but, as President J. L. Morrill noted in 1948, to be still "unique, distinct, and indispensable," the colleges must be willing to pioneer in new directions.

The Future

In addition to increased service in new directions, the Land-Grant Colleges will be called upon to expand in size far beyond their present level. The substantial increase in the birthrate following World War II, accompanied by an increase in personal and social income, has swelled beyond all expectations the number of American youth flocking to the college doors. Their talents will be needed to serve the vastly increased adult population in such fields as science, industry, education, business, and the professions. Partly because of their philosophy and largely because of their inability to find the resources necessary to expansion, the nation's private institutions no longer will be able to carry their current proportionate share of the load. As a result, the burden will fall heavily on the publicly-supported institutions, of which group the Land-Grant Colleges are important members. As a report to the Governor's Conference observed in 1952, "Public funds remain the major source of funds with which to finance future increases in the cost of providing higher education for American youth." [12] If the funds are not forthcoming, the colleges will have to reappraise their program and their standards. Without adequate support for all phases, the institutions will be forced to eliminate some services now regarded as essential. So, too, new methods of education will have to be found, regardless of the availability of funds. Many of the land-grant institutions have established off-campus community colleges to reach more students at less cost both to the students and to the institutions.

The future brings another national challenge. Some years ago President James Bryant Conant of Harvard University reached a conclusion of even greater force today and of tremendous significance to the Land-Grant Colleges. At the inauguration of the Cornell president, he declared that "during the next century of academic history, university education in this Republic will be largely in the hands of the tax-supported institutions. As they fare, so fares the cultural and intellectual life of the American people." [13]

In Conclusion

In this volume we have examined the emergence of a new type of higher education. In their endeavor to be part and parcel of American life, the Land-Grant Colleges have, in one form or another, come to mirror the major values of the American people. Another and earlier president of Harvard had written not long after the passage of the Morrill Act that "when the American University appears, it will not be a copy of foreign institutions, or a hot-bed plant, but the slow and natural growth of American social and political habits, and an expression of the average aims and ambitions of the better educated classes." [14] This, in essence, is what the Land-Grant Colleges and Universities have become.

As the nation grew, it turned to education as an instrument of progress. The institutions, founded through Federal initiative and under state control, responded to the challenge. They came to look upon their task so seriously that one of their presidents was led to conclude, "The supreme test of the cardinal American doctrine— that the destinies of free men, in a state of civilization, are directed and determined by that process men call education—is being made through such institutions as this. If the Land-Grant College fails, neither democracy's goal of education nor education's goal of democracy will be reached." [15] Born out of America's worship of education, the Land-Grant Colleges strengthened that worship. Partially through their efforts, higher education came to be regarded as not so much a luxury as a national necessity. Before long, America had taken for granted the assumption that each individual, regardless of his economic or social status, should be given the opportunity to develop his innate abilities to the ultimate benefit not only to himself but to the nation. Each man was worth educating as a person and as a citizen in keeping with the Judeo-Christian and democratic belief in his dignity and worth.

The result in the land-grant institutions has been the presence of a cross-section of American life. The institutions have become an academic melting pot of all classes and kinds. With higher education of qualified youth now deemed a national necessity, college education is regarded no longer as a privilege but as a right. As rights are guaranteed by the state, so college education should be at public expense if not otherwise available. To meet the demand, the colleges opened their doors to an increasing number of American youth to whom they would furnish subjects for study to suit the needs and tastes of each generation of a changing nation.

Americans thus have reflected their values in the development of these educational instruments. The colleges have emphasized the dignity of labor, the combination of liberal and practical education, social consciousness, a widening of opportunity in the democratization of education, the potentiality of science, the freedom of education through secular control, the necessity for citizenship training, the regard for the student and citizen as an individual, and the idea of a university serving all the people throughout their lives.

From small acorns the great oaks have grown. Many decades ago Ezra Cornell commented on the opening of that university that there is not "a single thing finished." Proudly, it seems, the Land-Grant Colleges still echo that, in their own institutions, as yet not a single thing is finished. When the day arrives that it is finished, we are led to observe, that day shall find the institutions deadened to the needs of American society and no longer useful to the American people. In their ability to serve the changing needs of a changing nation the Land-Grant Colleges and Universities have demonstrated their value.

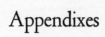

Appendixes

A. List of Land-Grant Colleges and Universities

Separate Colleges or Universities

(meaning not a part of a state university otherwise operating in the state, although the institution may be included in a state system of higher education)

	Main campus or headquarters
Alabama Polytechnic Institute	Auburn
Colorado State University	Fort Collins
Purdue University (Indiana)	Lafayette
Iowa State College of Agriculture and Mechanic Arts	Ames
Kansas State College of Agriculture and Applied Science	Manhattan
Massachusetts Institute of Technology	Cambridge
Michigan State University	East Lansing
Mississippi State College	State College
Montana State College	Bozeman
New Mexico College of Agriculture and Mechanic Arts	State College
North Carolina State College of Agriculture and Engineering	Raleigh
North Dakota Agricultural College	Fargo
Oklahoma Agricultural and Mechanical College	Stillwater
Oregon State College	Corvallis

Clemson Agricultural College of South Carolina	Clemson
South Dakota State College of Agriculture and Mechanic Arts	Brookings
Agricultural and Mechanical College of Texas	College Station
Utah State Agricultural College	Logan
Virginia Polytechnic Institute	Blacksburg
State College of Washington	Pullman

STATE OR TERRITORIAL UNIVERSITIES
(or parts thereof)

University of Alaska	College
University of Arizona	Tucson
University of Arkansas	Fayetteville
University of California	Berkeley
University of Connecticut	Storrs
University of Delaware	Newark
University of Florida	Gainesville
University of Georgia	Athens
University of Hawaii	Honolulu
University of Idaho	Moscow
University of Illinois	Urbana
University of Kentucky	Lexington
Louisiana State University	Baton Rouge
University of Maine	Orono
University of Maryland	College Park
University of Massachusetts	Amherst
University of Minnesota	Minneapolis
University of Missouri	Columbia
University of Nebraska	Lincoln
University of Nevada	Reno
University of New Hampshire	Durham
Rutgers University (The State University of New Jersey)	New Brunswick
Cornell University (New York)	Ithaca
Ohio State University	Columbus
Pennsylvania State University	University Park
University of Puerto Rico	Rio Piedras
University of Rhode Island	Kingston
University of Tennessee	Knoxville
University of Vermont	Burlington

West Virginia University	Morgantown
University of Wisconsin	Madison
University of Wyoming	Laramie

INSTITUTIONS ATTENDED PREDOMINANTLY BY NEGRO STUDENTS

Alabama Agricultural and Mechanical College	Normal
Agricultural, Mechanical and Normal College (Arkansas)	Pine Bluff
Delaware State College	Dover
Florida Agricultural and Mechanical University	Tallahassee
Fort Valley State College (Georgia)	Fort Valley
Kentucky State College	Frankfort
Southern University (Louisiana)	Baton Rouge
Maryland State College	Princess Anne
Alcorn Agricultural and Mechanical College (Mississippi)	Alcorn
Lincoln University (Missouri)	Jefferson City
Agricultural and Technical College of North Carolina	Greensboro
Langston University (Oklahoma)	Langston
South Carolina State College	Orangeburg
Tennessee Agricultural and Industrial State University	Nashville
Prairie View Agricultural and Mechanical College (Texas)	Prairie View
Virginia State College	Petersburg
West Virginia State College	Institute

OTHER MEMBERS OF THE AMERICAN ASSOCIATION OF LAND-GRANT COLLEGES AND STATE UNIVERSITIES

Connecticut Agricultural Experiment Station	New Haven
Georgia Institute of Technology	Atlanta
State University of New York	Albany
Texas Agricultural and Mechanical College System	College Station

B. Footnotes

Unless otherwise noted, *Proceedings* refer to the annual sessions of the Land-Grant College Association. See *Selected References* for changes in the name of the Association over the years.

1. THE BACKGROUND

1. Charles A. and Mary R. Beard, *A Basic History of the United States*, p. 245.

2. Carl L. Becker, *Cornell University: Founders and the Founding*, pp. 3–4.

3. Quoted in David Starr Jordan, *The Trend of the American University*, p. 86.

4. Becker, 17.

5. Andrew D. White, "The Need of Another University," *Forum*, 6 (January 1889), p. 466.

6. White, "The Need of Another University," 465.

7. William Watts Folwell, *Autobiography and Letters of a Pioneer of Culture*, quoted in Palmer O. Johnson, *Aspects of Land-Grant College Education*, p. 57.

8. Charles F. Thwing, *A History of Higher Education in America*, p. 258.

9. Writing in *American Farmer*, xii (1856), p. 69, and quoted in Alester G. Holmes and George R. Sherrill, *Thomas Green Clemson: His Life and Work*, p. 7.

10. Quoted in Elmer Ellsworth Brown, "The Origin of American State Universities," *University of California Publications in Education*, 3, 1 (April 10, 1903), p. 31.

11. Quoted in Earle D. Ross, *Democracy's College: The Land-Grant Movement in the Formative Stage*, p. 15.

12. *Proceedings of the Association of Land-Grant Colleges and Universities*, 45 (1931), p. 70.

13. From a paper by Clemson in 1859 on "The Necessity and Value of Scientific Instruction," *American Farmer*, xiv (1859), p. 275.

14. Eugene Davenport in *Proceedings*, 26 (1912), p. 159.

15. Quoted in Thwing, 421.

16. Henry Adams, *The Formative Years, A History of the United States during the Administrations of Jefferson and Madison*, quoted in William Edwin Sawyer, "The Evolution of the Morrill Act of 1862" (MS. Thesis, Boston University Library, 1948), p. 17.

17. *Albany Cultivator*, v (September 1838), p. 124.

18. Quoted by A. C. True in Report of the Bibliographer, *Proceedings*, 21 (1907), p. 18.

19. Louis F. Snow, *The College Curriculum in the United States*, p. 97.

20. Sawyer, 31.

21. A. C. True, *A History of Agricultural Education in the United States*, p. 7.

22. True, *A History of Agricultural Education*, p. 23.

23. Ross, *Democracy's College*, 17.

24. Ross, *Democracy's College*, 22.

25. *New York Weekly Tribune*, May 11, 1850.

26. Ross, *Democracy's College*, 27.

27. Burt E. Powell, *The Movement for Industrial Education and the Establishment of the University, 1840–1870*, Volume I of the Semi-Centennial History of the University of Illinois, p. 10.

28. Madison Kuhn, *Michigan State: The First Hundred Years, 1855–1955*, p. 20.

29. Quoted in W. J. Beal, *History of the Michigan Agricultural College*, pp. 23–24.

30. Beal, 139.

31. Beal, 138–139.

32. Ross, *Democracy's College*, 29.

33. Evan Pugh, *Endowment of Colleges for Agriculture and the Mechanic Arts*, p. 2.

34. Ross, *Democracy's College*, 31.

35. Barton Morgan, *A History of the Extension Service of Iowa State College*, p. 7.

36. Clemson, speaking on the importance of science in the development of agriculture, in an article on "Fertilizers" in the Patent Office Report of 1860, p. 150, and quoted in Holmes and Sherrill, 118.

37. Records of the Virginia Company, i, 220–268, quoted in Sawyer, 9.
38. Daniel Webster, Works, iii, p. 263, quoted in I. L. Kandel, Federal Aid for Vocational Education, p. 69.

2. THE FOUNDATION STONE, 1862

1. Prairie Farmer, xii, 3 (March 1852), p. 114, quoted in Fred H. Turner, Misconceptions Concerning the Early History of the University of Illinois, p. 5.
2. Mary Turner Carriel, The Life of Jonathan Baldwin Turner, pp. 121–128.
3. New York Tribune, February 26, 1853.
4. Jonathan B. Turner, "A Plan for an Industrial University for the State of Illinois," (Submitted to the Farmers' Convention at Granville, Illinois, November 18, 1851). Reprinted in Proceedings of the Society for the Promotion of Agricultural Science, xxviii, p. 68.
5. W. J. Kerr, Proceedings, 45 (1931). 71.
6. Morrill's letters to Ira Davis, quoted in Ross, Democracy's College, p. 48.
7. Kandel, Federal Aid, 7–8.
8. Morrill's comments quoted in Kandel, Federal Aid, 4–5.
9. Justin S. Morrill, State Aid to the U. S. Land Grant Colleges, n. p.
10. Congressional Globe, 46 Cong., 3 Sess., December 15, 1880.
11. Congressional Globe, 37 Cong., 2 Sess., Appendix 258.
12. Ross, Democracy's College, 46.
13. Congressional Globe, 34 Cong., 1 Sess., 530.
14. Congressional Globe, 35 Cong., 1 Sess., December 14, 1857.
15. Congressional Globe, 35 Cong., 2 Sess., 1414.
16. 12 Statutes at Large, 503–505 (1862).
17. "Our National Schools of Science," The North American Review, cv (October 1867), p. 504.
18. Sawyer, 221.
19. Becker, 31.
20. Justin S. Morrill, The Land-Grant Colleges, p. 10.
21. Earle D. Ross, "On Writing the History of Land-Grant Colleges and Universities," The Journal of Higher Education, xxiv, 8 (November 1953).
22. Proceedings, 57 (1943). 26–27.
23. Kandel, Federal Aid; 82.
24. Morrill, State Aid, 6 ff.
25. Morrill, The Land-Grant Colleges, 4 and 15.

26. R. A. Pearson, "The Place of the Mechanic Arts in Land-Grant Institutions," *Proceedings*, 29 (1915). 136.

27. A. J. Klein, dir., *Survey of Land-Grant Colleges and Universities*, i (1930), p. 797.

28. Quoted in Sawyer, 245.

29. Klein, *Survey*, i, 8.

30. "Our National Schools of Science," 506.

31. Becker, 36–37.

32. Edmund J. James, *The Origin of the Land Grant Act of 1862*, p. 13.

33. Samuel Eliot Morison and Henry Steele Commager, *The Growth of the American Republic*, ii, p. 196.

34. *Proceedings*, 37 (1923). 55.

35. Cornell University, *Account of the Proceedings at the Inauguration*, October 7, 1868, p. 6.

3. THE STRUGGLE, 1863–1879

1. Walter P. Rogers, *Andrew D. White and the Modern University*, p. 2.

2. W. Carson Ryan, *Studies in Early Graduate Education*, p. 5.

3. Evan Pugh, *A Report upon A Plan for the Organization of Colleges for Agriculture and the Mechanic Arts*, pp. 32–33.

4. "Our National Schools of Science," 498.

5. Rogers, 126.

6. Cornell University, *Account of the Proceedings*, 13. White quotes in his inaugural address this passage of Goldwin Smith's letter to him.

7. *Proceedings*, 45 (1931). 82–83.

8. C. R. Mann in *Proceedings*, 36 (1922). 255.

9. F. B. Mumford, *The Land-Grant College Movement*, p. 30.

10. Andrew D. White, *Address on Agricultural Education*, n. p.

11. *American Agriculturist*, xxvi (1867), p. 6, quoted in Ross, *Democracy's College*, 91.

12. Mumford, 29.

13. *Proceedings* (1885). 37.

14. Isaac Phillips Roberts, *Autobiography of a Farm Boy*, p. 109.

15. Mumford, 35.

16. Andrew Dickson White, *Scientific and Industrial Education in the United States*, p. 23.

17. Andrew D. White, *What Profession Shall I Choose, and How Shall I Fit Myself for It?*, pp. 16–17.

18. Andrew Dickson White, *Autobiography*, ii, pp. 341–342.

19. Dorothy Schaffter and Thomas Woody, "Education of Women," *Encyclopedia of Educational Research* (Revised Edition, 1950), p. 339.

20. Roberts, 93.

21. Cited in A. C. True, "Notes on the History of Agricultural Pedagogy in the United States," *Proceedings of the Society for the Promotion of Agricultural Science*, xxviii (1907), 91.

22. Cornell University, *Account of the Proceedings*, 7.

23. Rogers, 52, quoting Andrew D. White.

24. Ross, *Democracy's College*, 133–134.

25. Ross, *Democracy's College*, 114.

26. Quoted in Fred H. Turner, 25.

27. Beal, 35.

28. Roberts, 97–98.

29. Beal, 67–68.

30. Liberty Hyde Bailey in Introduction to Roberts, viii.

31. Ross, *Democracy's College*, 101.

32. Wayland Fuller Dunaway, *History of the Pennsylvania State College*, p. 38.

33. Roberts, 99.

34. Noah Porter, *The American Colleges and the American Public*, p. 9.

35. Porter, 273.

36. Roberts, 136.

37. Kuhn, 137.

38. White, *Address on Agricultural Education*, n. p.

39. Roberts, 96.

40. Pugh, *Endowment of Colleges*, 5.

41. Quoted in Kuhn, 139.

42. Ross, *Democracy's College*, 169.

4. THE IDEA TAKES SHAPE, 1880–1899

1. Wilson O. Clough, *A History of the University of Wyoming, 1887–1937*, p. 52.

2. E. A. Bryan, "Some Recent Changes in the Theory of Higher Education," *Proceedings*, 12 (1898). 89.

3. W. L. Broun in Presidential Address, *Proceedings*, 6 (1892). 62.

4. Roberts, 132.

5. *Proceedings*, 10 (1896). 75.

6. *Proceedings*, 10 (1896). 80.

7. Editorial comment in the *Laramie* (Wyoming) *Sentinel*, May 1, 1866, quoted in Clough, 21.

8. *Proceedings*, 12 (1898). 96.

9. Ross, "On Writing the History."

10. Speaking on "Home Economics in a College Course," *Proceedings*, 20 (1906). 93.

11. S. M. Tracy, "Agricultural Research," *Proceedings of the Society for the Promotion of Agricultural Science*, xxviii (1907). 37.

12. *Proceedings* (1885). 32–33.

13. Mumford, 92.

14. *Proceedings*, 2 (1889). 29.

15. Quoted in Association of Land-Grant Colleges and Universities, *The Land-Grant Institutions and Their Relationships to Federal, State and Local Governments*, (A Report to the Commission on Intergovernmental Relations, 1954), p. 10.

16. Report of the College of Agriculture, Cornell University, Bulletin 137, 1897, as cited in Ruby Green Smith, *The People's Colleges: A History of the New York State Extension Service in Cornell University and the State, 1876–1948*, p. 65.

17. George Francis James, ed., *Handbook of University Extension*, p. 314.

18. Beal, 100.

19. J. L. Hills, "The Builders of the Association," *Proceedings*, 42 (1928). 25.

5.   FORM AND SUBSTANCE, 1900–1914

1. Thwing, 456.

2. Franklin M. Reck, *The 4-H Story: A History of 4-H Club Work*, p. 6.

3. Association of Land-Grant Colleges and Universities, *The Land-Grant Institutions*, 27. McKinley's comment is quoted as a statement to a committee of the American Association of Agricultural Colleges and Experiment Stations in November, 1901.

4. Clough, 69, quoting Colonel Downey in an 1897 report at the time of his resignation as president of the Wyoming Board.

5. D. F. Houston, Secretary of Agriculture, at 1914 Association meeting, *Proceedings*, 28 (1914). 21.

6. *Proceedings*, 18 (1904). 59.

7. Eugene Davenport in *Proceedings*, 26 (1912). 161.

8. Liberty Hyde Bailey in Presidential Address, *Proceedings*, 21 (1907). 60.

9. *Proceedings*, 11 (1897). 95.

10. *Proceedings*, 14 (1900). 34–35.

11. *Proceedings*, 19 (1905). 69.

12. *Proceedings*, 18 (1904). 60.

13. W. E. Stone in *Proceedings*, 19 (1905). 94–95.

14. *Proceedings*, 19 (1905). 71.

15. V. O. Key, Jr., *The Administration of Federal Grants to States*, pp. 369–370, cited in George A. Works and Barton Morgan, *The Land Grant Colleges*, p. 35.

16. Eugene Davenport, "The Relations Between the Federal Department of Agriculture and Agricultural Colleges and Experiment Stations," *Proceedings*, 27 (1913). 125 and 130.

17. Andrew M. Soule, "Contributions of the Land-Grant Colleges and Universities to Our Social and Economic Progress," *Proceedings*, 44 (1930). 32 ff.

18. *Proceedings*, 19 (1905). 100.

19. *Proceedings*, 18 (1904). 60.

20. Mary Geisler Phillips in Smith, 352–353.

21. True, *A History of Agricultural Extension Work*, 60.

22. *Proceedings*, 25 (1911). 37.

23. Mumford, 133–134.

24. *Proceedings*, 25 (1911). 219.

25. Quoted in Reck. 67.

26. Excerpt from Report of the Commission in *Proceedings*, 23 (1909). 39.

27. *Proceedings*, 25 (1911). 34.

28. Senator Hoke Smith speaking in 1912 at an Association convention, *Proceedings*, 26 (1912). 18–19.

29. *Proceedings*, 45 (1931). 86.

30. *Proceedings*, 38 (1924). 272.

31. Dunaway, 292.

32. Kuhn, 197–198.

6.   THE RESPONSE TO CRISES, 1915–1937

1. Milton S. Eisenhower, "Responsibilities and Potentialities of the Land-Grant Colleges and Universities," *Proceedings*, 66 (1952). 28.

2. Klein, dir., *Survey*, i, 73.

3. *Proceedings*, 43 (1929). 167.

4. *Proceedings*, 30 (1916). 250.

5. Reported by F. D. Farrell, *Proceedings*, 54 (1940). 27.

6. *Proceedings*, 38 (1924). 391.

7. Ernest V. Hollis, "Graduate School," *Encyclopedia of Educational Research* (Revised Edition, 1950), ed. Walter S. Monroe, p. 512.

8. Hollis, 512.

9. W. J. Kerr, *Proceedings*, 45 (1931). 79–80.

10. Clarence Beaman Smith and Meredith Chester Wilson, *The Agricultural Extension System of the United States*, p. 40.

11. *Proceedings*, 49 (1935). 234.

12. Chester C. Davis, "The Extension Service and the A.A.A.," *Proceedings*, 48 (1934). 169.

13. *Proceedings*, 48 (1934). 41.

14. *Proceedings*, 52 (1938). 114.

15. True, *A History of Agricultural Extension Work*, 181–182. The survey was published as Circular 148, USDA, *The Farm Woman's Problem*.

16. Quoted by C. W. Warburton, *Proceedings*, 49 (1935). 262.

17. Jane S. McKimmon, "Home Demonstration Work—Its Beginning," in R. K. Bliss, ed., *The Spirit and Philosophy of Extension Work*, p. 68.

18. Reck, 133, 147, 211, 238.

19. Smith, 190.

20. Louis E. Reber, "University Extension in Land-Grant College," Chapter XIII of Part II, *Land-Grant College Education, 1910 to 1920*, p. 90.

21. *Proceedings*, 30 (1916). 38.

22. Speaking at the convention of 1924, *Proceedings*, 38 (1924). 57.

23. Speaking at the convention of 1932, *Proceedings*, 46 (1932). 50.

7. MATURITY, 1938–1956

1. Mumford, 63.

2. Report of Committee on Postwar Agricultural Policy, *Proceedings*, 59 (1945). 71.

3 *Proceedings*, 59 (1945), 73.

4. Commission on Intergovernmental Relations, *A Description of Twenty-five Federal Grant-in-Aid Programs*, p. 30.

5. *Proceedings*, 67 (1953). 225.

6. T. R. McConnell and Ruth E. Eckert, "The University Curriculum Survey," *Studies in Higher Education*, University of Minnesota Committee on Educational Research, Biennial Report, 1940–42, cited in Minnesota Commission on Higher Education, *Higher Education in Minnesota*, p. 329.

7. Robert M. Hutchins, *The Higher Learning in America*, p. 8.

8. President's Commission on Higher Education, *Higher Education for American Democracy*, i, p. 49.

9. Edmund Ezra Day, "General Education in the Land-Grant Institutions," *Proceedings*, 64 (1950). 245.

10. C. B. Hutchison, "The Liberal Education of the 'Industrial Classes,'" *Proceedings*, 58 (1944). 26.

11. Association of Land-Grant Colleges and Universities, *Some Educational Questions Confronting Land-Grant Colleges and Universities*, p. 11 ff.

12. Kuhn, 288.

13. General of the Army Omar N. Bradley, "Remarks on the World Military Situation," *Proceedings*, 66 (1952). 46.

14. Hollis P. Allen, *The Federal Government and Education*, p. 249.

15. Ruth Ecker, "The University Faculty Load Study," cited in Minnesota Commission, 340.

16. James R. Killian, Jr., "Industrial Research in Engineering Colleges: Its Benefits and Hazards," *Proceedings*, 62 (1948). 190.

17. United States Department of Agriculture and Association of Land-Grant Colleges and Universities, *Joint Committee Report on Extension Programs, Policies and Goals*, p. 20.

18. Commission on Intergovernmental Relations, *A Description of Twenty-Five*, 12.

19. Dunaway, 410.

20. Allen, 103.

21. A few of the Negro colleges evidently were members of the Association during the late eighties and nineties. The 1893 *Proceedings*, for instance, lists, among the "visitors and delegates," representatives from Hampton Institute and Alcorn, in the same manner as representatives from other colleges. The Treasurer's report for that year also shows dues received from Hampton and Alcorn. There is no indication, however, in what year they dropped out and for what reasons. Their names are not listed in any *Proceedings* after 1899.

8.   THE NEGRO LAND-GRANT COLLEGES

1. Gandy, *Proceedings*, 39 (1925). 99.

2. John W. Davis, "The Negro Land-Grant Colleges," *Journal of Negro Education*, 2 (1933), cited in Horace M. Bond, "Negro Education," *Encyclopedia of Educational Research* (Revised Edition, 1950), p. 786.

3. Works and Morgan, 25.

4. Works and Morgan, 79.

9.   SOME PHILOSOPHY AND SOME CONCLUSIONS

1. Becker, 194.

2. Council of State Governments, *Higher Education in the Forty-Eight States,* p. 20.

3. Edmund Ezra Day, *Primary Elements of the American Tradition,* p. 4.

4. USDA and ALGCU, *Joint Committee Report,* 61.

5. National Manpower Council, *A Policy for Scientific and Professional Manpower,* p. 248.

6. Allen, 219.

7. Commission on Intergovernmental Relations, *A Report to the President for Transmittal to the Congress,* p. 119–120.

8. Commission on Intergovernmental Relations, *A Study Committee Report on Federal Aid to Agriculture,* p. 10.

9. F. D. Farrell, "Lest We Forget," *Proceedings,* 54 (1940). 28.

10. A. L. Strand, "Land-Grant Colleges and the State," *Proceedings,* 67 (1953). 225.

11. Virgil M. Hancher, "Liberal Education in Professional Curricula," *Proceedings,* 67 (1953). 51.

12. Council of State Governments, 5.

13. Quoted by J. L. Morrill, *Proceedings,* 57 (1943). 67.

14. C. W. Eliot, "The New Education," *The Atlantic Monthly,* xxiii (February 1869), p. 216, and quoted in Rogers, 197.

15. Edward C. Elliott, *There Are Giants on the Earth in These Days,* pp. 5–6.

C. Selected References

GENERAL

ALLEN, H. K., in collaboration with RICHARD G. AXT, *State Public Finance and State Institutions of Higher Education in the United States*. (Published for the Commission on Financing Higher Education). New York: Columbia University Press, 1952.

ALLEN, HOLLIS P., *The Federal Government and Education*. (Subtitled: "The Original and Complete Study of Education for the Hoover Commission Task Force on Public Welfare.") New York: McGraw-Hill Co., 1950.

ANDERSON, WILLIAM, *The Nation and the States, Rivals or Partners?* Minneapolis: The University of Minnesota Press, 1955.

ARMSBY, HENRY H., "A Review of Proposals for Federal Support of Engineering Research in the College," *Engineering Experiment Station Record* (Bulletin of the Engineering Section of the Association of Land-Grant Colleges and Universities), 27:4, October, 1947, pp. 34–37.

ASSOCIATION OF AMERICAN AGRICULTURAL COLLEGES AND EXPERIMENT STATIONS, *Report of the Committee on Station Work*, 1887. Published by the Commissioner of Agriculture. Washington: Government Printing Office, 1888.

ASSOCIATION OF LAND-GRANT COLLEGES AND UNIVERSITIES, *Proceedings*, Published under varying names and auspices, as follows:

1885—*Proceedings* of a Convention of Delegates from Agricultural Colleges and Experiment Stations. Department of Agriculture Miscellaneous Report No. 9, 1885. Washington: Government Printing Office, 1885.

1887—*Proceedings* of the First Annual Convention of the American Association of Agricultural Colleges and Experiment Stations. Reconstructed from manuscript notes. Washington: Association of Land-Grant Colleges and Universities, 1941.

302

1889 (Second Convention) through 1909 (Twenty-third Convention) —*Proceedings* of the American Association of Agricultural Colleges and Experiment Stations. Published as Miscellaneous Reports or Bulletins of the United States Department of Agriculture, Office of Experiment Stations. Washington: Government Printing Office.

1910 (Twenty-Fourth Convention) through 1919 (Thirty-Fourth Convention)—*Proceedings* of the American Association of Agricultural Colleges and Experiment Stations. Published by the Association.

1920 (Thirty-Fourth Convention) through 1925 (Thirty-Ninth Convention)—*Proceedings* of the Association of Land-Grant Colleges. Published by the Association.

1926 (Fortieth Convention) through 1954 (Sixty-Eighth Convention) —*Proceedings* of the Association of Land-Grant Colleges and Universities. Published by the Association.

(Note: In 1955 the name of the Association was changed to American Association of Land-Grant Colleges and State Universities. *Proceedings* henceforth will carry this name.)

————, *The Land-Grant Institutions and Their Relationships to Federal, State and Local Governments*, A Report of the Commission on Intergovernmental Relations by the Association. Washington: Association of Land-Grant Colleges and Universities, 1954. (Mimeographed)

————, *Some Educational Questions Confronting the Land-Grant Colleges and Universities*. (Subtitle: "A Manual of Inquiry Concerning the Report of the President's Commission on Higher Education.") Washington: Association of Land-Grant Colleges and Universities, 1948.

ATWOOD, RUFUS B., "A Functional Program for the Negro Land Grant College," *The Negro College Quarterly*, 11:2, June, 1944.

BEARD, CHARLES A., and MARY R., *A Basic History of the United States*. Garden City, N. Y.: Garden City Books, 1952.

BEVIER, ISABEL, *Home Economics in Education*. Philadelphia: J. B. Lippincott Co., 1924.

BEVIER, ISABEL, and SUSANNAH USHER, *The Home Economics Movement: Part I*. Boston: Whitcomb & Barrows, 1912.

BITTNER, WALTON S., *The University Extension Movement*. United States Department of the Interior, Bureau of Education, Bulletin No. 84, 1919. Washington: Government Printing Office, 1920.

BLACKMAR, FRANK W., *The History of Federal and State Aid to Higher Education*, United States Department of the Interior, Bureau of Education, Circular No. 1, 1890. Washington: Government Printing Office, 1890.

BLISS, R. K., editor, *The Spirit and Philosophy of Extension Work* (as recorded in Significant Extension Papers). Published jointly by the Graduate School, United States Department of Agriculture, and the Epsilon Sigma Phi, National Honorary Extension Fraternity. Washington: 1952.

BOND, HORACE M., "Negro Education," Encyclopedia of Educational Research, Revised Edition, 1950, Walter S. Monroe, editor, pp. 777–795.

BREWER, WILLIAM H., "The First New York State Agricultural College and What Came Before It." Unpublished manuscript, Cornell University Library, n.d.

BRODY, ALEXANDER, The American State and Higher Education (The Legal, Political and Constitutional Relationships). Washington: American Council on Education, 1935.

BROWN, ELMER ELLSWORTH, "The Origin of American State Universities." University of California Publications in Education, Vol. 3, No. 1, April 10, 1903, pp. 1–45. Berkeley, Calif.: University of California Press, 1903.

BRUNNER, EDMUND DeS., IRWIN T. SAUNDERS, and DOUGLAS ENSMINGER, Farmers of the World: The Development of Agricultural Extension. New York: Columbia University Press, 1945.

BRUNNER, EDMUND DeS., and E. HSIN PAO YANG, Rural America and the Extension Service. New York: Columbia University Teachers College, 1949.

CHAPMAN, O. J., "A Historical Study of Negro Land-Grant Colleges in Relationship with Their Social, Economic, Political, and Educational Backgrounds and a Program for Their Improvement." Unpublished Doctor's dissertation, Ohio State University, 1940.

COFFMAN, LOTUS D., The State University, Its Work and Problems. Minneapolis: The University of Minnesota Press, 1934. (A selection from addresses delivered between 1921 and 1933.)

COMMISSION ON INTERGOVERNMENTAL RELATIONS, Reports. Washington: June 1955. Including the following publications:
A Survey Report on The Impact of Federal Grants-in-Aid on the Structure and Functions of State and Local Governments. Submitted to the Commission by the Governmental Affairs Institute.
Summaries of Survey Reports on The Administrative and Fiscal Impact of Federal Grants-in-Aid. Prepared from original survey reports submitted to the Commission by Management Consulting and Research Organizations.
A Description of Twenty-Five Federal Grant-in-Aid Programs. Submitted to the Commission.
A Study Committee Report on Natural Resources and Conservation.

Submitted to the Commission by the Study Committee on Natural Resources and Conservation.

A *Study Committee Report on Federal Aid to Agriculture.* Submitted to the Commission by the Study Committee on Federal Aid to Agriculture.

A *Report to the President for Transmittal to the Congress.* Final Report of the Commission.

CONFERENCE OF PRESIDENTS OF NEGRO LAND-GRANT COLLEGES, *Proceedings of the Twenty-eighth Annual Session,* October 17–18–19, 1950, U. S. Office of Education, Washington, D. C., and Called Session, March 21, 1951, Convention Hall, Atlantic City, New Jersey. Frankfort, Kentucky: Office of the Secretary of the Conference, n.d. (The *Proceedings* are titled: "The Negro Land Grant College at Mid-Century . . . In Retrospect . . . In Prospect.")

CONNECTICUT AGRICULTURAL EXPERIMENT STATION, THE, *75th Anniversary Proceedings.* September 28–29, 1950. n.p., n.d. (Presumably published by the Station.)

CORNELL UNIVERSITY, *Account of the Proceedings at the Inauguration,* October 7, 1868. Ithaca: University Press, 1889.

———, *Report of the Committee on Organization* (Presented to the Trustees of Cornell University, October 21st, 1866). Albany, New York: C. Van Benthuysen & Sons' Printing House, 1867.

COUNCIL OF STATE GOVERNMENTS, THE, *Higher Education in the Forty-Eight States* (A Report to the Governor's Conference, 1952). Chicago: The Council of State Governments, 1952.

CROSBY, DICK J., *Organization and Work of Agricultural Experiment Stations in the United States.* United States Department of Agriculture, Office of Experiment Stations. Washington: Government Printing Office, 1904.

CURTI, MERLE, *The Social Ideas of American Educators.* New York: Scribners, 1935.

DAVIDSON, JAY B., and HERBERT M. HAMLIN and PAUL C. TAFT, *A Study of the Extension Service in Agriculture and Home Economics in Iowa.* Ames, Iowa: Collegiate Press, 1933.

DAVIS, JOHN W., "The Negro Land-Grant College," *Journal of Negro Education,* 2:312–328, 1933.

———, "The Participation of Negro Land-Grant Colleges in Permanent Federal Educational Funds," *Journal of Negro Education,* 7:282–291, 1938.

DAY, EDMUND EZRA, *Primary Elements of the American Tradition.* Ithaca: Cornell University, 1942.

EDWARDS, NEWTON, and HERMAN G. RICHEY, *The School in the American Social Order*. New York: Houghton Mifflin Co., 1947.

ELIOT, CHARLES W., *The Trend to the Concrete and Practical in Modern Education*. New York: Houghton Mifflin Co., 1913.

ELLIOTT, EDWARD C., *There Are Giants on the Earth in These Days*. Corvallis, Oregon: Oregon State Agricultural College, 1930. (Commencement Address at the College, June 2, 1930.)

FINE, BENJAMIN, *Democratic Education*. New York: Thomas Y. Crowell Co., 1945.

FOERSTER, NORMAN, *The American State University: Its Relation to Democracy*. Chapel Hill, North Carolina: University of North Carolina Press, 1937.

FOREIGN OPERATIONS ADMINISTRATION, *Technical Cooperation in Agriculture*. Washington: Office of Public Reports, Foreign Operations Administration, n.d.

FOSTER, WILLIAM T., *Administration of the College Curriculum*. Boston: Houghton Mifflin Co., 1911.

GABRIEL, RALPH H., *Main Currents in American History*. New York: D. Appleton-Century Co., 1942.

GARBER, L. O., "History and Present Status of Military Training in Land-Grant Colleges." Unpublished Master's thesis, University of Illinois, 1926.

GATES, PAUL, *The Wisconsin Pine Lands of Cornell University: A Study in Land Policy and Absentee Ownership*. Ithaca: Cornell University Press, 1943.

GRAY, WILLIAM S., editor, *General Education: Its Nature, Scope and Essential Elements*. (Proceedings of the Institute for Administrative Officers of Higher Institutions, Volume VI). Chicago: University of Chicago Press, 1934.

HAGAN, WILLIAM A., "Veterinary Medical Education—Its Evolution and Present Status." Unpublished address given on the occasion of the dedication of the veterinary hospital building, University of Minnesota, St. Paul, October 25, 1950.

HALLIDAY, SAMUEL DUMONT, *History of the Agricultural College Land-Grant of July 2, 1862, Together with a Statement of the Condition of the Fund, Derived therefrom as it now exists in Each State of the Union*. Ithaca, N.Y.: Journal Book and Commercial Printing House, 1890.

HAMILTON, JOHN, *Farmers' Institutes in the United States*. United States Department of Agriculture, Office of Experiment Stations Publication. Washington: Government Printing Office, 1904.

HARDIN, CHARLES M., *Freedom in Agricultural Education.* Chicago: University of Chicago Press, 1955.

HARVARD COMMITTEE, *General Education in a Free Society.* Cambridge, MASS.: Harvard University Press, 1945. (Report of the Harvard Committee on the Objectives of a General Education in a Free Society.)

HAWLEY, R. D., "The Business Administration and Financial Management of a Land-Grant College." Unpublished Master's thesis, Boston University, 1938.

HAYES, CECIL B., *The American Lyceum: Its History and Contribution to Education.* United States Department of the Interior, Office of Education, Bulletin No. 12, 1932. Washington: Government Printing Office, 1932.

HOFSTADTER, RICHARD, and C. DEWITT HARDY, *The Development and Scope of Higher Education in the United States.* New York: Columbia University Press, 1952. (Published for the Commission on Financing Higher Education.)

HOFSTADTER, RICHARD, and WALTER P. METZGER, *The Development of Academic Freedom in the United States.* New York: Columbia University Press, 1955.

HOLLIS, ERNEST V., "Graduate School," *Encyclopedia of Educational Research,* Revised Edition, 1950, Walter S. Monroe, editor, pp. 510–519.

HOLMES, ALESTER G., and GEORGE R. SHERRILL, *Thomas Green Clemson: His Life and Work.* Richmond, Virginia: Garrett and Massie, Inc., 1937.

HOLMES, DWIGHT OLIVER WENDELL, *The Evolution of the Negro College.* Teachers College, Columbia University, Contributions to Education, No. 609. New York: Bureau of Publications, Teachers College, Columbia University, 1934.

HUTCHINS, ROBERT M., *The Higher Learning in America.* New Haven: Yale University Press, 1936.

IOWA STATE COLLEGE, *The Role of the Land-Grant College in Governmental Agricultural Programs.* Iowa State College Bulletin, Vol. XXXVIII, No. 2, June 8, 1938. Ames: Iowa State College, 1938. (Report prepared by a Committee of the Faculty.)

JAMES, EDMUND J., *The Origin of the Land Grant Act of 1862.* (Subtitle: "The so-called Morrill Act, and Some Account of its Author, Jonathan B. Turner"). University of Illinois Studies, Vol. IV, No. 1. Urbana, Illinois: University Press, 1910.

JAMES, GEORGE FRANCIS, editor, *Handbook of University Extension.* Philadelphia: American Society for the Extension of University Teaching, 1893. (Second Edition.)

JOHN, WALTON C., editor, *Land-Grant College Education, 1910 to 1920.* Survey by the Department of the Interior, Bureau of Education. Washington: Government Printing Office. Published in five volumes with titles and dates as follows:
Part I—*History and Education Objectives.*
   Bulletin, 1924, No. 30.
Part II—*The Liberal Arts and Sciences including Miscellaneous Subjects and Activities.* Bulletin, 1924, No. 37.
Part III—*Agriculture.*
   Bulletin, 1924, No. 37.
Part IV—*Engineering and Mechanic Arts.*
   Bulletin, 1925, No. 5.
Part V—*Home Economics.*
   Bulletin, 1925, No. 29.

JOHNSON, PALMER O., *Aspects of Land-Grant College Education.* Minneapolis: University of Minnesota Press, 1934.

JONES, LEWIS WEBSTER, *Inaugural Address* as President of the University of Arkansas, June 9, 1947. University of Arkansas Bulletin, Vol. 41, No. 15, October 1, 1947. Fayetteville, Arkansas: University of Arkansas, 1947.

JORDAN, DAVID STARR, *The Trend of the American University.* Stanford: Stanford University Press, 1929. (Includes addresses in 1887 and 1898, and an article in 1927.)

KANDEL, I. L., *Federal Aid for Vocational Education.* A Report to The Carnegie Foundation for the Advancement of Teaching, Bulletin No. 10. New York: Carnegie Foundation, 1917.

KELLY, F. J., director, *National Survey of the Higher Education of Negroes.* 3 vols. United States Office of Education, Miscellaneous No. 6, 1942. Washington: Government Printing Office, 1942.

————, and J. H. MCNEELY, *The State and Higher Education.* New York: The Carnegie Foundation for the Advancement of Teaching, 1933.

KELLY, ROBERT LINCOLN, *The American Colleges and the Social Order.* New York: The Macmillan Co., 1940.

KELSEY, LINCOLN DAVID, and CANNON CHILES HEARNE, *Cooperative Extension Work.* Ithaca, New York: Comstock Publishing Co., 1949.

KILE, ORVILLE MERTON, *The Farm Bureau Through Three Decades.* Baltimore, Md.: The Waverly Press, 1948.

KLEIN, A. J., director, *Survey of Land-Grant Colleges and Universities.*

United States Department of the Interior, Office of Education, Bulletin No. 9, 1930. 2 vols. Washington: Government Printing Office, 1930.

————, director, *Survey of Negro Colleges and Universities*. United States Department of the Interior, Bureau of Education, Bulletin No. 7, 1928. Washington: Government Printing Office, 1928.

LANE, D. A., JR., "The Development of the Present Relationship of the Federal Government to Negro Education," *Journal of Negro Education*, 7:273–281, 1938.

LIAUTARD, A. F. A., "History and Progress of Veterinary Medicine in the United States," *American Veterinary Review*, I:5–19, 1877.

McNEELY, J. H., *Higher Educational Institutions in the Scheme of State Government*. United States Office of Education, Bulletin No. 3, 1939. Washington: Government Printing Office, 1939.

MANN, C. R., editor, *A Study of Engineering Education*. Carnegie Foundation for the Advancement of Teaching, Bulletin No. 11, 1918, by a Joint Committee on Engineering Education of the National Engineering Societies. New York: Carnegie Foundation for the Advancement of Teaching, 1918.

MAYS, A. B., *The Concept of Vocational Education in the Thinking of the General Educator, 1845 to 1945*. University of Illinois Bureau of Educational Research, Bulletin No. 62. Urbana, Illinois: University of Illinois, 1946.

————, *Principles and Practices of Vocational Education*. New York: McGraw-Hill Book Co., 1948.

MEADOWS, JOHN CASSIUS, *The Functions of a State University*. Contributions to Education No. 28. Nashville: George Peabody College, 1927.

MINNESOTA COMMISSION ON HIGHER EDUCATION, *Higher Education in Minnesota*. Minneapolis: University of Minnesota Press, 1950.

MOORE, ROSS E., "Land-Grant Institutions and Technical Cooperation," *Turrialba*, 1:6, October 1951, pp. 276–277.

MORISON, SAMUEL ELIOT, and HENRY STEELE COMMAGER, *The Growth of the American Republic*. 2 vols. New York: Oxford University Press, 1940.

MORRILL, JUSTIN S., *The Land-Grant Colleges*, An Address delivered at the University of Vermont and State Agricultural College, June 28, 1893. Burlington, Vermont: 1893.

————, *State Aid to the U. S. Land-Grant Colleges*, An Address in Behalf of the University of Vermont and the State Agricultural College delivered in the Hall of Representatives at Montpelier on October 10, 1888. Burlington, Vermont: Free Press Association, 1888.

Morse, H. T., editor, *General Education in Transition*. Minneapolis: University of Minnesota Press, 1951.

Morton, John R., *University Extension in the United States*, University, Alabama: University of Alabama Press, 1953. (A Study by the National University Extension Association, Made with the Assistance of a Grant from The Fund for Adult Education.)

Mumford, Frederick B., *Fifty Years of Agriculture Experiment Station Work*. Columbia, Missouri: Missouri Agricultural Experiment Station, 1938. (An Address delivered at the Fiftieth Anniversary Exercises, June 21, 1938.)

————, *The Land-Grant College Movement*. Missouri Agricultural Experiment Station, Bulletin No. 419, 1940. Columbia, Missouri: Missouri Agricultural Experiment Station, 1940.

Nash, Willard L., *A Study of the Stated Aims and Purposes of the Departments of Military Sciences and Tactics and Physical Education in the Land-Grant Colleges of the United States*. Teachers College, Columbia University, Contributions to Education, No. 614. New York: Bureau of Publications, Teachers College, Columbia University, 1934.

National Association of State Universities, *Transactions and Proceedings*. Vols. I–LII, 1902–1954. Published by the Association.

National Manpower Council, *A Policy for Scientific and Professional Manpower*. May 18, 1953 Report of National Manpower Council, No. 2 of 3 studies. New York: Columbia University Press, 1953.

National Society for the Study of Education, *General Education in the American College*. 38th Yearbook, Part II. Bloomington, Illinois: Public School Publishing Co., 1939.

National University Extension Association, *Proceedings*. Vols. 1–35, 1915–1950. Bloomington, Indiana: National University Extension Association.

Organisation for European Economic Cooperation, *Agricultural Extension Services in the United States of America*. Paris, France: Organisation for European Economic Cooperation, 1951.

"Our National Schools of Science," *The North American Review*, Vol. CV, October 1867, pp. 495–520.

Parker, William Belmont, *The Life and Public Services of Justin Smith Morrill*. Boston: Houghton Mifflin Co., 1924.

Parks, W. Robert, "History, Philosophy, and Traditions of the Land-Grant College." Unpublished paper presented before the Agriculture Division Seminar, Iowa State College, October 4, 1955, by the Professor of Government.

PEOPLE'S COLLEGE, THE, *Prospectus*, 1852. In Cornell University Pamphlets, Vol. 3. Cornell University Library.

PORTER, NOAH, *The American Colleges and the American Public*. New Haven, Conn.: Charles C. Chatfield & Co., 1870.

POTTER, A. A., "Contributions of Land-Grant College Engineering Experiment Stations," *Engineering Experiment Station Record* (Bulletin of the Engineering Section of the Association of Land-Grant Colleges and Universities). Series 27, No. 4, October 1947, pp. 48–52.

PRESIDENT'S COMMISSION ON HIGHER EDUCATION, THE, *Higher Education for American Democracy*. 6 vols. bound in 1. Washington: Government Printing Office, 1947. (Also published in one volume by Harper & Brothers, New York, 1948.)

PUGH, EVAN, *Endowment of Colleges for Agriculture and the Mechanic Arts*. ("A Statement made by Dr. E. Pugh, of the Agricultural College of Pennsylvania, at a special meeting of the Judiciary Committee, at Harrisburg, convened March 3d, 1864, in reference to the proposition to deprive this College of its Endowment.") N.p., n.d. In Pennsylvania State University Library.

————, *A Report Upon A Plan for the Organization of Colleges for Agriculture and the Mechanic Arts* (with especial reference to the organization of the Agricultural College of Pennsylvania, in view of the endowment of this institution by the land scrip fund donated by Congress to the State of Pennsylvania.) Harrisburg, Pa.: Singerly & Myers, 1864.

REBER, LOUIS E., *University Extension in the United States*. United States Bureau of Education, Bulletin No. 19, 1914. Washington: Government Printing Office, 1914.

RECK, FRANKLIN M., *The 4-H Story: A History of the 4-H Club Work*. Sponsored by the National Committee on Boys and Girls Club Work. Ames, Iowa: The Iowa State College Press, 1951.

REISNER, EDWARD H., *Nationalism and Education Since 1789: A Social and Political History of Modern Education*. New York: The Macmillan Co., 1922.

ROBERTS, ISAAC PHILLIPS, *Autobiography of a Farm Boy*. Ithaca: Cornell University Press, 1946. (Reissued from original published in 1915.)

ROGERS, WALTER P., *Andrew D. White and the Modern University*. Ithaca: Cornell University Press, 1942.

ROSS, EARLE D., *Democracy's College: The Land-Grant Movement in the Formative Stage*. Ames, Iowa: Iowa State College Press, 1942.

————, "The Father of the Land Grant College," *Agricultural History*, XII, April 1938, pp. 151–186.

————, "The Land-Grant College: A Democratic Adaptation," *Agricultural History*, XV, January 1941.

————, "Lincoln and Agriculture," *Agricultural History*, III, 1929, pp. 510–566.

————, "On Writing the History of Land-Grant Colleges and Universities," *The Journal of Higher Education*, XXIV:8, November 1953.

RUSSELL, JOHN DALE, and Associates, *Vocational Education*. Staff Study No. 8 prepared for The Advisory Committee on Education. Washington: Government Printing Office, 1938.

RYAN, W. CARSON, *Studies in Early Graduate Education*. Carneigie Foundation for the Advancement of Teaching, Bulletin No. 30. New York: Carnegie Foundation, 1939.

SAWYER, WILLIAM EDWIN, "The Evolution of the Morrill Act of 1862." Unpublished Doctor's dissertation, Boston University Graduate School, 1948.

SCHAFFTER, DOROTHY, and THOMAS WOODY, "Education of Women," *Encyclopedia of Educational Research*, Revised Edition, 1950, Walter S. Monroe, editor, pp. 336–346.

SEMANS, HUBERT H., "The Administration of General Education Requirements in Selected Agricultural and Engineering Colleges." Unpublished Doctor's dissertation, University of Southern California, 1948.

SEXTON, BRENDAN, "A Responsibility Forgotten: The Relationship Between Land-Grant Colleges and the Labor Movement." Unpublished address given by the Director of Education, United Automobile Workers-Congress of Industrial Organizations, at 69th Annual Convention of Association of Land-Grant Colleges and Universities, East Lansing, Michigan, November 17, 1955.

SHEPARDSON, WHITNEY H., *Agricultural Education in the United States*. New York: The Macmillan Co., 1929.

SMITH, CLARENCE BEAMAN, and MEREDITH CHESTER WILSON, *The Agricultural Extension System of the United States*. New York: John Wiley & Sons, Inc., 1930.

SNOW, LOUIS F., *The College Curriculum in the United States*. New York: Teachers College, Columbia University, 1907.

SOCIETY FOR THE PROMOTION OF ENGINEERING EDUCATION, *Report of the Investigation of Engineering Education, 1923–29.* 2 vols. Pittsburgh: Society for the Promotion of Engineering Education, University of Pittsburgh. Vol. I published in 1930; Vol. II in 1934.

TEWKSBURY, DONALD G., *The Founding of American Colleges and Universities before the Civil War*. New York: Teachers College, Columbia University, 1932.

THWING, CHARLES F., A History of Higher Education in America. New York: D. Appleton Century Co., 1906.

TRACY, S. M., "Agricultural Research," Proceedings of the Society for the Promotion of Agricultural Science, XXVIII, 1907, pp. 31–42.

TRUE, ALFRED CHARLES, A History of Agricultural Education in the United States. United States Department of Agriculture, Miscellaneous Publication No. 36, July 1929. Washington: Government Printing Office, 1929.

———, A History of Agricultural Experimentation and Research in the United States, 1607–1925, including a History of the United States Department of Agriculture. United States Department of Agriculture, Miscellaneous Publication No. 251, 1937. Washington: Government Printing Office, 1937.

———, A History of Agricultural Extension Work in the United States, 1785–1923. United States Department of Agriculture, Miscellaneous Publication No. 15, October 1928. Washington: Government Printing Office, 1928.

———, "Notes on the History of Agricultural Pedagogy in the United States," Proceedings of the Society for the Promotion of Agricultural Science, XXVIII, 1907, pp. 84–106.

TURNER, JONATHAN B., "A Plan for an Industrial University for the State of Illinois," (Submitted to the Farmers' Convention at Granville, Illinois, November 18, 1851.) Reprinted in Proceedings of the Society for the Promotion of Agricultural Science, XXVIII, 1907, pp. 54–72.

UNITED STATES DEPARTMENT OF AGRICULTURE, AGRICULTURAL RESEARCH SERVICE, OFFICE OF EXPERIMENT STATIONS, Federal Legislation, Rulings, and Regulations Affecting the State Agricultural Experiment Stations. Miscellaneous Publication No. 515, Revised November 1954. Washington: Government Printing Office, 1954.

UNITED STATES DEPARTMENT OF AGRICULTURE AND ASSOCIATION OF LAND-GRANT COLLEGES AND UNIVERSITIES, Joint Committee Report on Extension Programs, Policies and Goals. August 1948. Washington: Government Printing Office, 1948.

UNITED STATES GOVERNMENT, FEDERAL SECURITY AGENCY, OFFICE OF EDUCATION, Land-Grant Colleges and Universities: What They Are and the Relation of the Federal Government to Them. Office of Education, Bulletin No. 15, 1951. Washington: Government Printing Office, 1951.

UNITED STATES STATUTES AT LARGE PERTAINING TO THE LAND-GRANT COLLEGES:

Morrill Act of 1862   12, 503–505   (1862)

Hatch Act	24, 440–442	(1887)
Second Morrill Act of 1890	26, 417–419	(1890)
Adams Act	34, 63–64	(1906)
Nelson Amendment	34, 1281–1282	(1907)
Smith-Lever Act	38, 372–375	(1914)
Purnell Act	43, 970–972	(1925)
Capper-Ketcham Act	45, 711–712	(1928)
Bankhead-Jones Act	49, 436–439	(1935)
Research and Marketing Act of 1946	60, 1082	(1946)

WHITE, ANDREW DICKSON, *Address on Agricultural Education*. Albany, N. Y.: Printing House of Charles Van Benthuysen and Sons, 1869.

———, *Autobiography*. 2 vols. New York: The Century Co., 1905.

———, "The Need of Another University," *Forum*, 6:465–473, January 1889.

———, *Scientific and Industrial Education in the United States*. New York: D. Appleton & Co., 1874. (An Address delivered before the New York State Agricultural Society.)

———, *What Profession Shall I Choose, and How Shall I Fit Myself for it?* (with a Brief Statement of Facilities Offered at the Cornell University.) Ithaca, N. Y.: n.p., 1884.

WOODWARD, CARL R., *The Curriculum of the College of Agriculture*. United States Department of the Interior, Bureau of Education, Bulletin No. 40, 1920. Washington: Government Printing Office, 1921.

WOODY, THOMAS, *A History of Women's Education in the United States*. 2 vols. New York: Science Press, 1929.

WORKS, GEORGE A., and BARTON MORGAN, *The Land-Grant Colleges*. Staff Study No. 10 prepared for The Advisory Committee on Education. Washington: Government Printing Office, 1939.

ZEHMER, GEORGE B., "The Development of University Extension Services in the United States," *Proceedings* of the Institute for Administrative Officers of Higher Institutions, XVII, 1945, pp. 50–67.

COLLEGE AND UNIVERSITY HISTORIES

BEAL, W. J., *History of the Michigan Agricultural College and Biographical Sketches of Trustees and Professors*. East Lansing, Mich.: Michigan Agricultural College, 1915.

BECKER, CARL L., *Cornell University: Founders and the Founding*. Ithaca: Cornell University Press, 1944.

BETTERSWORTH, JOHN K., *People's College: A History of Mississippi State*. University, Alabama: University of Alabama Press, 1953.

BRITTAIN, M. K., *The Story of Georgia Tech.* Chapel Hill, N. C.: University of North Carolina Press, 1948.

BROOKS, ROBERT PRESTON, *The University of Georgia: Under Sixteen Administrations, 1785–1955.* Athens, Georgia: University of Georgia Press, 1956.

CHITTENDEN, R. H., *History of the Sheffield Scientific School of Yale University, 1846–1922.* 2 vols. New Haven, Conn.: Yale University Press, 1928.

CLOUGH, WILSON O., *A History of the University of Wyoming, 1887–1937.* Laramie, Wyoming: University of Wyoming, 1937.

CRAWFORD, ROBERT PLATT, *These Fifty Years: A History of the College of Agriculture of the University of Nebraska.* Nebraska Agricultural Experiment Station, Circular No. 26, 1925. Lincoln, Nebraska: College of Agriculture, University of Nebraska, 1925.

CURTI, MERLE, and VERNON CARSTENSEN, *The University of Wisconsin: A History.* Madison, Wisconsin: University of Wisconsin Press, 1949.

DEMAREST, WILLIAM H. S., *A History of Rutgers College (1766–1924).* New Brunswick, New Jersey: Rutgers College, 1924.

DOTEN, S. B., *An Illustrated History of the University of Nevada.* Reno, Nevada: University of Nevada, 1924.

DUNAWAY, WAYLAND FULLER, *History of The Pennsylvania State College.* State College, Pa.: The Pennsylvania State College, 1946.

FERNALD, M. C., *History of the Maine State College and the University of Maine.* Orono, Maine: University of Maine, 1916.

FERRIER, W. W., *Origin and Development of the University of California.* Berkeley, Calif.: Gather Gate Book Co., 1930.

FLEMING, W. L., *Louisiana State University, 1860–1896.* Baton Rouge, La.: Louisiana State University, 1936.

GRAY, JAMES, *The University of Minnesota, 1851–1951.* Minneapolis: University of Minnesota Press, 1951.

HALE, HARRISON, *University of Arkansas, 1871–1948.* Fayetteville, Ark.: University of Arkansas Alumni Association, 1948.

HEPBURN, WILLIAM MURRAY, and LOUIS MARTIN SEARS, *Purdue University: Fifty Years of Progress.* Indianapolis: Hollenbeck Press, 1925.

HEWETT, WATERMAN THOMAS, *Cornell University, A History.* 3 vols. New York: The University Publishing Society, 1905.

HOPKINS, JAMES F., *The University of Kentucky: Origin and Early Years.* Lexington, Kentucky: University of Kentucky Press, 1951.

KUHN, MADISON, *Michigan State: The First Hundred Years, 1855–1955.* East Lansing, Mich.: The Michigan State University Press, 1955.

LINDSAY, JULIAN IRA, *Tradition Looks Forward: The University of Vermont: *A History, 1791–1904.* Burlington, Vermont: The University of Vermont and State Agricultural College, 1954.

LOCKMILLER, DAVID A., *History of the North Carolina State College of Agriculture and Engineering of the University of North Carolina, 1889–1939.* Raleigh, N. C.: The General Alumni Association of the North Carolina State College, 1939.

MCCLELLAN, J. H., and BLANCHE E. HYDE, *History of the Extension Service of Colorado State College, 1912–1941.* Fort Collins, Colo.: Extension Service, Colorado State College of Agriculture and Mechanic Arts, 1941.

MENDENHALL, THOMAS C., editor, *History of the Ohio State University.* 3 vols. Columbus, Ohio: Ohio State University Press, 1920–26.

MORGAN, BARTON, *A·History of the Extension Service of Iowa State College.* Ames, Iowa: Collegiate Press, Inc., 1934.

NEVINS, ALLEN, *Illinois.* New York: Oxford University Press, 1917.

NEW HAMPSHIRE, UNIVERSITY OF, *History of the University of New Hampshire.* Durham, N. H.: University of New Hampshire, 1941.

OSUNA, JUAN JOSE, *A History of Education in Puerto Rico.* Rio Piedras, Puerto Rico: Editorial de la Universidad de Puerto Rico, 1949.

OUSLEY, CLARENCE, *History of the Agricultural and Mechanical College of Texas.* Agricultural and Mechanical College of Texas, Bulletin, December 1, 1935. College Station, Texas: Agricultural and Mechanical College of Texas, 1935.

POWELL, BURT E., *The Movement for Industrial Education and the Establishment of the University, 1840–1870.* Volume 1 of Semi-Centennial History of the University of Illinois (subsequent volumes not completed). Urbana, Illinois: The University of Illinois, 1918.

POWERS, W. H., editor, *A History of South Dakota State College.* Brookings, South Dakota: South Dakota State College, 1931.

RAND, FRANK PRENTICE, *Yesterdays at Massachusetts State College, 1863–1933.* Amherst, Mass.: The Associate Alumni, Massachusetts State College, 1933.

REYNOLD, JOHN HUGH, and DAVID YANCEY THOMAS, *History of the University of Arkansas.* Fayetteville, Ark.: University of Arkansas, 1910.

RICKS, JOEL EDWARD, *The Utah State Agricultural College: A History of Fifty Years, 1888–1938.* Logan, Utah: The Deseret News Press, 1938.

ROSS, EARLE D., *A History of the Iowa State College of Agriculture and Mechanic Arts.* Ames, Iowa: Iowa State College Press, 1942.

SAVAGE, W. SHERMAN, *The History of Lincoln University.* Jefferson City, Missouri: Lincoln University, 1939.

SELLERS, JAMES B., *History of the University of Alabama*. Vol. I, 1818–1902. University of Alabama: University of Alabama Press, 1953.

SLATER, C. P., editor, *History of the Land-Grant Endowment in the University of Illinois*. Urbana, Ill.: University of Illinois, 1940.

SMITH, RUBY GREEN, *The People's Colleges: A History of the New York State Extension Service in Cornell University and the State, 1876–1948*. Ithaca: Cornell University Press, 1949.

THWAITES, R. G., editor, *The University of Wisconsin, Its History and Alumni*. Madison, Wis.: J. N. Purcell, 1900.

TURNER, FRED H., *Misconceptions Concerning the Early History of the University of Illinois*. Reprinted from the Transactions of the Illinois State Historical Society for 1932—Publication No. 39. Printed by authority of the State of Illinois.

WALTER, J. D., *History of the Kansas State Agricultural College*. Manhattan, Kansas: Printing Department of the Kansas State Agricultural College, 1909.

WILLARD, J. T., *History of the Kansas State College of Agriculture and Applied Science*. Manhattan, Kansas: Kansas State College Press, 1940.

WILLIAMSON, FREDERICK W., *Origin and Growth of Agricultural Extension in Louisiana, 1860–1948*. (Subtitle: "How it Opened the Road for Progress in Better Farming and Better Living.") Baton Rouge, Louisiana: Louisiana State University and Agricultural and Mechanical College, 1951.

WOODWARD, CARL R., and I. N. WALLER, *New Jersey's Agricultural Experiment Station, 1880–1930*. New Brunswick, N. J.: New Jersey Agricultural Experiment Station, 1932.

SELECTED REFERENCES

Index

319

Set in Linotype Electra
Format by Marguerite Swanton
Manufactured by The Haddon Craftsmen, Inc.
Published by HARPER & BROTHERS, New York